TEXAS LAW for the SOCIAL WORKER

A Sourcebook

J. RAY HAYS, Ph.D., J.D.
ROBERT McPHERSON, Ph.D.
VICKI HANSEN, LMSW-AP, ACSW

TEXAS LAW for the SOCIAL WORKER

A Sourcebook

EDITED BY

HAYS, MCPHERSON & HANSEN

NASW, TEXAS CHAPTER
National Association of Social Workers
AUSTIN, TX

Bayou Publishing
HOUSTON, TX

Printed in the United States of America
First Edition 10 9 8 7 6 5 4 3 2 1

Publisher's Cataloging-in-Publication
(Provided by Quality Books, Inc.)

Texas law for the social worker : a sourcebook / [edited by] J. Ray Hays, Robert McPherson, Vicki Hansen. -- 1st ed.
p. cm.
Includes index.
LCCN 2006935321
ISBN-13: 9781886298217
ISBN-10: 1886298211

1. Social workers--Legal status, laws, etc.--Texas.
I. Hays, J. Ray (James Ray), 1942- II. McPherson, Robert H. III. Hansen, Vicki, 1952-

KFT1549.5.Z9T49 2006 344.76403'13
QBI06-600426

Published by:

NASW, TEXAS CHAPTER
National Association of Social Workers

Bayou Publishing

National Association of Social Workers
Texas Chapter
810 West 11th Street., Suite 410
Austin, TX 78701-2010
(512) 474-1454
http://www.naswtx.org

Bayou Publishing
2524 Nottingham
Houston, TX 77005-1412
713-526-4558
http://www.bayoupublishing.com

CONTENTS AT A GLANCE

CONTENTS

INTRODUCTION

This book brings together into one source the legal rules that guide the practice of social work in Texas. We gathered those statutes that are most directly related to practice so that the practitioner can find in one place the guidance necessary for most legally related practice questions. In addition to statutory material, we included several other sources of legal guidance for the practitioner and student by adding case law, and a synopsis of the HIPAA security rule that came into effect in the spring of 2005.

The statutory material in this edition follows the organization of the statutory codes; that is, we have kept the classification scheme used by the Texas Legislature instead of attempting to organize the material in a more user friendly way. For example, the concept of privacy of mental health information is covered primarily in Chapter 611 of the Health and Safety Code. However, there are several other Texas statutes that deal with privacy of information, such as the Communicable Disease Act, Family Code, and alcohol and drug statues. We have included the statutory authority for the regulation of "telehealth" in this edition from the Occupation Code.

We have included three legal decisions in this book that are important for the practice of clinical social work. *Jaffee v. Redmond* for the first time gave the right of privacy to psychotherapy notes in federal court. We have also included two Texas legal decisions: *Thapar v. Zezulka* and *Abrams v. Jones*. *Thapar v. Zezulka* provides an excellent discussion of the duty to warn and duty to protect doctrine in Texas. We waited over 20 years in Texas to know the status of these duties. The Texas Supreme Court has now given practitioners guidance when a patient threatens another person. In this case, the Texas Supreme Court takes the position that courts should not second-guess the decision by a practitioner to tell law enforcement personnel or medical personnel about the danger presented by a patient. This gives a good deal of discretion to practitioners who are faced with a difficult situation and the decision is certainly pro-therapist. *Abrams v. Jones* concerns the privacy of information between a therapist, a child client, and the child's parents and provides a remedy for parents who request but are denied access to a child's records. Practitioners can draw guidance from this case about record keeping and the duty to parents and child clients.

Remember lawyers give opinions not answers. There are always "ifs," "ands," or "buts" in the law which most certainly keep lawyers fully employed. When you have a question about the legal aspects of practice use this text for reference but also get the consult from other professionals involved in your type of practice and do not hesitate to ask an attorney or our licensing board for advice. Your malpractice insurance carrier can provide consultation on matters that relate to many aspects of practice.

We are fortunate in Texas to be at the stage of professional development that we are. The continued growth of mental health practice is dependent not only on what we do in our offices but the shape of the laws that control practice. This volume represents the state of regulatory development. If you see areas where the rights and prerogatives of our patients and our profession can be enhanced, please take a proactive stance of being involved in positive change by contacting the Texas Chapter of NASW or your local area society.

I am grateful to each person who has made suggestions about inclusion of material in this book and to my co-editors, Bob McPherson and Vicki Hansen. Finally, a portion of the proceeds from the sale of this book goes to the National Association of Social Workers Texas Chapter.

—Ray Hays, Ph.D., J.D.
Diplomate in Clinical and Forensic Psychology, ABPP
Houston, Texas

About the Editors

J. Ray Hays, Ph.D., J.D., is a member of the faculty of the Menninger Department of Psychiatry and Behavioral Sciences, Baylor College of Medicine, where he is Chief of the Psychology Service at Ben Taub General Hospital. He has edited this series since its inception in 1985 after proposing the idea for the book to the Texas Psychological Association Executive Committee. He is a Diplomate in both Clinical and Forensic Psychology from the American Board of Professional Psychology and the American Board of Forensic Psychology. His doctorate is from the University of Georgia with an internship at the Texas Research Institute of Mental Sciences. His law degree is from the South Texas College of Law. He is a former Chair of the Texas State Board of Examiners of Psychologists, serving as member from 1975 to 1982, and former President and one of the first Fellows of the American Association of State Psychology Boards, now the Association of State and Provincial Psychology Boards. He has written, edited, or compiled nine books, sixteen book chapters, and over 100 scientific articles on a variety of psychological topics. He is the recipient of the Texas Psychological Association Award for Outstanding Contribution to Education.

Robert H. McPherson, Ph.D., is Executive Associate Dean for the College of Education at the University of Houston, former Chair of the Department of Educational Psychology, and former Director of Training for the counseling psychology program. He completed his doctorate at the University of Houston and his internship at Texas A&M. He teaches the supervision and mental health & public policy courses for the counseling psychology program. His research interests address supervision processes, as well as legal, ethical, and regulatory issues related to professional practice. He is a Fellow of the American Psychological Association, past president of the Texas and Houston Psychological Associations, and former chair of the Council of Counseling Psychology Training Programs. He has been inducted into the National Academies of Practice and is recipient of the American Psychological Association's Karl Heiser Award in recognition for his advocacy contributions on behalf of psychologists and their patients.

Vicki Hansen, LMSW-AP, ACSW, has served as the Executive Director of the Texas Chapter of the National Association of Social Workers since 1998. She is a Licensed Master Social Worker, Advanced Practitioner and a member of the NASW Academy of Certified Social Workers. She has participated in federal and foundation grants involving schools and service integration and developed parent participation materials used in Ohio and Florida. She was an organizer of a national symposium on the re-professionalization of public child welfare and was a contributing co-editor of a book of proceedings; was the Project Director of a 3-year grant from the Texas Cancer Council on developing cancer prevention materials for low-income, minority populations; served as an ombudsperson for the Texas Department of Health Strategic Health Partnership, as a participant for the TDH Bioterrorism Preparedness and Response Plan, and was a member of the Texas Social Work Licensing Revision Task Force. Vicki has served on the NASW national committee on Standards for Continuing Social Work Education and was recently appointed to the NASW Foundation Board of Directors. She is an adjunct faculty member of the University of Texas at San Antonio Social Work Program and has been an invited lecturer at many schools of social work across Texas. She was named the NASW Executive Director of the Year for 2005.

STATUTES

Texas Statutes

Civil Practice and Remedies Code

Sexual Exploitation by Mental Health Provider—§81

§81.001. Definitions

In this chapter:

(1) *"Mental health services"* means assessment, diagnosis, treatment, or counseling in a professional relationship to assist an individual or group in:

(A) alleviating mental or emotional illness, symptoms, conditions, or disorders, including alcohol or drug addiction;

(B) understanding conscious or subconscious motivations;

(C) resolving emotional, attitudinal, or relationship conflicts; or

(D) modifying feelings, attitudes, or behaviors that interfere with effective emotional, social, or intellectual functioning.

(2) *"Mental health services provider"* means an individual, licensed or unlicensed, who performs or purports to perform mental health services, including a:

(A) licensed social worker as defined by Section 505.002, Occupations Code;

(B) chemical dependency counselor as defined by Section 504.001, Occupations Code;

(C) licensed professional counselor as defined by Section 503.002, Occupations Code;

(D) licensed marriage and family therapist as defined by Section 505.002, Occupations Code;

(E) member of the clergy;

(F) physician who is practicing medicine as defined by Section 151.002, Occupations Code;

(G) psychologist offering psychological services as defined by Section 501.003, Occupations Code; or

(H) special officer for mental health assignment certified under Section 1701.404, Occupations Code.

(3) *"Patient"* means an individual who seeks or obtains mental health services. The term includes a person who has contact with a special officer for mental health assignment because of circumstances relating to the person's mental health.

(4) " *Sexual contact*" means:

(A) "*deviate sexual intercourse*" as defined by Section 21.01, Penal Code;

(B) "*sexual contact*" as defined by Section 21.01, Penal Code;

(C) "*sexual intercourse*" as defined by Section 21.01, Penal Code; or

(D) requests by the mental health services provider for conduct described by Paragraph (A), (B), or (C). "Sexual contact" does not include conduct described by Paragraph (A) or (B) that is a part of a professionally recognized medical treatment of a patient.

(5) "*Sexual exploitation*" means a pattern, practice, or scheme of conduct, which may include sexual contact, that can reasonably be construed as being for the purposes of sexual arousal or gratification or sexual abuse of any person. The term does not include obtaining information about a patient's sexual history within standard accepted practice while treating a sexual or marital dysfunction.

(6) "*Therapeutic deception*" means a representation by a mental health services provider that sexual contact with, or sexual exploitation by, the mental health services provider is consistent with, or a part of, a patient's or former patient's treatment.

(7) "*Mental health services,*" as defined by this section, provided by a member of the clergy does not include religious, moral, and spiritual counseling, teaching, and instruction.

§81.002. Sexual Exploitation Cause of Action

A mental health services provider is liable to a patient or former patient of the mental health services provider for damages for sexual exploitation if the patient or former patient suffers, directly or indirectly, a physical, mental, or emotional injury caused by, resulting from, or arising out of:

(1) sexual contact between the patient or former patient and the mental health services provider;

(2) sexual exploitation of the patient or former patient by the mental health services provider; or

(3) therapeutic deception of the patient or former patient by the mental health services provider.

§81.003. Liability of Employer

(a) An employer of a mental health services provider is liable to a patient or former patient of the mental health services provider for damages if the patient or former patient is injured as described by Section 81.002 and the employer:

(1) fails to make inquiries of an employer or former employer, whose name and address have been disclosed to the employer and who employed the mental health services provider as a mental health services provider within the five years before the date of disclosure, concerning the possible occurrence of sexual exploitation by the mental health services provider of patients or former patients of the mental health services provider; or

(2) knows or has reason to know that the mental health services provider engaged in the sexual exploitation of the patient or former patient and the employer failed to:

(A) report the suspected sexual exploitation as required by Section 81.006; or

(B) take necessary action to prevent or stop the sexual exploitation by the mental health services provider.

(b) An employer or former employer of a mental health services provider is liable to a patient or former patient of the mental health services provider for damages if . patient or former patient is injured as described by Section 81.002 and the employer or former employer:

(1) knows of the occurrence of the sexual exploitation by the mental health services provider of the patient or former patient;

(2) receives a specific request by an employer or prospective employer of the mental health services provider, engaged in the business of providing mental health services, concerning the possible existence or nature of sexual exploitation by the mental health services provider; and

(3) fails to disclose the occurrence of the sexual exploitation.

(c) An employer or former employer is liable under this section only to the extent that the failure to take the action described by Subsection (a) or (b) was a proximate and actual cause of damages sustained.

(d) If a mental health professional who sexually exploits a patient or former patient is a member of the clergy and the sexual exploitation occurs when the professional is acting as a member of the clergy, liability if any under this section is limited to the church, congregation, or parish in which the member of the clergy carried out the clergy member's pastoral duties:

(1) at the time the sexual exploitation occurs, if the liability is based on a violation of Subsection (a); or

(2) at the time of the previous occurrence of sexual exploitation, if the liability is based on a violation of Subsection (b).

(e) Nothing in Subsection (d) shall prevent the extension of liability under this section beyond the local church, congregation, or parish where the current or previous sexual exploitation occurred, as appropriate under Subsection (d), if the patient proves that officers or employees of the religious denomination in question at the regional, state, or national level:

(1) knew or should have known of the occurrences of sexual exploitation by the mental health services provider;

(2) received reports of such occurrences and failed to take necessary action to prevent or stop such sexual exploitation by the mental health services provider and that such failure was a proximate and actual cause of the damages; or

(3) knew or should have known of the mental health professional's propensity to engage in sexual exploitation.

§81.004. Damages

(a) A plaintiff who prevails in a suit under this section may recover actual damages, including damages for mental anguish even if an injury other than mental anguish is not shown.

(b) In addition to an award under Subsection (a), a plaintiff who prevails in a suit under this section may recover exemplary damages and reasonable attorney fees.

§81.005. Defenses

(a) It is not a defense to an action brought under Section 81.002 or 81.003 that the sexual exploitation of the patient or former patient occurred:

(1) with the consent of the patient or former patient;

(2) outside the therapy or treatment sessions of the patient or former patient; or

(3) off the premises regularly used by the mental health services provider for the therapy or treatment sessions of the patient or former patient.

(b) It is a defense to an action brought under Section 81.002 or 81.003 by a former patient that the person was not emotionally dependent on the mental health services provider when the sexual exploitation began and the mental health services provider terminated mental health services with the patient more than two years before the date the sexual exploitation began.

(c) A person is considered not emotionally dependent for purposes of this chapter if the nature of the patient's or former patient's emotional condition and the nature of the treatment provided by the mental health services provider are not such that the mental health services provider knows or has reason to believe that the patient or former patient is unable to withhold consent to the sexual exploitation.

§81.006. Reporting therapist-client sexual relationship

(a) If a mental health services provider or the employer of a mental health services provider has reasonable cause to suspect that a patient has been the victim of sexual exploitation by a mental health services provider during the course of treatment, or if a patient alleges sexual exploitation by a mental health services provider during the course of treatment, the mental health services provider or the employer shall report the alleged conduct not later than the 30th day after the date the person became aware of the conduct or the allegations to:

(1) the prosecuting attorney in the county in which the alleged sexual exploitation occurred; and

(2) any state licensing board that has responsibility for the mental health services provider's licensing.

(b) Before making a report under this section, the reporter shall inform the alleged victim of the reporter's duty to report and shall determine if the alleged victim wants to remain anonymous.

(c) A report under this section need contain only the information needed to:

(1) identify the reporter;

(2) identify the alleged victim, unless the alleged victim has requested anonymity; and

(3) express suspicion that sexual exploitation has occurred.

(d) Information in a report is privileged information and is for the exclusive use of the prosecuting attorney or state licensing board that receives the information. A person who receives privileged information may not disclose the information except to the extent that disclosure is consistent with the authorized purposes for which the person first obtained the information. The identity of an alleged victim of sexual exploitation by a mental health services provider may not be disclosed by the reporter, or by a person who has received or has access to a report or record, unless the alleged victim has consented to the disclosure in writing.

(e) A person who intentionally violates Subsection (a) or (d) is subject to disciplinary action by that person's appropriate licensing board and also commits an offense. An offense under this subsection is a Class C misdemeanor.

§81.007. Limited Immunity from Liability

(a) A person who, in good faith, makes a report required by Section 81.006 is immune from civil or criminal liability resulting from the filing of that report.

(b) Reporting under this chapter is presumed to be done in good faith.

(c) The immunity provided by this section does not apply to liability resulting from sexual exploitation by a mental health services provider of a patient or former patient.

§81.008. Admission of Evidence

(a) In an action for sexual exploitation, evidence of the plaintiff's sexual history and reputation is not admissible unless:

(1) the plaintiff claims damage to sexual functioning; or

(2) (A) the defendant requests a hearing before trial and makes an offer of proof of the relevancy of the history or reputation; and

(B) the court finds that the history or reputation is relevant and that the probative value of the evidence outweighs its prejudicial effect.

(b) The court may allow the admission only of specific information or examples of the plaintiff's conduct that are determined by the court to be relevant. The court's order shall detail the information or conduct that is admissible and no other such evidence may be introduced.

§81.009. Limitations

(a) Except as otherwise provided by this section, an action under this chapter must be filed before the third anniversary of the date the patient or former patient understood or should have understood the conduct for which liability is established under Section 81.002 or 81.003.

(b) If a patient or former patient entitled to file an action under this chapter is unable to bring the action because of the effects of the sexual exploitation, continued emotional dependence on the mental health services provider, or threats, instructions, or statements by the mental health services provider, the deadline for filing an action under this chapter is tolled during that period, except that the deadline may not be tolled for more than 15 years.

(c) This section does not apply to a patient or former patient who is a "child" or a "minor" as defined by Section 101.003, Family Code, until that patient or former patient has reached the age of 18. If the action is brought by a parent, guardian, or other person having custody of the child or minor, it must be brought within the period set forth in this section.

DECLARATION FOR MENTAL HEALTH TREATMENT—§137

§137.001. Definition

In this chapter:

(1) *'Adult'* means a person 18 years of age or older or a person under 18 years of age who has had the disabilities of minority removed.

(2) *'Attending physician'* means the physician, selected by or assigned to a patient, who has primary responsibility for the treatment and care of the patient.

(3) *'Declaration for mental health treatment'* means a document making a declaration of preferences or instructions regarding mental health treatment.

(4) *'Emergency'* means a situation in which it is immediately necessary to treat a patient to prevent:

(A) probable imminent death or serious bodily injury to the patient because the patient:

(i) overtly or continually is threatening or attempting to commit suicide or serious bodily injury to the patient; or

(ii) is behaving in a manner that indicates that the patient is unable to satisfy the patient's need for nourishment, essential medical care, or self-protection; or

(B) imminent physical or emotional harm to another because of threats, attempts, or other acts of the patient.

(5) *'Health care provider'* means an individual or facility licensed, certified, or otherwise authorized to administer health care or treatment, for profit or otherwise, in the ordinary course of business or professional practice and includes a physician or other health care provider, a residential care provider, or an inpatient mental health facility as defined by Section 571.003, Health and Safety Code.

(6) *'Incapacitated'* means that, in the opinion of the court in a guardianship proceeding under Chapter XIII, Texas Probate Code, or in a medication hearing under Section 574.106, Health and Safety Code, a person lacks the ability to understand the nature and consequences of a proposed treatment, including the benefits, risks, and alternatives to the proposed treatment, and lacks the ability to make mental health treatment decisions because of impairment.

(7) *'Mental health treatment'* means electroconvulsive or other convulsive treatment, treatment of mental illness with psychoactive medication as defined by Section 574.101, Health and Safety Code, or emergency mental health treatment.

(8) *'Principal'* means a person who has executed a declaration for mental health treatment.

§137.002. Eligible Persons; Period of validity

Persons who may execute declaration for mental health treatment; Period of validity.

(a) An adult who is not incapacitated may execute a declaration for mental health treatment. The preferences or instructions may include consent to or refusal of mental health treatment.

(b) A declaration for mental health treatment is effective on execution as provided by this chapter. Except as provided by Subsection (c), a declaration for mental health treatment expires on the third anniversary of the date of its execution or when revoked by the principal, whichever is earlier.

(c) If the declaration for mental health treatment is in effect and the principal is incapacitated on the third anniversary of the date of its execution, the declaration remains in effect until the principal is no longer incapacitated.

§137.003. Execution and Witnesses

(a) A declaration for mental health treatment must be signed by the principal in the presence of two or more subscribing witnesses.

(b) A witness may not, at the time of execution, be:

(1) the principal's health or residential care provider or an employee of that provider;

(2) the operator of a community health care facility providing care to the principal or an employee of an operator of the facility;

(3) a person related to the principal by blood, marriage, or adoption;

(4) a person entitled to any part of the estate of the principal on the death of the principal under a will, trust, or deed in existence or who would be entitled to any part of the estate by operation of law if the principal died intestate; or

(5) a person who has a claim against the estate of the principal.

(c) For a witness's signature to be effective, the witness must sign a statement affirming that, at the time the declaration for mental health treatment was signed, the principal:

(1) appeared to be of sound mind to make a mental health treatment decision;

(2) has stated in the witness's presence that the principal was aware of the nature of the declaration for mental health treatment and that the principal was signing the document voluntarily and free from any duress; and

(3) requested that the witness serve as a witness to the principal's execution of the document.

§137.004. Health Care Provider

Health care provider is to act in accordance with declaration for mental health treatment.

A physician or other health care provider shall act in accordance with the declaration for mental health treatment when the principal has been found to be incapacitated. A physician or other provider shall continue to seek and act in accordance with the principal's informed consent to all mental health treatment decisions if the principal is capable of providing informed consent.

§137.005. Limitation on Liability

(a) An attending physician, health or residential care provider, or person acting for or under an attending physician's or health or residential care provider's control is not subject to criminal or civil liability and has not engaged in professional misconduct for an act or omission if the act or omission is done in good faith under the terms of a declaration for mental health treatment.

(b) An attending physician, health or residential care provider, or person acting for or under an attending physician's or health or residential care provider's control does not engage in professional misconduct for:

   (1) failure to act in accordance with a declaration for mental health treatment if the physician, provider, or other person:

      (A) was not provided with a copy of the declaration; and

      (B) had no knowledge of the declaration after a good faith attempt to learn of the existence of a declaration; or

   (2) acting in accordance with a directive for mental health treatment after the directive has expired or has been revoked if the physician, provider, or other person does not have knowledge of the expiration or revocation.

§137.006. Discrimination in Relation to Execution of Declaration for Mental Health Treatment

A health or residential care provider, health care service plan, insurer issuing disability insurance, self-insured employee benefit plan, or nonprofit hospital service plan may not:

   (1) charge a person a different rate solely because the person has executed a declaration for mental health treatment;

   (2) require a person to execute a declaration for mental health treatment before:

      (A) admitting the person to a hospital, nursing home, or residential care home;

      (B) insuring the person; or

      (C) allowing the person to receive health or residential care;

   (3) refuse health or residential care to a person solely because the person has executed a declaration for mental health treatment; or

   (4) discharge the person solely because the person has or has not executed a declaration for mental health treatment.

§137.007. Use and effect of declaration for mental health treatment

(a) On being presented with a declaration for mental health treatment, a physician or other health care provider shall make the declaration a part of the principal's medical record. When acting in accordance with a declaration for mental health treatment, a physician or other health care provider shall comply with the declaration to the fullest extent possible.

(b) If a physician or other provider is unwilling at any time to comply with a declaration for mental health treatment, the physician or provider may withdraw from providing treatment consistent with the exercise of independent medical judgment and must promptly:

(1) make a reasonable effort to transfer care for the principal to a physician or provider who is willing to comply with the declaration;

(2) notify the principal, or principal's guardian, if appropriate, of the decision to withdraw; and

(3) record in the principal's medical record the notification and, if applicable, the name of the physician or provider to whom the principal is transferred.

§137.008. Disregard of Declaration for Mental Health Treatment

(a) A physician or other health care provider may subject the principal to mental health treatment in a manner contrary to the principal's wishes as expressed in a declaration for mental health treatment only:

(1) if the principal is under an order for temporary or extended mental health services under Section 574.034 or 574.035, Health and Safety Code, and treatment is authorized in compliance with Section 574.106, Health and Safety Code; or

(2) in case of an emergency when the principal's instructions have not been effective in reducing the severity of the behavior that has caused the emergency.

(b) A declaration for mental health treatment does not limit any authority provided by Chapter 573 or 574, Health and Safety Code:

(1) to take a person into custody; or

(2) to admit or retain a person in a mental health treatment facility.

(c) This section does not apply to the use of electroconvulsive treatment or other convulsive treatment.

§137.009. Conflicting or Contrary Provisions

(a) Mental health treatment instructions contained in a declaration executed in accordance with this chapter supersede any contrary or conflicting instructions given by:

(1) a durable power of attorney under Chapter 135; or

(2) a guardian appointed under Chapter XIII, Texas Probate Code, after the execution of the declaration.

(b) Mental health treatment instructions contained in a declaration executed in accordance with this chapter shall be conclusive evidence of a declarant's preference in a medication hearing under Section 574.106, Health and Safety Code.

§137.010. Revocation

(a) A declaration for mental health treatment is revoked when a principal who is not incapacitated:

(1) notifies a licensed or certified health or residential care provider of the revocation;

(2) acts in a manner that demonstrates a specific intent to revoke the declaration; or

(3) executes a later declaration for mental health treatment.

(b) A principal's health or residential care provider who is informed of or provided with a revocation of a declaration for mental health treatment immediately shall:

(1) record the revocation in the principal's medical record; and

(2) give notice of the revocation to any other health or residential care provider the provider knows to be responsible for the principal's care.

§137.011. Form of Declaration for Mental Health Treatment

The declaration for mental health treatment must be in substantially the following form:

DECLARATION FOR MENTAL HEALTH TREATMENT

I, ________________, being an adult of sound mind, willfully and voluntarily make this declaration for mental health treatment to be followed if it is determined by a court that my ability to understand the nature and consequences of a proposed treatment, including the benefits, risks, and alternatives to the proposed treatment, is impaired to such an extent that I lack the capacity to make mental health treatment decisions. 'Mental health treatment' means electroconvulsive or other convulsive treatment, treatment of mental illness with psychoactive medication, and preferences regarding emergency mental health treatment.

*(OPTIONAL PARAGRAPH)*I understand that I may become incapable of giving or withholding informed consent for mental health treatment due to the symptoms of a diagnosed mental disorder. These symptoms may include::

____

____

PSYCHOACTIVE MEDICATIONS

If I become incapable of giving or withholding informed consent for mental health treatment, my wishes regarding psychoactive medications are as follows:

❑ I consent to the administration of the following medications:

____

____

____

❑ I do not consent to the administration of the following medications:

____

____

____

❑ I consent to the administration of a federal Food and Drug Administration approved medication that was only approved and in existence after my declaration and that is considered in the same class of psychoactive medications as stated below:

____

____

____

Conditions or limitations:

____

____

Convulsive Treatment

If I become incapable of giving or withholding informed consent for mental health treatment, my wishes regarding convulsive treatment are as follows:

❑ I consent to the administration of convulsive treatment.

❑ I do not consent to the administration of convulsive treatment.

Conditions or limitations:

Preferences for Emergency Treatment

In an emergency, I prefer the following treatment FIRST (circle one)

Restraint Seclusion Medication.

In an emergency, I prefer the following treatment SECOND (circle one)

Restraint Seclusion Medication.

In an emergency, I prefer the following treatment THIRD (circle one)

Restraint Seclusion Medication.

❑ I prefer a male/female to administer restraint, seclusion, and/or medications.

Options for treatment prior to use of restraint, seclusion, and/or medications:

____

____

Conditions or limitations:

____

____

Additional Preferences or Instructions

Conditions or limitations:

Signature of Principal/ Date: ______________________

Statement of Witnesses

I declare under penalty of perjury that the principal's name has been represented to me by the principal, that the principal signed or acknowledged this declaration in my presence, that I believe the principal to be of sound mind, that the principal has affirmed that the principal is aware of the nature of the document and is signing it voluntarily and free from duress, that the principal requested that I serve as witness to the principal's execution of this document, and that I am not a provider of health or residential care to the principal, an employee of a provider of health or residential care to the principal, an operator of a community health care facility providing care to the principal, or an employee of an operator of a community health care facility providing care to the principal.

I declare that I am not related to the principal by blood, marriage, or adoption and that to the best of my knowledge I am not entitled to and do not have a claim against any part of the estate of the principal on the death of the principal under a will or by operation of law.

Witness Signature: ________________________________

Print Name: ________________________________

Date: ________________________________

Address: ________________________________

Witness Signature: ________________________________

Print Name: ________________________________

Date: ________________________________

Address: ________________________________

NOTICE TO PERSON MAKING A DECLARATION FOR MENTAL HEALTH TREATMENT

This is an important legal document. It creates a declaration for mental health treatment. Before signing this document, you should know these important facts:

This document allows you to make decisions in advance about mental health treatment and specifically three types of mental health treatment: psychoactive medication, convulsive therapy, and emergency mental health treatment. The instructions that you include in this declaration will be followed only if a court believes that you are incapacitated to make treatment decisions. Otherwise, you will be considered able to give or withhold consent for the treatments.

This document will continue in effect for a period of three years unless you become incapacitated to participate in mental health treatment decisions. If this occurs, the directive will continue in effect until you are no longer incapacitated.

You have the right to revoke this document in whole or in part at any time you have not been determined to be incapacitated. YOU MAY NOT REVOKE THIS DECLARATION WHEN YOU ARE CONSIDERED BY A COURT TO BE INCAPACITATED. A revocation is effective when it is communicated to your attending physician or other health care provider.

If there is anything in this document that you do not understand, you should ask a lawyer to explain it to you. This declaration is not valid unless it is signed by two qualified witnesses who are personally known to you and who are present when you sign or acknowledge your signature.

CODE OF CRIMINAL PROCEDURE

INCOMPETENCY TO STAND TRIAL—§46B

§46B.003. Incompetency; Presumptions

(a) A person is incompetent to stand trial if the person does not have:

(1) sufficient present ability to consult with the person's lawyer with a reasonable degree of rational understanding; or

(2) a rational as well as factual understanding of the proceedings against the person.

(b) A defendant is presumed competent to stand trial and shall be found competent to stand trial unless proved incompetent by a preponderance of the evidence.

§46B.004. Raising the Issue of Incompetency to Stand Trial

(a) Either party may suggest by motion, or the trial court may suggest on its own motion, that the defendant may be incompetent to stand trial. A motion suggesting that the defendant may be incompetent to stand trial may be supported by affidavits setting out the facts on which the suggestion is made.

(b) If evidence suggesting the defendant may be incompetent to stand trial comes to the attention of the court, the court on its own motion shall suggest that the defendant may be incompetent to stand trial.

(c) On suggestion that the defendant may be incompetent to stand trial, the court shall determine by informal inquiry whether there is some evidence from any source that would support a finding that the defendant may be incompetent to stand trial.

(d) If the court determines there is evidence to support a finding of incompetency, the court, except as provided by Article 46B.005(d), shall stay all other proceedings in the case.

§46B.005. Determining Incompetency to Stand Trial

(a) If after an informal inquiry the court determines that evidence exists to support a finding of incompetency, the court shall order an examination under Subchapter B to determine whether the defendant is incompetent to stand trial.

(b) Except as provided by Subsection (c), the court shall hold a hearing under Subchapter C before determining whether the defendant is incompetent to stand trial.

(c) The court is not required to hold a hearing if:

(1) neither party requests a jury trial on the issue of incompetency;

(2) neither party opposes a finding of incompetency; and

(3) the court does not, on its own motion, determine that a hearing is necessary to determine incompetency.

(d) If the issue of the defendant's incompetency to stand trial is raised after the trial begins, the court may determine the issue at any time before sentencing. If the determination is delayed until after the return of a verdict, the court shall make the determination as soon as reasonably possible after the return. If a verdict of not guilty is returned, the court may not determine the issue of incompetency.

§46B.007. Admissibility of Statements and Certain Other Evidence

A statement made by a defendant during an examination or hearing on the defendant's incompetency, the testimony of an expert based on that statement, and evidence obtained as a result of that statement may not be admitted in evidence against the defendant in any criminal proceeding, other than at:

(1) a hearing on the defendant's incompetency; or

(2) any proceeding at which the defendant first introduces into evidence a statement, testimony, or evidence described by this section.

SUBCHAPTER B
EXAMINATION

§46B.021. Appointment of Experts

(a) On a suggestion that the defendant may be incompetent to stand trial, the court may appoint one or more disinterested experts to:

(1) examine the defendant and report to the court on the competency or incompetency of the defendant; and

(2) testify as to the issue of competency or incompetency of the defendant at any trial or hearing involving that issue.

(b) On a determination that evidence exists to support a finding of incompetency to stand trial, the court shall appoint one or more experts to perform the duties described by Subsection (a).

(c) An expert involved in the treatment of the defendant may not be appointed to examine the defendant under this article.

(d) The movant or other party as directed by the court shall provide to experts appointed under this article information relevant to a determination of the defendant's competency, including copies of the indictment or information, any supporting documents used to establish probable cause in the case, and previous mental health evaluation and treatment records.

(e) The court may appoint as experts under this chapter qualified psychiatrists or psychologists employed by the local mental health authority or local mental retardation authority. The local mental health authority or local mental retardation authority is entitled to compensation and reimbursement as provided by Article 46B.027.

(f) If a defendant wishes to be examined by an expert of the defendant's own choice, the court on timely request shall provide the expert with reasonable opportunity to examine the defendant.

§46B.022. Experts: Qualifications

(a) To qualify for appointment under this subchapter as an expert, a psychiatrist or psychologist must:

(1) as appropriate, be a physician licensed in this state or be a psychologist licensed in this state who has a doctoral degree in psychology; and

(2) have the following certification or experience or training:

(A) as appropriate, certification by:

(i) the American Board of Psychiatry and Neurology with added or special qualifications in forensic psychiatry; or

(ii) the American Board of Professional Psychology in forensic psychology; or

(B) experience or training consisting of:

(i) at least 24 hours of specialized forensic training relating to incompetency or insanity evaluations;

(ii) for an appointment made before January 1, 2005, at least five years of experience before January 1, 2004, in performing criminal forensic evaluations for courts; or

(iii) for an appointment made on or after January 1, 2005, at least five years of experience before January 1, 2004, in performing criminal forensic evaluations for courts and eight or more hours of continuing education relating to forensic evaluations, completed in the 12 months preceding the appointment and documented with the court.

(b) In addition to meeting qualifications required by Subsection (a), to be appointed as an expert a psychiatrist or psychologist must have completed six hours of required continuing education in courses in forensic psychiatry or psychology, as appropriate, in either of the reporting periods in the 24 months preceding the appointment.

(c) A court may appoint as an expert a psychiatrist or psychologist who does not meet the requirements of Subsections (a) and (b) only if exigent circumstances require the court to base the appointment on professional training or experience of the expert that directly provides the expert with a specialized expertise to examine the defendant that would not ordinarily be possessed by a psychiatrist or psychologist who meets the requirements of Subsections (a) and (b).

§46B.024. Factors Considered in Examination

During an examination under this subchapter and in any report based on that examination, an expert shall consider, in addition to other issues determined relevant by the expert, the following:

(1) the capacity of the defendant during criminal proceedings to:

(A) rationally understand the charges against the defendant and the potential consequences of the pending criminal proceedings;

(B) disclose to counsel pertinent facts, events, and states of mind;

(C) engage in a reasoned choice of legal strategies and options;

(D) understand the adversarial nature of criminal proceedings;

(E) exhibit appropriate courtroom behavior; and

(F) testify;

(2) whether the defendant has a diagnosable mental illness or is a person with mental retardation;

(3) the impact of the mental illness or mental retardation, if existent, on the defendant's capacity to engage with counsel in a reasonable and rational manner; and

(4) if the defendant is taking psychoactive or other medication:

(A) whether the medication is necessary to maintain the defendant's competency; and

(B) the effect, if any, of the medication on the defendant's appearance, demeanor, or ability to participate in the proceedings.

§46B.025. Expert's Report

(a) An expert's report to the court must state an opinion on a defendant's competency or incompetency to stand trial or explain why the expert is unable to state such an opinion and must also:

(1) identify and address specific issues referred to the expert for evaluation;

(2) document that the expert explained to the defendant the purpose of the evaluation, the persons to whom a report on the evaluation is provided, and the limits on rules of confidentiality applying to the relationship between the expert and the defendant;

(3) in general terms, describe procedures, techniques, and tests used in the examination and the purpose of each procedure, technique, or test; and

(4) state the expert's clinical observations, findings, and opinions on each specific issue referred to the expert by the court, and state specifically any issues on which the expert could not provide an opinion.

(b) If in the opinion of an expert appointed under Article 46B.021 the defendant is incompetent to proceed, the expert shall state in the report:

(1) the exact nature of the deficits resulting from the defendant's mental illness or mental retardation, if any, that impact the factors listed in Article 46B.024, contributing to the defendant's incompetency; and

(2) prospective treatment options, if any, appropriate for the defendant.

(c) An expert's report may not state the expert's opinion on the defendant's sanity at the time of the alleged offense, if in the opinion of the expert the defendant is incompetent to proceed.

§46B.026. Report Deadline

(a) Except as provided by Subsection (b), an expert examining the defendant shall provide the report on the defendant' s competency or incompetency to stand trial to the court, the attorney representing the state, and the attorney representing the defendant not later than the 30th day after the date on which the expert was ordered to examine the defendant and prepare the report.

(b) For good cause shown, the court may permit an expert to complete the examination and report and provide the report to the court and attorneys at a date later than the date required by Subsection (a).

SUBCHAPTER C
COURT-ORDERED EXAMINATION AND REPORT

§46C.101. Appointment of Experts

(a) If notice of intention to raise the insanity defense is filed under Article 46C.051, the court may, on its own motion or motion by the defendant, the defendant's counsel, or the attorney representing the state, appoint one or more disinterested experts to:

(1) examine the defendant with regard to the insanity defense; and

(2) testify as to the issue of insanity at any trial or hearing involving that issue.

(b) The court shall advise an expert appointed under this article of the facts and circumstances of the offense with which the defendant is charged and the elements of the insanity defense.

§46C.102. Expert's Qualifications

(a) The court may appoint qualified psychiatrists or psychologists as experts under this chapter. To qualify for appointment under this subchapter as an expert, a psychiatrist or psychologist must:

(1) as appropriate, be a physician licensed in this state or be a psychologist licensed in this state who has a doctoral degree in psychology; and

(2) have the following certification or experience or training:

(A) as appropriate, certification by:

(i) the American Board of Psychiatry and Neurology with added or special qualifications in forensic psychiatry; or

(ii) the American Board of Professional Psychology in forensic psychology; or

(B) experience or training consisting of:

(i) at least 24 hours of specialized forensic training relating to incompetency or insanity evaluations;

(ii) at least five years of experience in performing criminal forensic evaluations for courts; and

(iii) eight or more hours of continuing education relating to forensic evaluations, completed in the 12 months preceding the appointment and documented with the court.

(b) In addition to meeting qualifications required by Subsection (a), to be appointed as an expert a psychiatrist or psychologist must have completed six hours of required continuing education in courses in forensic psychiatry or psychology, as appropriate, in the 24 months preceding the appointment.

(c) A court may appoint as an expert a psychiatrist or psychologist who does not meet the requirements of Subsections (a) and (b) only if exigent circumstances require the court to base the appointment on professional training or experience of the expert that directly provides the expert with a specialized expertise to examine the defendant that would not ordinarily be possessed by a psychiatrist or psychologist who meets the requirements of Subsections (a) and (b).

§46C.103. Competency to Stand Trail: Concurrent Appointment

(a) An expert appointed under this subchapter to examine the defendant with regard to the insanity defense also may be appointed by the court to examine the defendant with regard to the defendant's competency to stand trial under Chapter 46B, if the expert files with the court separate written reports concerning the defendant's competency to stand trial and the insanity defense.

(b) Notwithstanding Subsection (a), an expert may not examine the defendant for purposes of determining the defendant's sanity and may not file a report regarding the defendant's sanity if in the opinion of the expert the defendant is incompetent to proceed.

§46C.104. Order Compelling Defendant to Submit to Examination

(a) For the purposes described by this chapter, the court may order any defendant to submit to examination, including a defendant who is free on bail. If the defendant fails or refuses to submit to examination, the court may order the defendant to custody for examination for a reasonable period not to exceed 21 days. Custody ordered by the court under this subsection may include custody at a facility operated by the department.

(b) If a defendant who has been ordered to a facility operated by the department for examination remains in the facility for a period that exceeds 21 days, the head of that facility shall cause the defendant to be immediately transported to the committing court and placed in the custody of the sheriff of the county in which the committing court is located. That county shall reimburse the facility for the mileage and per diem expenses of the personnel required to transport the defendant, calculated in accordance with the state travel rules in effect at that time.

(c) The court may not order a defendant to a facility operated by the department for examination without the consent of the head of that facility.

§46C.105. Reports Submitted by Experts

(a) A written report of the examination shall be submitted to the court not later than the 30th day after the date of the order of examination. The court shall provide copies of the report to the defense counsel and the attorney representing the state.

(b) The report must include a description of the procedures used in the examination and the examiner's observations and findings pertaining to the insanity defense.

(c) The examiner shall submit a separate report stating the examiner's observations and findings concerning:

(1) whether the defendant is presently a person with a mental illness and requires court-ordered mental health services under Subtitle C, Title 7, Health and Safety Code; or

(2) whether the defendant is presently a person with mental retardation.

§46C.106. Compensation of Experts

(a) The appointed experts shall be paid by the county in which the indictment was returned or information was filed.

(b) The county in which the indictment was returned or information was filed shall reimburse a facility operated by the department that accepts a defendant for examination under this subchapter for expenses incurred that are determined by the department to be reasonably necessary and incidental to the proper examination of the defendant.

§46C.107. Examination by Expert of Defendant's Choice

If a defendant wishes to be examined by an expert of the defendant's own choice, the court on timely request shall provide the examiner with reasonable opportunity to examine the defendant.

EDUCATION CODE

STATEWIDE PLAN FOR SERVICES TO CHILDREN WITH DISABILITIES—§29

§29.001. Statewide Plan

The agency shall develop, and modify as necessary, a statewide design, consistent with federal law, for the delivery of services to children with disabilities in this state that includes rules for the administration and funding of the special education program so that a free appropriate public education is available to all of those children between the ages of three and 21. The statewide design shall include the provision of services primarily through school districts and shared services arrangements, supplemented by regional education service centers. The agency shall also develop and implement a statewide plan with programmatic content that includes procedures designed to:

(1) ensure state compliance with requirements for supplemental federal funding for all state-administered programs involving the delivery of instructional or related services to students with disabilities;

(2) facilitate interagency coordination when other state agencies are involved in the delivery of instructional or related services to students with disabilities;

(3) periodically assess statewide personnel needs in all areas of specialization related to special education and pursue strategies to meet those needs through a consortium of representatives from regional education service centers, local education agencies, and institutions of higher education and through other available alternatives;

(4) ensure that regional education service centers throughout the state maintain a regional support function, which may include direct service delivery and a component designed to facilitate the placement of students with disabilities who cannot be appropriately served in their resident districts;

(5) allow the agency to effectively monitor and periodically conduct site visits of all school districts to ensure that rules adopted under this section are applied in a consistent and uniform manner, to ensure that districts are complying with those rules, and to ensure that annual statistical reports filed by the districts and not otherwise available through the Public Education Information Management System under Section 42.006, are accurate and complete;

(6) ensure that appropriately trained personnel are involved in the diagnostic and evaluative procedures operating in all districts and that those personnel routinely serve on district admissions, review, and dismissal committees;

(7) ensure that an individualized education program for each student with a disability is properly developed, implemented, and maintained in the least restrictive environment that is appropriate to meet the student's educational needs;

(8) ensure that, when appropriate, each student with a disability is provided an opportunity to participate in career and technology and physical education classes, in addition to participating in regular or special classes; and

(9) ensure that each student with a disability is provided necessary related services; and

(10) ensure that an individual assigned to act as a surrogate parent for a child with a disability, as provided by 20 U.S.C. Section 1415(b) and its subsequent amendments, is required to:

(A) complete a training program that complies with minimum standards established by agency rule;

(B) visit the child and the child's school;

(C) consult with persons involved in the child's education, including teachers, caseworkers, court-appointed volunteers, guardians ad litem, attorneys ad litem, foster parents, and caretakers;

(D) review the child's educational records;

(E) attend meetings of the child's admission, review, and dismissal committee;

(F) exercise independent judgment in pursuing the child's interests;

(G) and exercise the child's due process rights under applicable state and federal law.

§29.002. Definition

In this subchapter, "*special services*" means:

(1) *special instruction*, which may be provided by professional and paraprofessional personnel in the regular classroom or in an instructional arrangement described by Section 42.151; or

(2) *related services*, which are developmental, corrective, supportive, or evaluative services, not instructional in nature, that may be required for the proper development and implementation of a student's individualized education program.

§29.003. Eligibility Criteria

(a) The agency shall develop specific eligibility criteria based on the general classifications established by this section with reference to contemporary diagnostic or evaluative terminologies and techniques. Eligible students with disabilities shall enjoy the right to a free appropriate public education, which may include instruction in the regular classroom, instruction through special teaching, or instruction through contracts approved under this subchapter. Instruction shall be supplemented by the provision of related services when appropriate.

(b) A student is eligible to participate in a school district's special education program if the student:

(1) is not more than 21 years of age and has a visual or auditory impairment that prevents the student from being adequately or safely educated in public school without the provision of special services; or

(2) is at least three but not more than 21 years of age and has one or more of the following disabilities that prevents the student from being adequately or safely educated in public school without the provision of special services:

(A) physical disability;

(B) mental retardation;

(C) emotional disturbance;

(D) learning disability;

(E) autism;

(F) speech disability; or

(G) traumatic brain injury.

§29.004. Comprehensive Assessment

A written report of a comprehensive individual assessment of a student for purposes of special education services shall be completed not later than the 60th calendar day following the date on which the referral for assessment was initiated by school personnel, the student's parent or legal guardian, or another appropriate person. The assessment shall be conducted using procedures that are appropriate for the student's most proficient method of communication.

§29.005. Individualized Education Program

(a) Before a child is enrolled in a special education program of a school district, the district shall establish a committee composed of the persons required under 20 U.S.C. Section 1401(20) to develop the child's individualized education program.

(b) The committee shall develop the individualized education program by agreement of the committee members or, if those persons cannot agree, by an alternate method provided by the agency. Majority vote may not be used to determine the individualized education program.

(c) If the individualized education program is not developed by agreement, the written statement of the program required under 20 U.S.C. Section 1401(20) must include the basis of the disagreement.

(d) If the child's parent is unable to speak English, the district shall:

(1) provide the parent with a written or audiotaped copy of the child's individualized education program translated into Spanish if Spanish is the parent's native language; or

(2) if the parent's native language is a language other than Spanish, make a good faith effort to provide the parent with a written or audiotaped

copy of the child's individualized education program translated into the parent's native language.

§30.001. Coordination of Services to Children with Disabilities

(a) In this section, "*children with disabilities*" means students eligible to participate in a school district's special education program under §29.003.

(b) The commissioner, with the approval of the State Board of Education, shall develop and implement a plan for the coordination of services to children with disabilities in each region served by a regional education service center. The plan must include procedures for:

(1) identifying existing public or private educational and related services for children with disabilities in each region;

(2) identifying and referring children with disabilities who cannot be appropriately served by the school district in which they reside to other appropriate programs;

(3) assisting school districts to individually or cooperatively develop programs to identify and provide appropriate services for children with disabilities;

(4) expanding and coordinating services provided by regional education service centers for children with disabilities; and

(5) providing for special services, including special seats, books, instructional media, and other supplemental supplies and services required for proper instruction.

(c) The commissioner may allocate appropriated funds to regional education service centers or may otherwise spend those funds, as necessary, to implement this section.

§37.0021. Use of Confinement, Restraint, Seclusion and Time-Out

(a) It is the policy of this state to treat with dignity and respect all students, including students with disabilities who receive special education services under Subchapter A, Chapter 29. A student with a disability who receives special education services under Subchapter A, Chapter 29, may not be confined in a locked box, locked closet, or other specially designed locked space as either a discipline management practice or a behavior management technique.

(b) In this section:

(1) "*Restraint*" means the use of physical force or a mechanical device to significantly restrict the free movement of all/part of a student's body.

(2 "*Seclusion*" means a behavior management technique in which a student is confined in a locked box, locked closet, or locked room:

(A) that is designed solely to seclude a person; and

(B) that contains less than 50 square feet of space.

(3) *"Time-out"* means a behavior management technique in which, to provide a student with an opportunity to regain self-control, the student is separated from other students for a limited period in a setting:

(A) that is not locked; and

(B) from which the exit is not physically blocked by furniture, a closed door held shut from the outside, or another inanimate object.

(c) A school district employee or volunteer or an independent contractor of a district may not place a student in seclusion. This subsection does not apply to the use of seclusion in a court-ordered placement, other than a placement in an educational program of a school district, or in a placement or facility to which the following law, rules, or regulations apply:

(1) the Children's Health Act of 2000, Pub. L. No. 106-310, any subsequent amendments to that Act, any regulations adopted under that Act, or any subsequent amendments to those regulations;

(2) 40 T.A.C. Sections 720.1001-720.1013; or

(3) 25 T.A.C. Section 412.308(e).

(d) The commissioner by rule shall adopt procedures for the use of restraint and time-out by a school district employee or volunteer or an independent contractor of a district in the case of a student with a disability receiving special education services under Subchapter A, Chapter 29. A procedure adopted under this subsection must:

(1) be consistent with:

(A) professionally accepted practices and standards of student discipline and techniques for behavior management; and

(B) relevant health and safety standards; and

(2) identify any discipline management practice or behavior management technique that requires a district employee or volunteer or an independent contractor of a district to be trained before using that practice or technique.

(e) In the case of a conflict between a rule adopted under Subsection

(d) and a rule adopted under Subchapter A, Chapter 29, the rule adopted under Subsection (d) controls.

(f) For purposes of this subsection, "weapon" includes any weapon described under Section 37.007(a)(1). This section does not prevent a student's locked, unattended confinement in an emergency situation while awaiting the arrival of law enforcement personnel if:

(1) the student possesses a weapon; and

(2) the confinement is necessary to prevent the student from causing bodily harm to the student or another person.

(g) This section and any rules or procedures adopted under this section do not apply to:

(1) a peace officer while performing law enforcement duties;

(2) juvenile probation, detention, or corrections personnel; or

(3) an educational services provider with whom a student is placed by a judicial authority, unless the services are provided in an educational program of a school district.

§38.016. Psychotropic Drugs and Psychiatric Evaluations or Examinations

(a) In this section:

(1) "*Parent*" includes a guardian or other person in parental relation.

(2) "*Psychotropic drug*" means a substance that is:

(A) used in the diagnosis, treatment, or prevention of a disease or as a component of a medication; and

(B) intended to alter perception, emotion, or behavior.

(b) A school district employee may not:

(1) recommend that a student use a psychotropic drug; or

(2) suggest any particular diagnosis; or

(3) use the refusal by a parent to consent to administration of a psychotropic drug to a student, or to a psychiatric evaluation or examination of a student as grounds, by itself, for prohibiting the child from attending a class or participating in a school-related activity.

(c) Subsection (b) does not:

(1) prevent an appropriate referral under the child find system required under 20 U.S.C. Section 1412, as amended; or

(2) prohibit a school district employee who is a registered nurse, advanced nurse practitioner, physician, or certified or appropriately credentialed mental health professional from recommending that a child be evaluated by an appropriate medical practitioner; or

3) prohibit a school employee from discussing any aspect of a child's behavior or academic progress with the child's parent or another school district employee.

(d) The board of trustees of each school district shall adopt a policy to ensure implementation and enforcement of this section.

(e) An act in violation of Subsection (b) does not override the immunity from personal liability granted in Section 22.051 or other law or the district's sovereign and governmental immunity.

Administrative Code

(Title 19, Part 2, Chapter 89, Subchapter 89, Subchapter AA, Division 2)

Rule 89.1053 Procedures for Use of Restraint and Time-Out

(a) **Requirement to Implement**

In addition to the requirements of 34 Code of Federal Regulations (CFR), §300.346(a)(2)(i) and (c), school districts and charter schools must implement the provisions of this section regarding the use of restraint and time-out. In accordance with the provisions of Texas Education Code (TEC), §37.0021 (Use of Confinement, Restraint, Seclusion, and Time-Out), it is the policy of the state to treat with dignity and respect all students, including students with disabilities who receive special education services under TEC, Chapter 29, Subchapter A.

(b) **Definitions**

(1) "*Emergency*" means a situation in which a student's behavior poses a threat of:

(A) imminent, serious physical harm to the student or others; or

(B) imminent, serious property destruction.

(2) "*Restraint*" means the use of physical force or a mechanical device to significantly restrict the free movement of all or a portion of the student's body.

(3) "*Time-out*" means a behavior management technique in which, to provide a student with an opportunity to regain self-control, the student is separated from other students for a limited period in a setting:

(A) that is not locked; and

(B) from which the exit is not physically blocked by furniture, a closed door held shut from the outside, or another inanimate object.

(c) **Use of Restraint**

A school employee, volunteer, or independent contractor may use restraint only in an emergency as defined in subsection (b) of this section and with the following limitations.

(1) Restraint shall be limited to the use of such reasonable force as is necessary to address the emergency.

(2) Restraint shall be discontinued at the point at which the emergency no longer exists.

(3) Restraint shall be implemented in such a way as to protect the health and safety of the student and others.

(4) Restraint shall not deprive the student of basic human necessities.

(d) **Training on Use of Restraint**

Training for school employees, volunteers, or independent contractors shall be provided according to the following requirements.

(1) Not later than April 1, 2003, a core team of personnel on each campus must be trained in the use of restraint, and the team must include a campus administrator or designee and any general or special education personnel likely to use restraint.

(2) After April 1, 2003, personnel called upon to use restraint in an emergency and who have not received prior training must receive training within 30 school days following the use of restraint.

(3) Training on use of restraint must include prevention and de-escalation techniques and provide alternatives to the use of restraint.

(4) All trained personnel shall receive instruction in current professionally accepted practices and standards regarding behavior management and the use of restraint.

(e) **Documentation and Notification on Use of Restraint**

In a case in which restraint is used, school employees, volunteers, or independent contractors shall implement the following documentation requirements.

(1) On the day restraint is utilized, the campus administrator or designee must be notified verbally or in writing regarding the use of restraint.

(2) On the day restraint is utilized, a good faith effort shall be made to verbally notify the parent(s) regarding the use of restraint.

(3) Written notification of the use of restraint must be placed in the mail or otherwise provided to the parent within one school day of the use of restraint.

(4) Written documentation regarding the use of restraint must be placed in the student's special education eligibility folder in a timely manner so the information is available to the ARD committee when it considers the impact of the student's behavior on the student's learning and/or the creation or revision of a behavioral intervention plan (BIP).

(5) Written notification to the parent(s) and documentation to the student's special education eligibility folder shall include the following:

(A) name of the student;

(B) name of the staff member(s) administering the restraint;

(C) date of the restraint and the time the restraint began and ended;

(D) location of the restraint;

(E) nature of the restraint;

(F) a description of the activity in which the student was engaged immediately preceding the use of restraint;

(G) the behavior that prompted the restraint;

(H) the efforts made to de-escalate the situation and alternatives to restraint that were attempted; and

(I) information documenting parent contact and notification.

(f) Clarification Regarding Restraint

The provisions adopted under this section do not apply to the use of physical force or a mechanical device which does not significantly restrict the free movement of all or a portion of the student's body. Restraint that involves significant restriction as referenced in subsection (b)(2) of this section does not include:

(1) physical contact or appropriately prescribed adaptive equipment to promote normative body positioning and/or physical functioning;

(2) limited physical contact with a student to promote safety (e.g., holding a student's hand), prevent a potentially harmful action (e.g., running into the street), teach a skill, redirect attention, provide guidance to a location, or provide comfort;

(3) limited physical contact or appropriately prescribed adaptive equipment to prevent a student from engaging in ongoing, repetitive self-injurious behaviors, with the expectation that instruction will be reflected in the individualized education program (IEP) as required by 34 CFR §300.346(a)(2)(i) and (c) to promote student learning and reduce and/or prevent the need for ongoing intervention; or

(4) seat belts and other safety equipment used to secure students during transportation.

(g) Use of Time-Out

A school employee, volunteer, or independent contractor may use time-out in accordance with subsection (b)(3) of this section with the following limitations.

(1) Physical force or threat of physical force shall not be used to place a student in time-out.

(2) Time-out may only be used in conjunction with an array of positive behavior intervention strategies and techniques and must be included in the student's IEP and/or BIP if it is utilized on a recurrent basis to increase or decrease a targeted behavior.

(3) Use of time-out shall not be implemented in a fashion that precludes the ability of the student to be involved in and progress in the general curriculum and advance appropriately toward attaining the annual goals specified in the student's IEP.

(h) **Training on Use of Time-Out**

Training for school employees, volunteers, or independent contractors shall be provided according to the following requirements.

(1) Not later than April 1, 2003, general or special education personnel who implement time-out based on requirements established in a student's IEP and/or BIP must be trained in the use of time-out.

(2) After April 1, 2003, newly-identified personnel called upon to implement time-out based on requirements established in a student's IEP and/or BIP must receive training in the use of time-out within 30 school days of being assigned the responsibility for implementing time-out.

(3) Training on the use of time-out must be provided as part of a program which addresses a full continuum of positive behavioral intervention strategies, and must address the impact of time-out on the ability of the student to be involved in and progress in the general curriculum and advance appropriately toward attaining the annual goals specified in the student's IEP.

(4) All trained personnel shall receive instruction in current professionally accepted practices and standards regarding behavior management and the use of time-out.

(i) **Documentation on Use of Time-Out**

Necessary documentation or data collection regarding the use of time-out, if any, must be addressed in the IEP or BIP. The admission, review, and dismissal (ARD) committee must use any collected data to judge the effectiveness of the intervention and provide a basis for making determinations regarding its continued use.

(j) **Student Safety**

Any behavior management technique and/or discipline management practice must be implemented in such a way as to protect the health and safety of the student and others. No discipline management practice may be calculated to inflict injury, cause harm, demean, or deprive the student of basic human necessities.

(k) **Data Reporting**

Beginning with the 2003-2004 school year, with the exception of actions covered by subsection (f) of this section, data regarding the use of restraint must be electronically reported to the Texas Education Agency in accordance with reporting standards specified by the Agency.

(l) **Excluded Provisions**

The provisions adopted under this section do not apply to:

(1) a peace officer while performing law enforcement duties;

(2) juvenile probation, detention, or corrections personnel; or

(3) an educational services provider with whom a student is placed by a judicial authority, unless the services are provided in an educational program of a school district.

RULES RELATING TO THE LICENSING AND REGULATION OF SOCIAL WORKERS[1]

(TITLE 22—EXAMINING BOARDS, PART 34, CHAPTER 781)

ALERT: Rules guiding the social work profession can be changed at any time. It is the licensee's responsibility to visit the Texas State Board of Social Worker Examiners website on a regular basis to check for any changes to the rules. Inclusion of the most recent approved set of rules (5/26/06) in this book in no way guarantees that they are the most current rules. http://www.dshs.state.tx.us/socialwork/default.shtm

---

SUBCHAPTER A. GENERAL PROVISIONS.

§781.101. Purpose and Scope

(a) The purpose of this chapter is to implement the provisions in the Social Work Practice Act (Act), Occupations Code Chapter 505, concerning the licensure and regulation of social workers.

(b) The Act restricts the use of the titles "social worker," "licensed master social worker," "licensed social worker," "licensed baccalaureate social worker," "licensed clinical social worker" or "social work associate" or any other title that implies licensure or certification in professional social work services.

(c) A person not represented to the public, directly or indirectly, as a social worker is exempt from this chapter.

(d) This chapter covers the organization, administration, and general procedures and policies of the Texas State Board of Social Worker Examiners.

(e) The Act and this chapter apply to every licensee even if the licensee is involved in activities or services exempt under the Act, §505.003.

§781.102. Definitions

The following words and terms, when used in this chapter, shall have the following meanings, unless the context clearly indicates otherwise.

(1) *Accredited colleges* or universities—An educational institution that is accredited by an agency recognized by the Texas Higher Education Coordinating Board.

(2) *Act*—The Social Work Practice Act, Occupations Code, Chapter 505.

---

1 Texas State Board of Social Worker Examiners •Department of State Health Services •1100 West 49th Street •Austin, TX 78756-3183 •512/719-3521 •800/232-3162 •Fax: 512/834-6677 • lsw@dshs.state.tx.us • http://www.dshs.state.tx.us/socialwork/

(3) *ALJ*—A person within the State Office of Administrative Hearings who conducts hearings under this chapter on behalf of the board.

(4) *Agency*—A public or private employer, contractor or business entity providing social work services.

(5) *AMEC*—alternative method of examining competency, as referenced in Occupations Code, §505.356(3).

(6) *APA*—The Administrative Procedure Act, Government Code, Chapter 2001.

(7) *Association of Social Work Boards* (ASWB)—National organization representing regulatory boards of social work. Administers the national examinations utilized in the assessment for licensure.

(8) *Board*—Texas State Board of Social Worker Examiners.

(9) *Case record*—Any information related to a client and the services provided to that client, however recorded and stored.

(10) *Client*—An individual, family, couple, group or organization that seeks or receives social work services from a person identified as a social worker who is either licensed or unlicensed by the board. An individual, family, couple, group or organization remains a client until the formal termination of services.

(11) *Clinical social work*—A specialty within the practice of social work that requires the application of social work theory, knowledge, methods, ethics, and the professional use of self to restore or enhance social, psychosocial, or biopsychosocial functioning of individuals, couples, families, groups, and/or persons who are adversely affected by social or psychosocial stress or health impairment. The practice of Clinical Social Work requires the application of specialized clinical knowledge and advanced clinical skills in the areas of assessment, diagnosis, and treatment of mental, emotional, and behavioral disorders, conditions and addictions, including severe mental illness in adults and serious emotional disturbances in children. Treatment methods include the provision of individual, marital, couple, family, and group therapy and psychotherapy. Clinical social workers are qualified to use the Diagnostic and Statistical Manual of Mental Disorders (DSM), the International Classification of Diseases (ICD), and other diagnostic classification systems in assessment, diagnosis, and other activities.

(12) *Clinical supervision*—An interactional professional relationship between a supervisor and a social worker that provides evaluation and direction over the supervisee's practice of clinical social work and promotes continued development of the social worker's knowledge, skills, and abilities to engage in the practice of clinical social work in an ethical and competent manner.

(13) *Confidential information*—Individually identifiable information obtained from a client or records relating to a client, including

the client's identity, demographic information collected from an individual, that relates to the past, present, or future physical or mental health or condition of an individual; the provision of social work services to an individual; the past, present, or future payment for the provision of social work services to an individual; and identifies the individual or with respect to which there is a reasonable basis to believe the information can be used to identify the individual which is not discloseable under applicable law or court rules of evidence. Client information is "confidential" if it is intended to be disclosed to third persons to further the interest of the client in the diagnosis, examination, evaluation, or treatment, or those reasonably necessary for the transmission of the communication, or those who are participating in the diagnosis, examination, evaluation, or treatment under the direction of the professional, including members of the patient's family.

(14) *Completed application*—The official social work application form, fees and all supporting documentation which meets the criteria set out in this title (relating to Required Application Materials).

(15) *Contested case*—A proceeding in accordance with the APA and this chapter, including, but not limited to, rule enforcement and licensing, in which the legal rights, duties, or privileges of a party are to be determined by the board after an opportunity for an adjudicative hearing.

(16) *Counseling*—A method used by social workers to assist individuals, couples, families or groups in learning how to solve problems and make decisions about personal, health, social, educational, vocational, financial, and other interpersonal concerns.

(17) *Consultation*—To provide advice, opinions and to confer with other professionals regarding social work practice.

(18) *Continuing education*—Formal or informal education or trainings, which are oriented to maintain, improve or enhance social work practice.

(19) *Council on Social Work Education* (CSWE)—The national organization that accredits social work education schools and programs.

(20) *Department*—Department of State Health Services.

(21) *Detrimental to the client*—An act or omission of a professional responsibility that is damaging to the physical, mental, or financial status of the client.

(22) *Direct practice*—The provision of services, research, system linkage, system development, maintenance and enhancement of social and psychosocial functioning of clients.

(23) *Dual relationship*—Dual or multiple relationships occur when social workers relate to clients in more than one capacity, whether it be before,

during or after the professional, social, or business relationship. Dual or multiple relationships can occur simultaneously or consecutively.

(24) *Endorsement*—The process whereby the board reviews requirements for licensure completed while under the jurisdiction of a different regulatory board from another state. The board may accept, deny or grant partial credit for requirements completed in a different jurisdiction.

(25) *Examination*—A standardized test or examination of social work knowledge, skills and abilities, which has been approved by the board.

(26) *Exploitation*—An unequal balance is inherent in the client/professional relationship and may be present in the professional/professional relationship. To use this power imbalance for the personal benefit of the professional at the expense of the client or another professional is exploitation. Exploitation may take financial, business, emotional, sexual, verbal, religious and/or relational forms.

(27) *Exploitive behavior*—A pattern, practice or scheme of conduct that can reasonably be construed as being primarily for the purposes of meeting the needs or being to the benefit of the social worker rather than in the best interest of the client or at the expense of another professional. Exploitation may take financial, business, emotional, sexual, verbal, religious and/or relational forms.

(28) *Family systems*—An open, on-going, goal-seeking, self-regulating, social system. Certain features such as its unique structuring of gender, race, nationality and generation set it apart from other social systems. Each individual family system is shaped by its own particular structural features (size, complexity, composition, life stage), the psychobiological characteristics of its individual members (age, race, nationality, gender, fertility, sexual orientation, health and temperament) and its socio-cultural and historic position in its larger environment.

(29) *Formal hearing*—A hearing or proceeding in accordance with this chapter, including a contested case as defined in this section to address the issues of a contested case.

(30) *Flagrant*—Obviously inconsistent with what is right or proper as to appear to be a flouting of law or morality.

(31) *Fraud*—Any misrepresentation or omission by a social worker related to professional qualifications, services, or related activities or information that benefits the social worker.

(32) *Full-time experience*—Social work services totaling 30 or more hours per week.

(33) *Group supervision*—Supervision that involves a minimum of two and no more than six supervisees in a supervision hour.

(34) *Health care professional*—A licensee or any other person licensed, certified, or registered by the State of Texas in a health related profession.

(35) *Home study*—A formal written evaluation or social study to determine what is the best interest of a minor child or other dependent person.

(36) *Independent practice*—The practice of social work services outside the jurisdiction of an organizational setting, after completion of all applicable supervision requirements, in which the social worker assumes responsibility and accountability for the nature and quality of the services provided to clients in exchange for direct payment or third party reimbursement.

(37) *Indirect practice*—Work on behalf of the client utilizing negotiation, education, advocacy, administration, research, policy development and resource location that does not involve immediate or personal contact with the clients being served.

(38) *Individual supervision*—Supervision of one supervisee during the supervision session.

(39) *Investigator*—A professional utilized by the board in the investigation of allegations of professional misconduct.

(40) *LBSW*—Licensed Baccalaureate Social Worker.

(41) *LCSW*—Licensed Clinical Social Worker.

(42) *License*—A regular, provisional, or temporary license or recognition issued by the board unless the content of the rule indicates otherwise.

(43) *Licensee*—A person licensed or recognized by the board to perform professional social work practice.

(44) *LMSW*—Licensed Master Social Worker.

(45) *LMSW-AP*—Licensed master social worker-advanced practitioner.

(46) *Non-clinical social work*—The areas of social work practice that include community organization, planning, administration, teaching, research, administrative supervision, non-clinical consultation and other related social work activities.

(47) *Part-time*—Social work services totaling less than 30 hours per week.

(48) *Party*—Each person, governmental agency, or officer or employee of a governmental agency named by the ALJ as having a justiciable interest in the matter being considered, or any person, governmental agency, or officer or employee of a governmental agency meeting the requirements of a party as prescribed by applicable law.

(49) *Persistently*—Existing for a long or longer than usual time or continuously.

(50) *Person*—An individual, corporation, partnership, or other legal entity.

(51) *Pleading*—Any written allegation filed by a party concerning its claim or position.

(52) *Psychotherapy*—The use of treatment methods utilizing a specialized, formal interaction between a clinical social worker and an individual, couple, family, or group in which a therapeutic relationship is established, maintained and sustained to understand intrapersonal, interpersonal and psychosocial dynamics, and the diagnosis and treatment of mental, emotional, and behavioral disorders, conditions and addictions.

(53) *Reciprocity*—The granting of an official license based on the current status of licensure in a different jurisdiction. Reciprocity is granted based on the formal written agreement between the board and regulatory body in the other jurisdiction.

(54) *Recognition*—Authorization from the board to engage in the independent or specialty practice of social work services.

(55) *Rules*—Provisions in this chapter specifying the implementation of statute and operations of the board and individuals affected by the Act.

(56) *Sexual contact*—Any touching or behavior that can be construed as sexual in nature.

(57) *Sexual exploitation*—A pattern, practice or scheme of exploitative behavior, which may include sexual contact.

(58) *Social Work Case Management*—The use of a biopsychosocial perspective to assess, evaluate, implement, monitor and advocate for services on behalf of and in collaboration with the identified client.

(59) *Social worker*—A person licensed under the Act.

(60) *Social work practice*—Services and actions performed as an employee, independent practitioner, consultant, or volunteer for compensation or pro bono to effect changes in human behavior, a person's emotional responses, interpersonal relationships, and the social conditions of individuals, families, groups, organizations, and communities. For the purpose of this definition, the practice of social work is guided by special knowledge, acquired through formal social work education development and behavior within the context of the social environment, and methods to enhance the functioning of individuals, families, groups, communities, and social welfare organizations. Social work practice involves the disciplined application of social work values, principles, and methods, including psychotherapy, marriage and family therapy, couples therapy, group therapy, case management, supervision of social work services, counseling, assessment, and evaluation. Social work practice may also be referred to as social work services, of social welfare policies and services, social welfare systems and resources, human services.

(61) *Supportive counseling*—The methods used by social worker to help individuals create and maintain adaptive patterns. Such methods may include building community resources and networks, linking clients with services and resources, educating clients and informing the public, helping clients identify and build strengths, leading community groups, and providing reassurance and support. This type of social work is not considered clinical social work.

(62) *Supervisor*—A person meeting the requirements set out in §781.302 of this title (relating to Supervisor Requirements), to supervise a licensee towards the LCSW, LMSW-AP or Independent Practice recognition.

(63) *Supervision*—The professional interaction between a supervisor and a social worker in which the supervisor evaluates and directs the services provided by the social worker and promotes continued development of the social worker's knowledge, skills and abilities to provide social work services in an ethical and competent manner.

(64) *Supervision hour*—A supervision hour is a minimum of 60 minutes in length.

(65) *Telepractice*—Interactive service delivery where the client resides in one location and the professional in another.

(66) *Termination*—The end of professional services, meetings, and billing for services.

(67) *Texas Open Meetings Act*—Government Code, Chapter 551.

(68) *Texas Public Information Act*—Government Code, Chapter 552.

(69) *Waiver*—The suspension of educational, professional, and/or examination requirements for applicants who meet the criteria for licensure under special conditions based on appeal to the board.

SUBCHAPTER B. THE BOARD

§781.201. Board Rules

(a) The purpose of this section is to delineate the board's procedures for the submission, consideration, and disposition of a petition to the board to adopt a rule.

(b) Submission of the petition.

(1) Any person may petition the board to adopt a rule.

(2) The petition shall be in writing; shall state the petitioner's name, address, and phone number; and shall contain the following:

(A) a brief explanation of a justification for the proposed rule;

(B) the text of the proposed rule prepared in a manner to indicate the words to be added or deleted from the current text, if any;

(C) a statement of the statutory or other authority under which the rule is to be promulgated; and

(D) the public benefit anticipated as a result of adopting the rule or the anticipated injury or inequity which could result from the failure to adopt the proposed rule.

(3) The petition shall be filed with the board office.

(4) The board office may determine the petition does not contain the information described in paragraph (2) of this subsection and shall return the petition to the petitioner.

(c) Consideration and disposition of the petition.

(1) Except as otherwise provided in subsection (d) of this section, the executive director shall submit a completed petition to the board for consideration.

(2) Within 60 days after receipt of the petition, the board shall deny the petition or institute rulemaking procedures in accordance with the APA, the Government Code, Chapter 2001. The board may deny parts of the petition or institute rulemaking procedures on parts of the petition.

(3) If the board denies the petition, the board shall give the petitioner written notice of the board's denial, including the board's reasons for the denial.

(4) If the board initiates rule-making procedures, the version of the rule that the board proposes may differ from the version proposed by the petitioner.

(d) Subsequent petitions to adopt the same or similar rules. All initial petitions for the adoption of a rule shall be presented to and decided by the board in accordance with the provisions of subsections (b) and (c) of this section. The board may refuse to consider a subsequent petition for the adoption of the same or similar rules submitted within six months after the date of an initial position.

§781.202. Board Meetings

(a) The board shall hold at least one meeting each year and additional meetings as necessary.

(b) The chairperson may call a meeting after consultation with board members or by a majority of members so voting at a meeting.

(c) Meetings shall be announced and conducted under the provisions of the Texas Open Meetings Act.

(d) The chairperson may invite comments or statements from non-board members on all agenda items, but may limit the time allotted to each individual. The board may not act on comments or statements related to issues not on the agenda.

(e) Interpreters and other reasonable accommodations necessary to facilitate public participation will be made available as requested. The executive director must receive notice that reasonable accommodations will be needed at least 10 days in advance of the board or committee meeting.

§781.203. Board Training

A person who is appointed to and qualifies for office as a member of the board may not vote, deliberate, or be counted as a member in attendance at a meeting of the board until the person completes a training program that meets the requirements established in the Act.

§781.204. Transaction of Official Board Business.

(a) The board may transact official business only when in a legally constituted meeting with a quorum present. A quorum of the board necessary to conduct official business is five members.

(b) The board shall not be bound in any way by any statement or action on the part of any board or staff member except when a statement or action is pursuant to specific instructions of the board.

(c) Robert's Rules of Order Revised shall be the basis of parliamentary decisions except as otherwise provided in this chapter.

§781.205. Board Agendas

(a) The executive director shall be responsible for preparing and submitting an agenda to each member of the board prior to each meeting which includes items requested by members, items required by law, and other matters of board business which have been approved for discussion by the chairperson.

(b) Requests for items to be placed on the agenda must be submitted to the executive director at least 30 days in advance of the scheduled meeting.

(c) The official agenda of a meeting shall be filed with the Texas Secretary of State as required by law.

§781.206. Board Minutes

(a) The minutes of a board meeting are official only when affixed with the original signature of the chairperson.

(b) Drafts of the minutes of each meeting shall be forwarded to each member of the board for review and comments or corrections prior to approval by the board.

(c) The official minutes of the board meetings shall be kept in the office of the executive director and shall be available to any person desiring to examine them.

§781.207. Elections

(a) At the first meeting following the last day of January of each year, the board shall elect a vice-chair.

(b) A vacancy, which occurs in the office of vice-chair, may be filled at any meeting.

§781.208. Officers of the Board

(a) Chair.

(1) The chair shall preside at all meetings of the full board at which he or she is in attendance and perform all duties prescribed by law or this chapter.

(2) The chair is authorized by the board to make day-to-day decisions regarding board activities in order to facilitate the responsiveness and effectiveness of the board.

(b) Vice-chair.

(1) The vice-chair shall perform the duties of the chair in case of the absence or disability of the chair.

(2) In case the office of the chair becomes vacant, the vice-chair shall serve until a successor is appointed.

§781.209. Committees of the Board

(a) The board or the chair may establish committees deemed necessary to carry out board responsibilities.

(b) The chair shall appoint members of the board to serve on committees and shall appoint the committee chairs.

(c) Only members of the board may be appointed to board committees.

(d) Committee chairs shall make regular reports to the board in interim written reports or at regular meetings.

(e) Committees may direct all reports or other materials to the executive director for distribution.

(f) Committees shall meet when called by the committee chair or when so directed by the board or the board chair.

(g) Each committee shall consist of least one public member and one professional member, unless the board authorizes otherwise. At least one public member of the board shall be appointed to any board committee established to review a complaint filed with the board or review an enforcement action against a license holder related to a complaint filed with the board.

§781.210. Executive Director

(a) The executive director of the board shall be an employee of the department who serves as the administrator of board activities.

(b) The executive director serves at the will of the board.

(c) The executive director shall keep the minutes of the meetings and proceedings of the board and shall be the custodian of the files and records of the board unless the board designates another custodian.

(d) The executive director shall exercise general supervision over persons employed in the administration of the Act. The executive director may delegate responsibilities to other staff members when appropriate.

(e) The executive director shall be responsible for the investigation and presentation of complaints.

(f) The executive director shall be responsible for all correspondence for the board and obtain, assemble, or prepare reports and information that the board may direct, or as authorized or required by the department or other agency with appropriate statutory authority.

(g) The executive director shall have the responsibility of assembling and evaluating materials submitted by applicants for licensure and renewal. Determinations made by the executive director that propose denial of licensure are subject to the approval of the appropriate committee of the board or the board which shall make the final decision on the eligibility of the applicants.

§781.211. Reimbursement for Expenses

(a) A board member is entitled to per diem in the same amount set for state employees by the General Appropriations Act and travel expenses to and from meetings.

(b) Payment to members of per diem and transportation expenses shall be on official department vouchers.

§781.212. Official Records of the Board

(a) Records that are public may be reviewed by inspection or duplication, or both in accordance with the Texas Public Information Act. Confidential records will not be made available.

(b) When any person's request would be unreasonably disruptive to the ongoing business of the office or when the safety of any record is at issue, physical access by inspection may be denied and the requester will be provided the option of receiving copies at the requester's cost.

(c) Applicable costs of duplication shall be paid by the requester at the time of or before the duplicated records are sent or given to the requester. The charge for copies shall be the same as set by the department for copies.

(d) The rules of procedure for inspection and duplication of public records contained in the Texas Public Information Act shall apply to requests received by the board.

§781.213. Impartiality and Non-discrimination

(a) The board shall make all decisions in the discharge of its statutory authority without regard to any person's age, gender, race, color, religion, national origin, disability, sexual orientation, or political affiliation.

(b) Any board member who is unable to be impartial in the determination of an applicant's eligibility for licensure or in a disciplinary action against a licensee shall so declare this to the board and shall not participate in any board proceedings involving that applicant or licensee.

§781.214. Applicants with Disabilities

(a) The board shall comply with applicable provisions of the Americans with Disabilities Act.

(b) Applicants with disabilities shall inform the board in advance of any reasonable accommodations needed.

§781.215. The License

(a) The board shall prepare and provide to each licensee a license, which contains the licensee's name and license number.

(b) Regular licenses shall be signed by the board chairperson and executive director and be affixed with the seal of the board.

(c) Temporary and provisional licenses shall be printed on board letterhead and signed by the executive director.

(d) All licenses issued by the board remain the property of the board and must be surrendered to the board on demand. The board maintains jurisdiction over a licensee until the license is returned to the board.

§781.216. Roster of Licensees

(a) The board shall publish a roster of licensees at its discretion.

(b) The roster of licensees shall include, but not be limited to, the name and address of current licensees.

(c) The board shall mail a copy of the roster to each licensee, and upon request, copies to other state agencies and the general public.

§781.217. Fees

(a) The following are the board's fees:

  (1) application fee for all licenses or specialty recognition—$20;

  (2) license fee for LBSW, or LMSW—$60 biennially;

  (3) renewal fee for LBSW or LMSW—$80 biennially;

  (4) license fee for LCSW—$100 biennially;

  (5) renewal fee for LCSW—$100 biennially;

  (6) additional license fee for specialty recognition (AP or Independent Practice)—$20 biennially;

  (7) additional or replacement license fee—$10;

  (8) fee for late renewal:

    (A) 1-90 days—renewal fee plus fee equal to one-half the current contracted examination fee rounded to the nearest dollar amount; or

    (B) 91 days, but less than one year—renewal fee plus fee equal to the current contracted examination fee rounded to the nearest dollar amount.

(9) inactive status fee—$30 biennially;

(10) returned check fee—$25;

(11) written license verification fee—$10 per verification copy;

(12) specialty license verification fee—$10 per verification copy;

(13) student loan default reinstatement fee—$35;

(14) continuing education sponsor application fee—$50 annually;

(15) delinquent child support administrative fee—$35;

(16) legislatively mandated fees per licensee for the operation of the Office of Patient Protection per application and renewal as legislatively established;

(17) legislatively mandated fees per licensee for the boards participation in the Texas On-line per application and renewal as legislatively established;

(18) approved supervisor fee—$25 annually;

(19) AMEC participant administrative fee—Fee equal to the current contract examination fee;

(20) Petition for re-examination fee—$20 per petition; and

(21) Temporary license fee—$30.

(b) Fees paid to the board by applicants are not refundable except in accordance with §781.305 of this title (relating to Application for Licensure).

(c) Remittances submitted to the board in payment of fees may be in the form of a personal check, cashier's check, or money order; however, repayment of funds after a returned check, including the returned check fee, must be in the form of a cashier's check or money order.

(d) A license which is issued by the board, but for which a check is returned (for example, insufficient funds, account closed, or payment stopped) i s invalid. A license will be considered expired and the licensee in violation of board rules until the receipt and processing of the renewal fee and returned check fee by the board.

SUBCHAPTER C. LICENSES AND LICENSING PROCESS

§781.301. Qualifications for Licensure

(a) The following education and experience is required for the specified licenses and specialty recognitions:

(1) *Licensed Clinical Social Worker (LCSW).*

(A) Must be licensed as an LMSW.

(B) Obtain 3000 hours of Board approved supervised professional full-time clinical employment experience over a minimum two-year period, but within a maximum four-year period or its equivalent if the experience was completed in another state.

(C) Complete a minimum of 100 hours of face-to-face supervision, over the course of the 3000 hours of full-time experience, with a board-approved supervisor. Supervised experience must have occurred within the five previous calendar years occurring from the date of application.

(D) Passing score on the clinical exam administered nationally by ASWB.

(2) *Licensed Master Social Worker (LMSW).*

(A) A doctoral or master's degree in social work from a CSWE accredited social work program.

(B) Passing score on the intermediate or master's exam administered nationally by ASWB.

(3) *Licensed Master Social Worker-Advanced Practitioner (LMSW-AP).*

(A) Must be licensed as an LMSW.

(B) Obtain 3000 hours of Board approved supervised professional full-time non-clinical employment experience over a minimum two-year period, but within a maximum four-year period or its equivalent if the experience was completed in another state.

(C) Complete a minimum of 100 hours of face-to-face supervision, over the course of the 3000 hours of full-time experience, with a board-approved supervisor. Supervised experience must have occurred within the five previous calendar years occurring from the date of application.

(D) Passing score on the advanced or advanced generalist examination administered nationally by ASWB.

(4) *Licensed Baccalaureate Social Worker (LBSW).*

(A) A baccalaureate degree in social work from a CSWE accredited social work program.

(B) Passing score on the basic exam administered nationally by ASWB.

(b) Only a person who is licensed and has been recognized by the board for independent practice is qualified for the independent practice of social work.

(1) A LCSW may provide any clinical or non-clinical social work services in either an employment or independent practice setting.

(2) An LMSW-AP, LBSW or LMSW recognized for independent practice must restrict his or her independent practice to the provision of non-clinical social work services.

(3) A licensee must not engage in any independent practice that falls within the definition of social work practice (relating to definitions) without being licensed and recognized by the board unless the person is licensed in another profession and acting solely within the scope of that license. The person may not use the titles "licensed clinical social worker," "licensed master social worker," "licensed social worker," "licensed baccalaureate social worker," or "social work associate" or any other title or initials that states or implies licensure or certification in social work unless one holds the appropriate license or recognition.

(4) A licensee who is not recognized for independent practice may not provide direct social work services to clients from a location that she or he owns or leases and that is not owned or leased by an employer or other legal entity with responsibility for the client. This does not preclude in home services such as in home health care or the use of telephones or other electronic media to provide services in an emergency.

(c) Applicants for a license must complete the board's jurisprudence examination and submit proof of completion at the time of application. The jurisprudence examination must have been completed no more than six months prior to the date of application.

§781.302. Supervision for LCSW or LMSW-AP

A LMSW who plans to apply for the LCSW or LMSW-AP must:

(1) submit a supervisory plan to the board for approval by the appropriate committee of the board or executive director within 30 days of initiating supervision. If the LMSW fails to submit a supervisory plan, then the LMSW will need to submit documentation regarding dates, times and summary of all supervisory sessions at the time the LMSW makes application for the LCSW or LMSW-AP;

(2) submit a current job description from the agency in which the social worker is employed with a verification of authenticity from the agency director or their designee on agency letterhead;

(3) submit a supervision verification form to the board within 30 days of the end of each supervisory plan with each supervisor. If the supervisor does not recommend the supervisee for recognition as an AP or LCSW, the supervisor must provide specific reasons for not recommending the supervisee. The board may consider the supervisor's reservations in its evaluation of qualifications of the supervisee; and

(4) submit a new supervisory plan within 30 days of changing supervisors. Only one supervisory plan may be in place at any time.

(5) A person who has obtained only the temporary license may not begin the supervision process until the issuance of the regular license.

§781.303. Independent Practice Recognition

A LBSW or LMSW who seeks to obtain board approval for the recognition of independent practice shall meet requirements and parameters set by the board.

(1) To qualify for the recognition of independent practice, as a LBSW, an individual, after licensure, shall obtain 3000 hours of Board approved supervised full-time experience over a minimum two-year period, but within a maximum four-year period or its equivalent if the experience was completed in another state. Supervised experience must have occurred within the five previous calendar years occurring from the date of application.

(2) To qualify for the recognition of independent practice, as a LMSW, an individual, after licensure, shall obtain 3000 hours of Board approved supervised full-time experience over a minimum two-year period, but within a maximum four-year period or its equivalent if the experience was completed in another state. Supervised experience must have occurred within the five previous calendar years occurring from the date of application.

(3) To qualify for independent practice the licensee must complete a minimum of 100 hours of face-to-face supervision, over the course of the 3000 hours of full-time experience, with a board approved supervisor. A licensee who plans to apply for independent practice recognition shall:

(A) submit a supervisory plan to the board for approval by the appropriate committee of the board or executive director within 30 days of initiating supervision. If the licensee fails to submit a supervisory plan, then the licensee will need to submit documentation regarding dates, times and summary of all supervisory sessions at the time the licensee makes application for the upgrade.

(B) submit a current job description from the agency the social worker is employed in with a verification of authenticity from the agency director or their designee on agency letterhead.

(C) submit a supervision verification form to the board within 30 days of the end of each supervisory plan with each supervisor. If the supervisor does not recommend the supervisee for recognition as an independent practice, the supervisor must provide specific reasons for not recommending the supervisee. The board may consider the supervisor's reservations in its evaluation of qualifications of the supervisee.

(D) submit a new supervisory plan within 30 days of changing supervisors.

(E) An individual providing supervision to a LBSW shall be a LBSW,

LMSW, LMSW-AP or LCSW. An individual providing supervision to a LMSW shall be a LMSW, LMSW-AP or LCSW. In addition to the required licensure, the supervisor shall be board-approved and have attained the recognition of independent practice.

(4) A person who has obtained only the temporary license may not begin the supervision process until the issuance of the regular license.

(5) The board may use the twenty common law factors developed by the Internal Revenue Service (IRS) as part of their determination process regarding whether a worker is an independent contractor or an employee.

(A) No instructions to accomplish a job.

(B) No training by the hiring company.

(C) Others can be hired by the independent contractor (sub-contracting).

(D) Independent contractor's work is not essential to the company's success or continuation.

(E) No time clock.

(F) No permanent relationship between the contractor and company.

(G) Independent contractors control their own workers.

(H) Independent contractor should have enough time available to pursue other jobs.

(I) Independent contractor determines location of work.

(J) Independent contractor determines order of work.

(K) No interim reports.

(L) No hourly pay.

(M) Independent contractor often works for multiple firms.

(N) Independent contractor is often responsible for own business expenses.

(O) Own tools.

(P) Significant investment.

(Q) Services available to the public by having an office and assistants; having business signs; having a business license; listing their services in a business directory; or advertising their services.

(R) Profit or loss possibilities.

(S) Can't be fired.

(T) No compensation if the job isn't done.

§781.304. Recognition as an Approved Supervisor and Supervision Process

A person who wishes to be an approved supervisor must file a request with the board.

(1) A supervisor must:

(A) be a LBSW, LMSW, LCSW or LMSW-AP in good standing or hold the equivalent social work license or certification in another state;

(B) take professional responsibility for the social work services provided within the supervisory plan;

(C) have completed a supervisor's training program acceptable to the board;

(D) currently be engaged in the practice of social work and self-identified as a social worker;

(E) submit the required documentation and fee to the board for approval; and

(F) pay the annual Approved Supervisor fee as listed in §781.217 of this title (relating to Fees).

(2) On receipt of the request and verification of qualifications, the board will issue a letter of approval to a qualified supervisor.

(3) A supervisor must maintain the qualifications described in subsection (a) of this section while he or she is providing supervision.

(4) Supervisory sessions may be in one-on-one sessions or in a combination of individual and group sessions.

(A) There can be no more than six individuals in a supervision group.

(B) Supervision shall be spread out over the experience of the supervisee.

(C) Supervision shall be accomplished in one or two hour blocks not exceeding 10 hours per month.

(D) Supervision must be face-to-face meetings between the supervisor and supervisee unless the executive director of the board or a committee of the board has granted an exception allowing an alternate form of supervision due to geographical difficulties or physical disabilities. If an alternate form of supervision is approved, limits may be set on the amount of alternate supervision to assure sufficient interaction between the supervisor and supervisee.

(5) Supervision must extend over a full 3000 hours. Supervision must average one hour per 30-40 hours of social work services over the full period. Individuals who work less than 30 hours per week will be credited for experience and supervision in proportion to the average hours worked per week.

(6) A social worker may contract for supervision with written approval of the employing agency. A copy of the approval must accompany the supervisory plan submitted to the board.

(7) A board-approved supervisor may not charge or collect a fee or anything of value from his or her employee or contract employee for the supervision services provided to the employee or contract employee.

(8) The supervisor must be responsible for establishing all conditions of exchange with the clients served by her or his supervisee.

(9) Supervision completed before the effective date of this chapter will be evaluated on the basis of the rules in effect at the time the supervision plan or verification is submitted to the board.

(10) A supervisor may not be "employed by" or "under the employment supervision of" the person whom he or she is supervising.

(11) A supervisor may not be related within the second degree by affinity (marriage) or within the third degree by consanguinity (blood or adoption) to the person whom he or she is supervising.

(12) During the period of supervised experience, a supervisee may be employed on a salary basis or volunteer within an established supervisory setting. The established settings must be structured with clearly defined job descriptions and areas of responsibility. The board may require that the applicant provide documentation of all work experience.

(13) All supervision submitted in fulfillment of the board's requirements must have been on a formal basis arranged prior to the period of supervision. Supervisory arrangements must include all specific conditions agreed to by the supervisor and supervisee.

(14) No payment for services will be made directly by a client to the supervisee.

(15) Client records are the responsibility of the agency and shall remain the property of the agency and not the property of the supervisee.

(16) A supervisor shall submit billing reflective of the services provided and the provider of that service. All billing documents for services provided by the supervisee shall reflect the license held by the supervisee and that the licensee is under supervision.

§781.305. Application for Licensure

(a) An application for licensure must be on the official form designated by the board. Application packets, which include the application form, are available on request.

(b) The application process begins when the completed application form and fee are received in the board office.

(c) Receipt of an application form will be acknowledged by a letter from the executive director within 15 working days of receipt. The letter will include:

(1) the licensing or recognition category requested;

(2) deficiencies in documented qualifications, if any; and

(3) additional documentation necessary for examination approval. This could include transcripts, supervisory references and other documents, which verify qualifications.

(d) A letter approving the applicant to sit for the examination will be mailed within 15 working days of the receipt of all required documentation.

(e) If an applicant fails to fully document his or her qualifications and/or fails to pass the examination within 12 months of filing the application, his or her application will be voided and reapplication may be required. If the applicant fails the examination, reexamination will be required prior to the expiration of the application.

(f) If the applicant passes the examination, the executive director shall mail a notice of approval stating the fee for initial licensure.

(g) When the applicant has met all other qualifications for licensure and on receipt of the license fee in the board office, licensure for the LCSW, LMSW, LBSW, or specialty recognition will be immediately granted.

(h) In the event an application is not processed in the time periods stated in this section, the applicant has the right to request reimbursement of all fees paid in that particular application process. Application for reimbursement shall be made, in writing, to the executive director. If the executive director does not agree that the time period has been violated or finds that good cause existed for exceeding the time period, the request will be denied. The executive director will respond to the request for refund within 30 days from the date it is received. Good cause for exceeding the time period is considered to exist if the number of applications for license or license renewal exceeds by 15% or more the number of applications processed in the same calendar quarter the preceding year; another public or private entity relied upon by the board in the application process caused the delay; or any other condition exists giving the board good cause for exceeding the time period.

(i) If a request for reimbursement under this section is denied by the executive director, the applicant may appeal to the chairperson of the board for a timely resolution of any dispute arising from a violation of the time periods. The applicant shall give written notice to the chairperson at the address of the board that he or she requests full reimbursement of all fees paid because his or her application was not processed within the applicable time period. The executive director shall submit a written report of the facts related to the processing of the application and of any good cause for exceeding the applicable time period. The chairperson shall provide written notice of the chairperson's decision to the applicant and the executive director. An appeal shall be decided in the applicant's favor if the applicable time period was exceeded and good cause was not established. If the appeal is decided in favor of the applicant, full reimbursement of all fees paid in that particular application process shall be made.

§781.306. Required Documentation of Qualifications for Licensure

(a) Application form. An applicant for licensure must submit a completed official application form made under oath with all requested information.

(b) Education verification.

(1) The applicant's education must be documented by official college transcripts. Educational requirements must be met by completion of educational programs at colleges or universities accredited by CSWE.

(2) Degrees for licensure as a LBSW or LMSW must be from programs accredited or in candidacy for accreditation by CSWE. (Current written verification of a program's CSWE candidacy status must be on file with the board.) College or university degrees from outside of the United States and its territories must be from programs judged by the CSWE to be equivalent to a CSWE accredited program in the United States.

(c) Experience verification.

(1) *Experience required for licensure* or for specialty recognition must meet the requirements of §781.301 of this title (relating to qualifications for licensure). Private, independent practice within the scope of the definition of professional social work practice will not be counted as experience in this subsection. Required written documentation includes:

(A) names and addresses of supervisors;

(B) beginning and ending dates of supervision;

(C) job description;

(D) average number of hours of social work activity per week; and

(E) evaluations from each supervisor.

(2) *Written documentation of experience* must include verification of the following:

(A) administrative authority over the applicant's provision of social work services;

(B) the applicant's compensation status for services; and

(C) the employment status as reflected in all advertising, informational material, and written policy.

(3) The board shall credit part-time experience on a prorated basis.

(4) Experience must have been in a position with primary responsibility for providing social work services, under the supervision of a qualified

supervisor, and satisfactorily performed as indicated by written evaluations. Supervised experience must have occurred within the five previous calendar years occurring from the date of application.

(5) The applicant must maintain and upon request, provide to the board documentation of employment status, pay vouchers, or supervisory evaluations.

(d) *References.* An applicant must list on the official application the names and addresses of three individuals familiar with the applicant's professional qualifications. The board may contact the references for verification of the applicant's qualifications and fitness.

(e) *Jurisprudence examination.* Applicants for a license must complete the board's jurisprudence examination and submit proof of completion at the time of application. The jurisprudence examination must have been completed no more than six months prior to the date of application.

§781.307. Fitness of Applicants for Licensure

(a) In determining the fitness of an applicant, the board shall consider all of the following:

(1) the skills and abilities of an applicant to provide adequate social work services to clients;

(2) the ethical behavior of an applicant in relationships with other professionals and clients; and

(3) the applicant's worthiness of public trust and confidence.

(b) The board may consider a person, who has committed any act that would have been a violation of the Act or this chapter had the person been licensed at the time the act was committed, as unworthy of public trust and confidence.

(c) Surrender of a social work license within the previous five years while under investigation for professional misconduct shall be considered evidence that the person is unworthy of public trust and confidence.

(d) Revocation of a social work license within the previous five years for professional misconduct shall be considered evidence that the person is unworthy of public trust and confidence.

(e) A surrender or revocation, which occurred more than five years before application, may also be considered in determining fitness.

§781.308. Materials Considered in Determination of Fitness of Applicants

In determining the fitness of applicants, the board shall consider the following:

(1) evaluations of supervisors or instructors;

(2) statements from persons submitting references for the applicant;

(3) evaluations of employers and/or professional associations;

(4) allegations of clients;

(5) transcripts or findings from official court, hearing, or investigative proceedings; and

(6) any other information which the board considers pertinent to determining the fitness of an applicant.

§781.309. Finding of Non-Fitness

(a) The substantiation of any of the following items related to an applicant may be, as the board determines, the basis for the denial of a license, license renewal or recognition:

(1) lack of the necessary skills and abilities to provide adequate social work services;

(2) any misrepresentation in the application for licensure or license renewal or any other materials submitted to the board;

(3) the violation of any provision of the Act in effect at the time of application which is applicable to an unlicensed person; or

(4) the violation of any provision of the code of ethics or standards of practice which would have applied if the applicant had been a licensee at the time of the violation.

(b) The board may require an applicant for licensure or licensure renewal to obtain a criminal background check from an agency designated by the board and provide the board an official copy of that report. The board may consider the information on the report in determining the applicant's eligibility for licensure or licensure renewal. Failure to obtain the background check within 30 days of the request from the board is grounds for the denial of the application for licensure or licensure renewal.

§781.310. Provisional Licenses

(a) The board may grant a provisional license as a social worker to a person who holds, at the time of application, a license or certificate as a social worker or social work associate issued by another state, the District of Columbia, or a territory of the United States that is acceptable to the board. An applicant for a provisional license must:

(1) submit a written request for a provisional license along with a completed application;

(2) be licensed in good standing as a social worker or social work associate in another state, the District of Columbia, or territory of the United States that has licensing requirements that are substantially equivalent to the regular licensing requirements of the Act;

(3) have passed an equivalent examination accepted by another state, District of Columbia, or territory for licensure or certification as a social worker; and

(4) be sponsored by a person who holds a license issued by the board with whom the provisional licensee may practice.

(b) An applicant for a provisional license may be excused from the requirement of subsection (a)(4) of this section if the board determines that compliance with that subsection constitutes a hardship to the applicant.

(c) The provisional licensee shall use the appropriate licensing title or initials followed by the word "provisional".

(d) The provisional license shall be issued for the same category or level of license or certificate as the applicant held in the other state, District of Columbia, or territory of the United States.

(e) The board must complete the processing of a provisional licensee's application for a regular license not later than the 180th day after the date the provisional license is issued or at the time licenses are issued following the successful completion of the examination, whichever is later. The person holding a provisional license must file all evidence of his or her academic and experience requirements within this time period. The board office shall evaluate the information received and may issue a deficiency letter during this period. If the documentation received during this period does not show that the person meets the education and experience requirements set out in this chapter, the application shall be proposed for denial.

(f) A provisional license is valid until the date the board issues a license or denies the provisional licensee's application for a license.

(g) The board shall issue a regular license to the holder of a provisional license if:

(1) the provisional licensee passes the examination required by §505.354 of the Act; and

(2) the board verifies that the provisional licensee has the education and experience requirements for a regular license.

(h) The board shall consider only states, the District of Columbia, and territories of the United States as acceptable for the purposes of licensure by endorsement.

§781.311. Temporary License

(a) Prior to examination, an applicant for licensure may obtain a temporary license as a social worker as long as the applicant meets all the requirements, with the exception of the examination, for the level of license sought.

(1) A person holding a temporary license must take the designated examination within six months of issuance of the temporary license.

(2) The temporary license is valid until the results of the first qualifying examination are made available (i.e., the first examination taken by the temporary licensee or the end of the six months from issuance of the license if the examination is not taken, whichever is earlier).

(3) A person holding a temporary license must display the license at the licensee's place of business and must use the appropriate licensed title or initials followed by the word "Temporary" in all professional use of the licensee's name.

(4) Should the applicant take and fail the exam, the temporary license is no longer valid. The applicant must cease and desist from the use of the temporary license and title immediately.

(5) Should the applicant pass the exam the board will issue the license or specialty recognition in accordance with §781.305(g) of this title (relating to Application For Licensure).

(b) A person who failed the examination and is without a valid temporary license may retake the examination under §781.312 of this title (relating to Examination Requirement).

(c) A temporary license will not be granted to an applicant who has held a temporary license for the same license category within the previous five years.

(d) An applicant for LCSW or specialty recognition is not eligible for a temporary or provisional license.

(e) Applicants requesting a temporary license must submit the application form and temporary fee required by the board.

§781.312. Examination Requirement

(a) An applicant for licensure or recognition must pass an examination designated by the board.

(b) If an applicant fails the first examination, the individual may retake the examination no more than two additional times. An applicant who has failed the examination three times must request in writing to the board to retake the examination a fourth time. The board may order the applicant to complete one or more social work educational courses as a prerequisite to retaking the examination. The applicant must submit the form and pay the petition for re-examination fee required by the board prior to each additional exam administration.

(c) An applicant who fails the exam must wait the required timeframe between exam administrations. The board or executive director may waive the waiting period if petition in writing providing justification of the waiver in accordance with board policy.

(d) If an applicant fails the examination on the fourth attempt, the person's application will be voided and reapplication may be required. The applicant will not be permitted to reapply for licensure for a period of not less than one year.

(e) The board may waive the examination for an applicant with a valid certificate or license from another state if the certificate or license was issued before January 1, 1986, if petitioned in writing.

Alert: For updates after 5/26/2006, visit Texas State Board of Social Worker Examiners web site:

§781.313. Alternate Method of Examining Competency (AMEC) Program

(a) An applicant who has taken an examination within the previous 12 months and who has failed the examination on two or more occasions by fewer than five points may submit a written petition to the board for a probated license as a LBSW, or LMSW. The last examination must be within the past 12 months. The applicant must complete the application for participation, pay the administrative fee and submit the memorandum of understanding and the findings of facts documentation to the board for consideration.

(b) The board will consider the interest of the public in its review of the petition and will issue its decision in writing with in 90 days of receiving all required materials from the applicant.

(c) The written decision will include the following:

(1) a statement of the reason(s) the petition for a probated license is denied; or

(2) the terms of participation under which the license is granted.

(d) The participant must complete the professional portfolio, quarterly reports and other requirements within the required timeframe as mandated by the board.

(e) The AMEC program must be completed in no less then 12 consecutive calendar months and no more then 24 consecutive calendars months from the date of agreed order issued by the board unless prior approval is received from the board or its designee.

(f) An AMEC participant must remain under supervision until the board has reviewed the required documents submitted and issued a final order regarding the issuance of a regular license by the board. Continued reports from the supervisor may be required at the discretion of the board or its designee.

(g) The board may grant a regular license to an applicant who successfully completes the terms of participation to the satisfaction of the board.

§781.314. Issuance of Licenses

(a) The board issues licenses indicating the professional social work title, whether LBSW, LMSW, LMSW-AP or LCSW, granted to applicants who have met all of the qualifications established by the board.

(b) The license title or its initials must be included in all professional uses of the licensee's name as required by the Act, §505.351.

(c) A licensee shall display the license issued by the board in a prominent place in all locations of practice.

(d) A copy of the Code of Conduct listed in §781.401 of this title (relating to Code of Conduct) is issued with the license. The copy of the Code of Conduct also includes information regarding the client complaint process. The copy of the Code of Conduct must be displayed in all locations of practice.

(e) The board will make available its client information brochure on the board's Internet website. The board may provide copies to each licensee approved for independent practice. The licensee shall make these brochures available to all clients.

(f) A licensee who offers social work services on the Internet must include a statement that the licensee is licensed by the State of Texas and provide a copy of the code of ethics with the information on how to contact this board by mail or telephone.

(g) Upon request of the client, a licensee shall provide information regarding their license category and how to contact the board.

§781.315. Application Denial

(a) The board shall deny an application if all of the requirements for licensure or recognition are not met. An applicant shall be notified when the license or recognition is proposed for denial.

(b) A person whose application for licensure or recognition is denied is entitled to a formal hearing as set out in Subchapter G of this chapter (relating to Formal Hearings).

§781.316. Required Reports to the Board

(a) A licensee shall make written reports to the board office within 30 days of the following:

  (1) a change of mailing address, place of employment or business or home phone number;

  (2) an arrest or conviction of the licensee;

  (3) the filing of a criminal case against the licensee;

  (4) a criminal conviction, other than a Class C misdemeanor traffic offense, of the licensee;

  (5) the settlement of or judgment rendered in a civil lawsuit filed against the licensee and relating to the licensee's professional social work practice; or

  (6) complaints against, investigations involving or actions against the licensee done by a licensing or certification body related to health or mental health services when known by the licensee.

(b) The information received under subsection (a) of this section may be used by the board to determine whether a licensee remains fit to hold a license.

(c) Failure to make a report as required by subsection (a) of this section is grounds for disciplinary action by the board.

§781.317. Surrender of License

(a) *Surrender by licensee.*

  (1) A licensee may at anytime voluntarily offer to surrender his or her license for any reason, without compulsion.

(2) The license may be delivered to the board office by hand or mail. The licensee must cease practice as a social worker pending action from the board on the surrender of the licensee's license.

(3) If there is no complaint pending, the board office may accept the surrender and void the license.

(b) *Formal disciplinary action.*

(1) When a licensee has offered the surrender of his or her license after a complaint has been filed, the board shall consider whether to accept the surrender of the license.

(2) When the board has accepted such a surrender, the surrender is deemed to be the result of a formal disciplinary action and a board order shall be prepared accepting the surrender.

(3) In order to accept a surrender, the board may require the licensee to agree to certain findings of fact and conclusions of law, including the making of an admission of a violation of the Act or this chapter.

(4) Surrender of a license without acceptance thereof by the board or a licensee's failure to renew the license shall not deprive the board of jurisdiction against the licensee under the Act or any other statute.

(c) *Reinstatement.* A license, which has been surrendered by the licensee and accepted by the board, may not be reinstated; however, a person may apply for a new license in accordance with the Act and this chapter.

§781.318. Issuance of Licenses to Certain Out-Of-State Applicants

(a) Notwithstanding any other licensing requirement of this chapter or the Act:

(1) the board may not require an applicant who is licensed in good standing in another state to pass a licensing examination conducted by the board under the Act if an applicant with substantially equivalent experience who resides in this state would not be required to take the licensing examination; and

(2) the board may issue a license to an applicant who is currently licensed in another state to independently practice social work if:

(A) after an assessment, the board determines that the applicant:

(i) demonstrates sufficient experience and competence;

(ii) has passed the jurisprudence examination conducted by the board under Occupations Code, §505.3545; and

(iii) at the time of the application, is in good standing with the regulatory agency of the state in which the applicant is licensed; and

(B) the applicant presents to the board credentials that the applicant obtained from a national accreditation organization and the board determines that the requirements to obtain the credentials are sufficient to minimize any risk to public safety.

(b) When assessing the experience and competence of an applicant for the purposes of this section, the board may take into consideration any supervision received by the applicant in another state or jurisdiction if the board determines that the supervision would be taken into consideration for the purpose of licensing or certification in the state or jurisdiction in which the applicant received the supervision.

SUBCHAPTER D. CODE OF CONDUCT AND PROFESSIONAL STANDARDS OF PRACTICE

§781.401. Code of Conduct

(a) A social worker must observe and comply with the code of conduct and standards of practice set forth in this Subchapter. Any violation of the code of conduct or standards of practice will constitute unethical conduct or conduct that discredits or tends to discredit the profession of social work and is grounds for disciplinary action.

(1) A social worker shall not refuse to do or refuse to perform any act or service for which the person is licensed solely on the basis of a client's age, gender, race, color, religion, national origin, disability, sexual orientation, or political affiliation.

(2) A social worker shall truthfully report or present her or his services, professional credentials and qualifications to clients or potential clients.

(3) A social worker shall only offer those services that are within his or her professional competency, and the services provided shall be within accepted professional standards of practice and appropriate to the needs of the client.

(4) A social worker shall strive to maintain and improve her or his professional knowledge, skills and abilities.

(5) A social worker shall base all services on an assessment, evaluation or diagnosis of the client.

(6) A social worker shall provide the client with a clear description of services, schedules, fees and billing at the initiation of services.

(7) A social worker shall safeguard the client's rights to confidentiality within the limits of the law.

(8) A social worker shall be responsible for setting and maintaining professional boundaries.

(9) A social worker shall not have sexual contact with a client or a person who has been a client.

(10) A social worker shall refrain from providing service while impaired due to the social worker's physical or mental health or the use of medication, drugs or alcohol.

(11) A social worker shall not exploit his or her position of trust with a client or former client.

(12) A social worker shall evaluate a client's progress on a continuing basis to guide service delivery and will make use of supervision and consultation as indicated by the client's needs.

(13) A social worker shall refer a client for those services that the social worker is unable to meet and terminate service to a client when continued service is no longer in the client's best interest.

(b) The grounds for disciplinary action of a social worker shall be based on the code of conduct or standards of practice in effect at the time of the violation.

§781.402. Standards of Practice of Professional Social Work

(a) *Practice of Baccalaureate Social Work*—The application of social work theory, knowledge, methods, ethics and the professional use of self to restore or enhance social, psychosocial, or biopsychosocial functioning of individuals, couples, families, groups, organizations and communities. Baccalaureate Social Work is basic generalist practice that includes interviewing, assessment, planning, intervention, evaluation, case management, information and referral, problem solving, supervision, consultation, education, advocacy, community organization and the development, implementation, and administration of policies, programs and activities.

(b) *Practice of Clinical Social Work*—A specialty within the practice of social work that requires the application of social work theory, knowledge, methods, ethics, and the professional use of self to restore or enhance social, psychosocial, or biopsychosocial functioning of individuals, couples, families, groups, and/or persons who are adversely affected by social or psychosocial stress or health impairment. The practice of Clinical Social Work requires the application of specialized clinical knowledge and advanced clinical skills in the areas of assessment, diagnosis, and treatment of mental, emotional, and behavioral disorders, conditions and addictions, including severe mental illness in adults and serious emotional disturbances in children. The practice of Clinical Social Work acknowledges the practitioners ability to engage in Baccalaureate Social Work practice and Master's Social Work Practice. Treatment methods include the provision of individual, marital, couple, family, and group therapy and psychotherapy. Clinical social workers are qualified to use the Diagnostic and Statistical Manual of Mental Disorders (DSM), the International Classification of Diseases (ICD), and other diagnostic classification systems in assessment, diagnosis, and other activities. The practice of Clinical Social Work may include independent clinical practice and the provision of clinical supervision.

(c) *Practice of Master's Social Work*—is the application of social work theory, knowledge, methods and ethics and the professional use of self to restore or enhance social, psychosocial, or biopsychosocial functioning of individuals, couples, families, groups, organizations and communities. Master's Social Work practice requires the application of specialized knowledge and advanced practice skills in the areas of assessment, treatment planning, implementation and evaluation, case management, information and referral, supervision, consultation, education, research, advocacy, community organization and the development, implementation, and administration of policies, programs and activities. The Practice of Master's Social Work may include the Practice of Clinical Social Work under clinical supervision. The practice of Master's Social Work acknowledges the practitioners ability to engage in Baccalaureate Social Work practice.

(d) *Independent Practice*—The practice of social work outside the jurisdiction of an organizational setting, after completion of all applicable supervision requirements, in which the social worker assumes responsibility and accountability for the nature and quality of the services provided to clients.

(e) *Private Practice*—The provision of clinical social work in independent practice wherein the practitioner is solely responsible for the welfare of the client and the services rendered.

§781.403. General Standards of Practice

The scope of this section establishes standards of professional conduct required of a social worker. The licensee, following applicable statutes.

(1) Shall not knowingly offer or provide professional services to an individual concurrently receiving professional services from another mental health services provider except with that provider's knowledge. If a licensee learns of such concurrent professional services, the licensee shall take immediate and reasonable action to inform the other mental health services provider.

(2) Shall terminate a professional relationship when it is reasonably clear that the client is not benefiting from the relationship. When professional services are still indicated, the licensee shall take reasonable steps to facilitate the transfer to an appropriate referral or source.

(3) Shall not evaluate any individual's mental, emotional, or behavioral condition unless the licensee has personally interviewed the individual or the licensee discloses with the evaluation that the licensee has not personally interviewed the individual.

(4) May not persistently or flagrantly over treat a client.

(5) Shall not aid and abet the unlicensed practice of social work by a person required to be licensed under the Act.

(6) Shall not participate in any way in the falsification of applications for licensure. Nor shall an applicant for licensure participate in any way in the falsification of applications for licensure.

(7) Shall ensure that the individual has been informed of the following before or at the time of the individual's initial appointment with the licensee:

(A) qualifications of the provider and any intent to delegate service provision;

(B) any restrictions placed on the license by the board;

(C) the limits on confidentiality and privacy; and

(D) fees and arrangements for payment.

(8) Shall ensure that the individual has been informed of any changes to the items in paragraph (7) of this subsection prior to initiating the change.

(9) If bartering for services, has the responsibility to assure that the market value of the barter does not exceed the customary charge for the service.

§781.404. Relationships with Clients

(a) A social worker shall make known to a prospective client the important aspects of the professional relationship, which can include but is not limited to office procedures, after-hours coverage, fees and arrangements for payment that might affect the client's decision to enter into the relationship.

(b) No commission or rebate or any other form of remuneration shall be given or received by a social worker for the referral of clients for professional services.

(c) A social worker shall not use relationships with clients to promote, for personal gain or for the profit of an agency, commercial enterprises of any kind.

(d) A social worker shall not engage in activities that seek to primarily meet the social worker's personal needs or personal gain instead of the needs of the client.

(e) A social worker shall be responsible for setting and maintaining professional boundaries.

(f) A social worker shall keep accurate records of services to include, but not be limited to, dates of services, types of services, progress or case notes and billing information for a minimum of five years for an adult client and five years beyond the age of 18 years of age for a minor, or in compliance with applicable laws or professional standards.

(g) A social worker shall bill clients or third parties for only those services actually rendered or as agreed to by mutual written understanding.

(h) A social worker shall terminate services when in the licensee's professional opinion the client either has met the service goals or is not benefiting from those services. When services to the client are still indicated, the licensee shall take reasonable steps to facilitate the transfer to an appropriate referral or sources.

(i) A licensee shall not make any false, misleading, deceptive, fraudulent or exaggerated claim or statement about the licensee's services, including, but not limited to:

(1) the effectiveness of services;

(2) the licensee's qualifications, capabilities, background, training, experience, education, professional affiliations, fees, products, or publications; or

(3) the practice or field of social work.

(j) A licensee shall not make any false, misleading, deceptive, fraudulent or exaggerated claims or statement about the services of an organization or agency, including, but not limited to, the effectiveness of services, qualifications, or products.

(k) If the licensee learns that any false, misleading, deceptive, fraudulent or exaggerated claims or statement about the services, qualifications or products have been made, the licensee shall take all available steps to correct the inappropriate claims and to prevent their reoccurrence. As appropriate, the licensee may notify the board in writing about these claims.

(l) A licensee shall provide social work intervention only in the context of a professional relationship.

(m) Telepractice may be used as part of the social work process. Social workers engaging in Telepractice must adhere to each provision of this chapter as well as those in the jurisdictions where the services take place.

(n) The licensee shall not provide social work to previous or current:

(1) family members;

(2) personal friends;

(3) educational associates;

(4) business associates; or

(5) individuals whose welfare might be jeopardized by a dual relationship.

(o) The licensee shall follow agency policy related to accepting from or giving gifts to clients or relatives of clients. If no agency policy exists, no gift with a value in excess of $25 may be accepted or given.

(p) The licensee may not borrow or lend money or items of value to clients or relatives of clients.

(q) The licensee shall take reasonable precautions to protect individuals from physical or emotional harm resulting from interaction within individual and group settings.

(r) A licensee shall not promote the licensee's personal or business activities that are unrelated to the current professional relationship.

(s) A licensee shall set and maintain professional boundaries. Dual relationships with clients should be avoided. It is the responsibility of the social worker to ensure the safety of the client if a dual relationship arises.

§781.405. Sexual Misconduct

(a) For the purpose of this section, the following terms shall have the following meanings.

(1) *Sexual contact*—Any touching or behavior that can be construed as sexual in nature or as defined by the Texas Penal Code, §21.01.

(2) *Therapeutic deception*—A representation by a licensee that sexual contact with, or sexual exploitation or exploitative behavior by, the licensee is consistent with, or a part of, a client's or former client's social work services.

(b) A licensee shall not engage in sexual contact or sexual exploitation with a person who is:

(1) a client or former client;

(2) being supervised by the licensee; or

(3) a student at an educational institution at which the licensee provides professional or educational services.

(c) A licensee shall not practice therapeutic deception of a person who is a client or former client.

(d) It is not a defense to a disciplinary action under subsections (a)-(c) of this section if the person was no longer emotionally dependent on the licensee when the sexual exploitation began, the sexual contact occurred, or the therapeutic deception occurred. It is also not a defense that the licensee terminated services with the person before the date the sexual exploitation began, the sexual contact occurred or the therapeutic deception occurred.

(e) It is not a defense to a disciplinary action under subsections (a)-(c) of this section if the sexual contact, sexual exploitation, or therapeutic deception with the person occurred:

(1) with the consent of the client;

(2) outside the appointments with the client; or

(3) off the premises used by the licensee for the appointments with the client.

(f) Examples of sexual contact are those activities and behaviors described in the Texas Penal Code, §21.01.

(g) A licensee shall report sexual misconduct in accordance with Texas Civil Practice and Remedies Code, Chapter 81. If a licensee has reasonable cause to suspect that a client has been the victim of sexual exploitation, sexual contact, or therapeutic deception by another licensee or a mental health services provider, or if a client alleges sexual exploitation, sexual contact, or therapeutic deception by another licensee or a mental health services provider, the licensee shall report the alleged conduct not later than the 30th day after the date the licensee became aware of the conduct or the allegations to:

(1) the prosecuting attorney in the county in which the alleged sexual exploitation, sexual contact or therapeutic deception occurred; and

(2) the board if the conduct involves a licensee and any other state licensing agency which licenses the mental health services provider.

(3) Before making a report under this subsection, the licensee shall inform the alleged victim of the licensee's duty to report and shall determine if the alleged victim wants to remain anonymous.

(4) A report under this subsection need contain only the information necessary to:

(A) identify the licensee;

(B) identify the alleged victim, unless the alleged victim has requested anonymity;

(C) express suspicion that sexual exploitation, sexual contact, or therapeutic deception occurred; and

(D) provide the name of the alleged perpetrator.

(h) The following may constitute sexual exploitation if done for the purpose of sexual arousal or gratification or sexual abuse of any person who is or has been a recipient of professional services from the licensee for the purpose of engaging in the practice of baccalaureate, clinical or master's social work services in an independent or private practice setting:

(1) sexual harassment, sexual solicitation, physical advances, verbal or nonverbal conduct that is sexual in nature, and:

(A) is not bound in the therapeutic modality for the purpose of the professional services rendered;

(B) is offensive or creates a hostile environment, and the licensee knows or is told this; or

(C) is sufficiently severe or intense to be abusive to a reasonable person in the context.

(2) any behavior, gestures, or expressions which may reasonably be interpreted as inappropriately seductive or sexual;

(3) inappropriate sexual comments about or to a person, including making sexual comments about a person's body;

(4) making sexually demeaning comments about an individual's sexual orientation;

(5) making comments about potential sexual performance except when the comment is pertinent to the issue of sexual function or dysfunction in counseling;

(6) requesting details of sexual history or sexual likes and dislikes when not necessary for counseling of the individual;

(7) initiating conversation regarding the sexual problems, preferences, or fantasies of the licensee;

(8) kissing or fondling;

(9) making a request to date;

(10) any other deliberate or repeated comments, gestures, or physical acts not constituting sexual intimacies, but of a sexual nature;

(11) any bodily exposure of genitals, anus or breasts;

(12) encouraging another to masturbate in the presence of the licensee; or

(13) masturbation by the licensee when another is present.

§781.406. Professional Representation

(a) A social worker shall not misrepresent any professional qualifications or associations.

(b) A social worker shall not misrepresent any agency or organization by presenting it as having attributes, which it does not possess.

(c) A social worker shall not make unreasonable, misleading, deceptive, fraudulent, exaggerated, or unsubstantiated claims about the efficacy of any services.

(d) A social worker shall not encourage, or within the social worker's power, allow a client to hold exaggerated ideas about the efficacy of services provided by the social worker.

§781.407. Testing

(a) A social worker shall make known to clients the purposes and explicit use to be made of any testing done as part of a professional relationship.

(b) A social worker shall not appropriate, reproduce, or modify published tests or parts thereof without the acknowledgment and permission of the publisher.

(c) A social worker shall not administer any test without the appropriate training and experience to administer the test.

(d) A social worker must observe the necessary precautions to maintain the security of any test administered by the social worker or under the social worker's supervision.

§781.408. Drug and Alcohol Use

A licensee shall not:

(1) use alcohol or drugs in a manner which adversely affects the licensee's ability to practice social work;

(2) use illegal drugs of any kind; or

(3) promote, encourage, or concur in the illegal use or possession of alcohol or drugs.

§781.409. Client Records and Record Keeping

Following applicable statutes, the licensee shall:

(1) keep accurate and legible records of the dates of services, types of services, progress or case notes, intake assessment, treatment plan, and billing information;

(2) retain and dispose of client records in such a way that confidentiality is maintained;

(3) in independent practice, establish a plan for the custody and control of the licensee's client mental health records in the event of the licensee's death or incapacity, or the termination of the licensee's professional services;

(4) keep client records for five years for adult clients and five years beyond the age of 18 for minor clients;

(5) at the request of a client, a client's guardian, or a client's parent (sole managing, joint managing or possessory conservator) if the client is a minor, provide, in plain language, a written explanation of the types of treatment and charges for counseling treatment intervention previously made on a bill or statement for the client (this requirement applies even if the charges are to be paid by a third party);

(6) comply with the requirements of Texas Health and Safety Code, Chapter 611, concerning the release of mental health records; and

(7) be responsible for services rendered when providing approval by signature for services rendered by another individual who may or may not be licensed.

§781.410. Billing and Financial Relationships

(a) A licensee shall not intentionally or knowingly offer to pay or agree to accept any remuneration directly or indirectly, overtly or covertly, in cash or in kind, to or from any person, firm, association of persons, partnership, corporation, or entity for securing or soliciting clients or patronage for or from any health care professional.

(b) In accordance with the provisions of the Act, §505.451, a licensee is subject to disciplinary action if the licensee directly or indirectly offers to pay or agrees to accept remuneration to or from any person for securing or soliciting a client or patronage.

(c) A licensee employed or under contract with a chemical dependency facility or a mental health facility, shall comply with the requirements in the Texas Health and Safety Code, §164.006, relating to soliciting and contracting with certain referral sources. Compliance with the Treatment Facilities Marketing Practices Act, Texas Health and Safety Code, Chapter 164, shall not be considered as a violation of state law relating to illegal remuneration.

(d) A licensee shall bill clients and/or third parties for only those services actually rendered by the licensee.

(e) Relationships between a licensee and any other person used by the licensee to provide services to a client shall be so reflected on billing documents.

(f) A licensee may not knowingly or flagrantly overcharge a client.

(g) A licensee may not submit to a client and/or a third payor a bill for services that the licensee knows were not provided or knows were improper, unreasonable or unnecessary, with the exception of a missed appointment.

§781.411. Client Confidentiality

(a) Communication between a licensee and client and the client's records, however created or stored, are confidential under the provisions of the Texas Health and Safety Code, Chapter 181, Texas Health and Safety Code, Chapter 611, and other state or federal statutes or rules, including court room rules of evidence, where such statutes or rules apply to a licensee's practice.

(b) A licensee shall not disclose any communication, record, or identity of a client except as provided in Texas Health and Safety Code, the Health Insurance Portability and Accountability Act (HIPAA), and/or other state or federal statutes or rules, as applicable.

(c) A licensee shall comply with Texas Health and Safety Code, Chapter 611, concerning access to mental health records.

(d) A licensee shall have written permission for release of information for clients. The written release should include:

  (1) name and identifying information of the client;

  (2) the purpose of the release of information;

  (3) whom the information is being released to;

  (4) duration the release is intended to be enforced; and

  (5) the signature of the client or guardian representative.

(e) The written release of information should be maintained in the permanent client record and should be reviewed and update regularly.

(f) A licensee shall report information if required by any of the following statutes:

  (1) Texas Family Code, Chapter 261, concerning abuse or neglect of minors;

  (2) Texas Human Resources Code, Chapter 48, concerning abuse, neglect, or exploitation of elderly or disabled persons;

  (3) Texas Health and Safety Code, §161.131 et seq., concerning abuse, neglect, and illegal, unprofessional, or unethical conduct in an in-patient mental health facility, a chemical dependency treatment facility

or a hospital providing comprehensive medical rehabilitation services; and

(4) Texas Civil Practice and Remedies Code, §81.006, concerning sexual exploitation by a mental health services provider.

(g) A social worker shall follow the rules of confidentiality set forth in the Health and Safety Code, Chapter 611, and other applicable laws.

(h) A licensee may take reasonable action to inform medical or law enforcement personnel if the professional determines that there is a probability of imminent physical injury by the client to the client or others, or there is a probability of immediate mental or emotional injury to the client in accordance with the Texas Health and Safety Code, Chapter 611.

§781.412. Licensees and the Board

(a) Any person licensed as a social worker is bound by the provisions of the Act and this chapter.

(b) A social worker shall report alleged misrepresentations or violations of this chapter to the board's executive director.

(c) The licensee shall report any and all name changes, address changes, or employment setting changes to the board within 30 days.

(d) The board is not responsible for any lost or misdirected mail if sent to the address last reported by the licensee.

(e) The board may ask any applicant for licensure as a social worker, whose file contains negative references of good moral character, to come before the board for an interview before the licensure process may proceed.

(f) The board may consider the failure of a social worker to respond to a request from the board or executive director for information or other correspondence as unprofessional conduct and grounds for disciplinary proceedings in accordance with this chapter.

§781.413. Assumed Names

(a) An individual practice by a social worker may be incorporated in accordance with the Professional Corporation Act, or other applicable law.

(b) When an assumed name is used in any practice of social work, the name of the social worker must be listed in conjunction with the assumed name. An assumed name used by a social worker must not be false, deceptive, or misleading.

§781.414. Consumer Information

(a) A licensee shall inform each client of the name, address, and telephone number of the board for the purpose of reporting violations of the Act or this chapter on a sign prominently displayed in the primary place of business; or

(b) The board shall make consumer information available to the public.

§781.415. Display of License Certificate

(a) A social worker shall display the license certificate, issued by the board, in a prominent place at each location of practice.

(b) A social worker shall display only an original of the license certificate issued by the board.

(c) A social worker shall not make any alteration on a license certificate issued by the board.

(d) A social worker shall not display a license certificate issued by the board, which has been reproduced or is expired, suspended, or revoked.

(e) A licensee who elects to copy or allow to be copied a license certificate issued by the board takes full responsibility for the use or misuse of the reproduced license.

§781.416. Advertising and Announcements

(a) Information used by a social worker in any advertisement or announcement of services shall not contain information which is deceptive, inaccurate, incomplete, or out of context.

(b) The board imposes no restrictions on the advertising medium a social worker uses, including personal appearances, use of personal voice, size or duration of the advertisement or use of a trade name.

(c) All advertisements or announcements of professional services which a licensee offers, including telephone directory listings, shall clearly state the social worker's licensure designation.

(d) A social worker shall not include in advertising or announcements any information or any reference to certification in a field outside of social work or membership in any organization, if that information might confuse or mislead the public as to the services or legal recognition of the social worker.

(e) Information used by a licensee in any advertisement or announcement shall not contain information, which is false, inaccurate, misleading, incomplete, out of context, deceptive or not readily verifiable. Advertising includes, but is not limited to, any announcement of services, letterhead, business cards, commercial products, and billing statements.

(f) A licensee who retains or hires others to advertise or promote the licensee's practice remains responsible for the statements and representations made.

§781.417. Research and Publications

(a) In research with a human subject, a social worker is responsible for the subject's welfare throughout a project, shall obtain informed consent and take reasonable precautions so that the subject shall suffer no injurious emotional, physical or social effect.

(b) A social worker shall disguise data obtained from a professional relationship for the purposes of education or research to ensure full protection of the identity of the subject client.

(c) When conducting and reporting research, a social worker must give recognition to previous work on the topic as well as observe all copyright laws.

(d) A social worker must give due credit through joint authorship, acknowledgment, footnote statements, Internet sources or other appropriate means to those who have contributed significantly to the social worker's research or publication.

§781.418. Provision of Court Ordered Home Studies, Adoption Studies or Custody Evaluations

(a) The role of social worker is to assist the parties, their children and the court by maintaining a posture that is both critical and impartial.

(b) Social workers performing such evaluations are required to provide written reports to the parties and the court and to testify under oath as to the factual issues and expert opinions. The social worker should maintain a copy of the report for his/her records in accordance with client records retention as required by §781.409(4) of this title (relating to Client Records and Record Keeping).

(c) Social workers should not use or review previous custody evaluations or home studies in making a recommendation unless instructed to do so by the court or by consent of all parties requesting the evaluation.

(d) The social worker should not perform an evaluation of a child or family in a case where the social worker has previously served or is currently serving in another professional role which may compromise the social worker's objectivity.

(e) Social workers performing evaluations for the Department of Family and Protective Services (DFPS) must meet the criteria established by that agency's Independent Pre-Adoptive Home Screening and Post-Placement Adoptive Report Rules at 40 Texas Administrative Code, Part 19, Chapter 745.

SUBCHAPTER E. LICENSE RENEWAL AND CONTINUING EDUCATION

§781.501. General

(a) A license must be renewed biennially.

(b) A person who holds a license must have fulfilled any continuing education requirements prescribed by this chapter in order to renew a license.

(c) Each person who holds a license is responsible for renewing the license and shall not be excused from paying penalty fees for late renewal. Failure to receive notice from the board does not waive payment of penalty fees.

(d) The board may deny the renewal of the license of a licensee who is in violation of the Act, or this chapter, at the time of application for renewal.

(e) A person whose license has expired shall not use the terms or titles described in the Act, §505.351. The person shall return his or her license to the board.

(f) The deadlines established for renewals, late renewals, and penalty fees are based on the postmarked date of the documentation submitted by the licensee.

(g) The board shall deny renewal if required by the Education Code, §57.491 (relating to Defaults on Guaranteed Student Loans).

(h) The board upon receipt of a final court or attorney general's order will suspend a license due to failure to pay child support per the Family Code, Chapter 232. The individual must pay the reinstatement fee set out in §781.217 of this title (relating to Fees).

(i) A license must be renewed and in good standing prior to the licensee obtaining a different category of licensure.

§781.502. Staggered Renewals

The board shall use a staggered system for license renewals.

(1) The renewal date of a license shall be the last day of the licensee's birth month.

(2) License fees will be prorated if the licensee's initial renewal date, as determined by the board, occurs less than 12 months after the original date of licensure.

(3) Prorated fees shall be rounded off to the nearest dollar.

§781.503. License Renewal

(a) At least 45 days prior to the expiration of a license, the board will send notice to a licensee that includes the expiration date of the license, a schedule of the renewal and penalty fees, and continuing competency activities needed to complete the renewal requirements.

(b) A license renewal form shall be furnished to licensees eligible for renewal. The form shall require the licensee to provide current addresses; telephone numbers; continuing education completed; a signed statement regarding any civil lawsuits, criminal cases and convictions or any complaints against, investigations involving, or actions against the licensee by any licensing or certification body; and a statement of continuing compliance with the Act and this chapter.

(c) The executive director will respond in writing to the application for renewal within 15 working days of initial receipt and of receipt of a completed application (if the initial application is deficient) notifying the applicant that his or her license is renewed, that the application is deficient, or that renewal is proposed for denial. Failure to process a renewal application in the time periods stated shall be governed by §781.305(h) and (i) of this title (relating to Application for Licensure).

(d) The board shall renew the license of a social worker whom has met all requirements for renewal including payment of all fees and submission of documentation of completion of all required continuing education.

(e) If a licensee has made timely and sufficient application for renewal, the license does not expire until the board has acted on the renewal. If the licensee claims to have made timely and sufficient application and is otherwise eligible for license renewal, his or her license will be considered to be current until the renewal is issued or until the board office receives the information that timely and sufficient application was not made.

(f) A licensee who has been recommended for disciplinary action must file a timely and complete application for license renewal. If the licensee fails to pay all fees or to document completion of required continuing education he or she must cease all social work practice until all requirements for license renewal are complete.

(g) The board may deny the renewal of a license if the licensee is a party to a formal disciplinary action. A formal action commences when the notice described in §781.602(c) of this title (relating to Disciplinary Action and Notices) is mailed by the board.

(h) A license that is not revoked or suspended as a result of formal proceedings shall be renewed provided that all other requirements are met.

(i) In the case of delay in the license renewal process because of formal disciplinary action, penalty fees shall not apply.

(j) If a complaint against a licensee is in process on the date that his or her license renewal is due:

   (1) a notice will be sent to the licensee, certified mail return receipt requested to the mailing address on file with the board, requiring the licensee to renew his or her license or return his or her license to the board;

   (2) the notice will state that the complaint process will continue until its final resolution or if the license is renewed; and

   (3) unless the return receipt is received by the board, receipt of the notice will be presumed to have occurred as provided in §781.602 of this title.

(k) The board may refuse to renew the license of a person who fails to pay an administrative penalty imposed in accordance with the Act unless the enforcement of the penalty is stayed or a court has ordered that the administrative penalty is not owed.

(l) For all licenses renewed between January 1, 2007 and December 31, 2008, the jurisprudence training course must be completed each renewal period in order to renew the license. Completion of the jurisprudence training course shall count as three hours of the continuing education requirement for professional ethics and social work values, as referenced in §781.508(b) of this title (relating to Hour Requirements for Continuing Education).

§781.504. Late Renewal

(a) A person who fails to meet all the requirements to renew his or her license by the renewal date ceases to be licensed.

(b) A person who renews a license after the expiration date but on or before 90 days after the expiration date shall pay the renewal fee and appropriate penalty fees.

(c) If a person has not renewed a license for more than 30 days after the date of expiration, the board shall inform the person of the expiration date of the license and the amount of the fee required for renewal.

(d) The board shall notify a person whose license is expired that the person may not practice social work or otherwise violate the Act.

(e) A person whose license was not renewed on or before 90 days from the expiration date may renew within one year of the expiration date by paying the appropriate renewal and penalty fees.

(f) If a person did not have the required continuing education at the time of expiration of the license, the person shall file evidence of completion of the required continuing education before the license can be renewed.

(g) The continuing education may have been earned during the continuing education period or within the one-year period following expiration.

(h) The evidence of continuing education shall be the completed continuing education form and other documentation required by the board.

(i) On or after one year from the expiration date, a person may no longer renew the license and must reapply by submitting a new application, paying the required fees, and meeting the current requirements for the license including passing the licensure examination.

§781.505. Inactive Status

(a) A licensee whose license has not lapsed, but who is not employed to provide social work services in Texas, is eligible for inactive status. The request for inactive status may be made to the board at any time prior to the lapse of the license.

(b) No continuing education is required of a licensee while on inactive status.

(c) The inactive status fee and any applicable renewal fee and penalty fee for late renewal must be paid prior to the date the license lapses.

(d) A person must notify the board in writing to reactivate the person's status. Reactivation status shall begin on the first day of the month following payment of the license fee. The license fee shall be prorated to the next renewal date in accordance with §781.502 of this title (relating to Staggered Renewals).

§781.506. Emeritus Status

(a) A licensee who is at least 55 years of age, or disabled, and who is not engaged in professional social work practice, is eligible for an emeritus license. The request for emeritus status must be submitted in writing to the board.

(b) On receipt of the request the board will issue an emeritus license that will remain valid for the lifetime of the licensee. No renewal fee or continuing education will be required.

(c) The emeritus licensee may only use his or her emeritus title in the provision of social work services as a volunteer. The emeritus social worker may not receive any compensation for social work services.

(d) An emeritus license can be reinstated to an active license without being subject to the additional penalty for late renewal of a license. To be eligible for a new license, the person would be required to submit an updated application and the application and license fee. Submission of verification of education, supervision, and examination score is not required.

§781.507. Active Military Duty

(a) A licensee on active duty with the Armed Forces of the United States who is not practicing in the State of Texas at the time of renewal is exempt from the renewal requirement and may, within one year of his or her return to Texas or release from active duty, whichever occurs first, request reinstatement of his or her license.

(b) The board will issue a license on receipt of the request for reinstatement, documentation of his or her active duty status at the time the license expired, and the fee for the current license. No continuing education will be required prior to reinstatement and no penalty fees will be charged.

§781.508. Hour Requirements for Continuing Education

(a) A licensee must complete a total of 30 clock-hours of continuing education biennially obtained from board approved continuing education providers.

(b) As part of the required 30 clock-hours, a licensee must complete a minimum of six clock-hours of continuing education in professional ethics and social work values during the biennial renewal period.

(c) A clock-hour is defined as 60 minutes of standard time.

(d) A licensee may earn credit for ethics as a presenter or a participant.

(e) On petition by a licensee, the executive director may waive part, but not all, of the continuing education renewal requirements for good and just cause or may permit the licensee an additional period of time in which to complete all continuing education requirements. In all cases, the decision of the executive director may be appealed to the Professional Development Committee of the board. Should the committee overturn the decision of the executive director, the committee may elect to waive the late fees accrued or determine that the late fees should be paid by the licensee. Should the decision of the executive director be upheld by the committee and the licensee be denied in the appeal, all late fees accrued will apply.

§781.509. Types of Acceptable Continuing Education

Continuing education undertaken by a licensee shall be acceptable to the board as credit hours if the education falls in one or more of the following categories:

(1) participating in institutes, seminars, workshops, conferences, independent study programs, post graduate training programs, college academic or continuing education courses which are related to or enhance the practice of social work and are offered or sponsored by a board approved provider;

(2) teaching or presenting the activities described in paragraph (1) of this section;

(3) writing a published work or making a presentation directed toward or applicable to the profession of social work;

(4) providing professional guidance as a field instructor for social work interns in connection with a college or university accredited by or in candidacy status with CSWE; or

(5) providing supervision to a social worker participating in the program in accordance with §781.313 of this title (relating to the Alternative Method of Examining Competency (AMEC) Program); or

(6) completion of the board's jurisprudence training course no more than once per renewal period, unless the board directs otherwise.

§781.510. Activities Unacceptable as Continuing Education

The board will not give credit hours for:

(1) education incidental to the regular professional activities of a social worker such as learning occurring from experience or research;

(2) organizational activity such as serving on committees or councils or as an officer in a professional organization;

(3) meetings and activities such as in service programs which are required as a part of one's job unless the in service training is a type of acceptable continuing education under §781.509 of this title (relating to Types of Acceptable Continuing Education);

(4) college academic courses which are audited or not taken for credit; or

(5) any experience which does not fit the types of acceptable continuing education in §781.509 of this title.

§781.511. Approval of Continuing Education Sponsor

(a) A sponsor must be approved under this section to offer continuing education programs.

(b) A person seeking approval as a continuing education sponsor shall file an application on board forms and include the continuing education sponsor application fee. Governmental agencies shall be exempt from paying this fee.

(c) Entities that receive automatic status without application or fee as approved providers are:

(1) accredited colleges and universities;

(2) a national or statewide association, board or organization representing members of the social work profession;

(3) nationally accredited health or mental health facilities; or

(4) a person or agency approved by any state or national organization in a related field such as medicine, psychiatry, psychology, sociology, marriage and family therapy, and similar field of human service practice.

(d) The applicant shall certify on the application that:

(1) all programs offered by the sponsor for credit hours from the board will comply with the criteria in this section; and

(2) the sponsor will be responsible for verifying attendance at each program and provide a certificate of attendance as set forth in subsection (k) of this section.

(e) A program offered by a sponsor for credit hours from the board shall:

(1) contribute to the advancement, extension and enhancement of the professional skills and knowledge of the licensee in the practice of social work;

(2) be developed and presented by persons who are appropriately knowledgeable in the subject matter of the program and training techniques;

(3) specify the course objectives, course content and teaching methods to be used;

(4) specify the number of credit hours; and

(5) specify the number of credit hours in ethics and values separately and as part of the total hours credited.

(f) The sponsor must document each program's compliance with subsection (d) of this section and maintain that documentation for a period of three years.

(g) The executive director will review the continuing education sponsor application and notify the applicant of any deficiencies or grant approval and indicate the continuing education sponsor approval number to be noted on all certificates of attendance.

(h) Each continuing education program shall provide a mechanism for evaluation of the program by the participants. The evaluation may be completed on-site immediately following the program presentation or an evaluation questionnaire may be distributed to participants to be completed and returned to the sponsor by mail. The sponsor and the instructor, together, shall review the evaluation outcomes and revise subsequent programs accordingly. The sponsor shall keep all evaluations for three years and allow the board to review the evaluations on request.

(i) An approved sponsor may subcontract with individuals or organizations to provide continuing education programs. The sponsor must insure that the subcontractor meets all requirements of this section. The Sponsor will provide a listing of subcontractors utilized as part of the renewal process.

(j) To maintain approval as a sponsor, each sponsor shall submit to the board annually an application for renewal of the approved provider status and a application fee if applicable.

(k) It shall be the responsibility of a sponsor to provide each participant in a program with a legible certificate of attendance. The certificate of attendance shall contain:

(1) the name of the sponsor and approval number;

(2) the name of the participant;

(3) the title of the program;

(4) the number of credit hours given, including ethics hours credited;

(5) the date and place of the program;

(6) the signature of the sponsor or its representative; and

(7) board contact information.

(l) The sponsor shall maintain attendance records for not less than two years.

(m) The sponsor shall be responsible for assuring that no licensee receives continuing education credit for time not actually spent attending the program.

(n) Upon the failure of a sponsor to comply with any of the requirements of this section, the board, after notice to the sponsor and a due process hearing, may revoke the sponsor's approval status.

(o) The board may evaluate any approved sponsor or applicant at any time to ensure compliance with requirements of this section.

(p) Complaints regarding continuing education programs offered by approved providers may be submitted in writing to the executive director.

§781.512. Removal of Continuing Education Sponsorship Status

(a) The board retains the right to remove the approval status of a continuing education sponsor.

(b) The board may remove a sponsor who is not in compliance with board requirements at the time of renewal.

(c) A sponsor removed by the board may reapply the 91st day following the board action.

(d) The executive director shall review complaints regarding the compliance with board requirements of a continuing education sponsor for possible action.

(e) Sponsors removed or denied may request a review by the Professional Development Committee.

(f) Continuing education hours received from a sponsor who has been removed or denied by the board but accepted by another licensing or approval entity shall not be acceptable for use of renewal of the social worker license.

(g) Continuing education hours received from sponsors who failed to meet the renewal requirements of the board shall not be acceptable for use in the renewal of the social worker's license.

(h) Fees paid by a sponsor who has been removed or denied are non-refundable.

(i) The Professional Development Committee shall review reapplication by a formerly approved or denied sponsor.

§781.513. Acceptance of Continuing Education Approved by Another Licensing Board

(a) A licensee may request in writing that the board consider approval of continuing education hours provided by a non-approved provider. The licensee shall submit documentation as specified in §781.511(e) of this title (relating to Approval of Continuing Education Sponsor) for the board to review and a fee equal to the continuing education sponsor application fee.

(b) The executive director will review the documentation and notify the licensee in writing whether the program(s) are acceptable as credit hours. In all cases, the decision of the executive director may be appealed to the Professional Development Committee of the board.

§781.514. Credit Hours Granted

The board will grant the following credit hours toward the continuing education requirements for license renewal.

(1) One credit hour will be given for each hour of participation in a continuing education program by an approved provider.

(2) Credit may be earned, post-licensure, through successfully completing postgraduate training programs (e.g., intern, residency, or fellowship programs) or successfully completing social work related courses which are part of the curriculum of a graduate school of social work at a rate of five credit hours per each semester hour or its equivalent not to exceed 10 hours per renewal period. A licensee may complete the ethics requirement in §781.508(a)(2) of this title (relating to Hour Requirements for Continuing Education) only through a course specifically designated as an ethics course.

(3) Credit may be earned for teaching social work courses in an accredited college or university. Credit will be applied at the rate of five credit hours for every course taught, not to exceed 15 hours per renewal period. A licensee may complete the ethics requirement in §781.508(a)(2) of this title only through teaching a course specifically designated as an ethics course.

(4) A field instructor for a social work intern will be granted five credit hours for each college semester completed, not to exceed 20 credit hours per renewal period.

(5) A presenter of a continuing education program or an author of a published work, which imparts social work knowledge and skills, may be granted five credit hours for each original or substantially revised presentation or publication, not to exceed 10 credit hours per renewal period.

(6) Credit hours may be earned by successful completion of an independent study program directly related to social work offered or approved by an approved provider. With the exception of persons residing outside the United States, a maximum of 10 credit hours for independent study programs will be accepted per renewal period.

(7) A licensee may carry over to the next renewal period up to 10 credit hours earned in excess of the continuing education renewal requirements. Continuing education earned during the licensee's birth month may be used for the current renewal or for the following year.

(8) For all licenses renewed between January 1, 2007 and December 31, 2008, the jurisprudence training course must be completed in order to renew the license. Completion of the jurisprudence training course shall count as three hours of the continuing education requirement in professional ethics and social work values, as referenced in §781.508(b) of this title.

§781.515. Continuing Education Documentation

(a) Credit hours must be listed on the license renewal form supplied by the board. Failure to submit the form or failure to complete the required continuing education is grounds for denial of the application for license renewal.

(b) A random sample of renewal applications will be selected for review.

(c) Documentation of continuing education listed on the renewal form must be retained for three years.

(d) A licensee who is selected for review will be notified by mail and required to submit acceptable documentation of the continuing education listed on the continuing education report form. Acceptable documentation includes the following:

(1) copies of continuing education certificates of attendance or other form of verification from the provider of the continuing education program;

(2) grade reports or transcripts verifying the completion of a college course;

(3) letters from the dean or department head or his or her authorized representative verifying the teaching or field instructor assignment;

(4) letters from the program sponsor verifying participation as a presenter in a continuing education program or a copy of the program; or

(5) copies of continuing education programs and other documentation as necessary to establish the relevance of its content to social work practice for any continuing education program which does not have an approved provider number.

(e) All forms of verification must include the subject, date(s), credit hours given and name of the sponsor, board issued sponsor approval number or other identifying sponsor information and board contact information (if applicable).

SUBCHAPTER F. COMPLAINTS AND VIOLATIONS

§781.601. Purpose

The purpose of this Subchapter is to set out grounds for denial of an application or discipline of a licensee and the procedures for reporting alleged violations of the Act or this chapter.

§781.602. Disciplinary Action and Notices

(a) The board shall revoke, suspend, suspend on an emergency basis, or deny a license or order of recognition, place on probation a person whose license or order of recognition has been suspended, or reprimand a person with a license or order of recognition for any of the following reasons:

(1) violation of any provision of the Act;

(2) violation of any rule adopted by the board;

(3) failure to cooperate in the investigation of a complaint filed under the provisions of this chapter;

(4) physical or mental incompetency to perform social work services as determined by the board;

(5) provision of false or misleading information to the board regarding his or her qualifications for licensure or renewal or to an inquiry by the board;

(6) any of the grounds described in the Act, §505.021(a); or

(7) violation of law or rules of another health or mental health profession resulting in disciplinary action by the regulatory body of that profession.

(b) Prior to institution of formal disciplinary proceedings against a licensee, the board shall give written notice to the licensee by certified mail, return receipt requested or registered mail. The notice of violation letter will include the facts or conduct alleged to warrant revocation, suspension, or reprimand and the severity level from the sanction guide. The licensee shall be given the opportunity, as described in the notice, to show compliance with all requirements of the Act and this chapter.

(c) The licensee or applicant must request, in writing, a formal hearing within 10 days of receipt of the notice, or the right to a hearing shall be waived and the license or recognition shall be denied, revoked, suspended, probated, or reprimanded.

(d) Receipt of a notice under subsection (b) or (c) of this section is presumed to occur on the tenth day after the notice is mailed to the last address known to the board unless another date is reflected on a United States Postal Service return receipt or other official receipt.

(e) The licensee will be considered to have received notice of board disciplinary action if the notice is mailed to the last address provided in writing to the board by the licensee.

(f) If a notice is mailed to the last known address of the licensee, and the licensee fails to respond to the notice within 10 days from receipt of the notice, the licensee will be considered to have waived his or her right to a hearing in the matter.

(g) If it appears to the board that a person who is not licensed under this chapter is violating this chapter, a rule adopted under this chapter, or another state statute or rule relating to the practice of social work, the board after notice and opportunity for a hearing, as described in this section, may issue a cease and desist order prohibiting the person from engaging in the activity. A violation of an order under this subsection constitutes grounds for the imposition of an administrative penalty by the board.

§781.603. Complaint Procedures

(a) A person wishing to report an alleged violation of the Act or this chapter by a licensee or other person shall notify the executive director. The initial notification may be in writing, by telephone, or by personal visit to the board office.

(b) The executive director will be responsible for the receipt and processing of complaints. The executive director will maintain a log of the receipt, investigation and disposition of all complaints. The board chairperson will appoint an ethics committee to work with the executive director.

(c) The board office shall not accept a complaint if the official form is not filed within five years of the date of termination of the professional-client relationship which gave rise to the alleged violations or five years from the date the complainant learned the behavior of the social worker was a violation of the rules and/or law. If the client was a minor at the time of the alleged violation, this time limitation does not begin to run until the client reaches the age of 18 years. A complainant shall be notified of the non-acceptance of untimely complaints.

(d) The board may waive the time limitation in cases of egregious acts or continuing threats to public health or safety when presented with specific evidence that warrants such action.

(e) On receipt of a complaint, the executive director shall send an acknowledgment letter. If the complaint is not in the form of a sworn statement, a copy of applicable rules, and an official form will be included with the letter of acknowledgment and further action on the complaint may, at the discretion of the executive director, be delayed until a sworn statement is received. The executive director may accept an anonymous complaint or a complaint that is not a sworn statement if there is sufficient information for the investigation; however, the executive director shall then complete a complaint form under oath.

(f) Within 15 days of the receipt of a complaint, the executive director shall review the complaint to assure that there is sufficient information to initiate an investigation and that the allegations contained in the complaint fall within the board's jurisdiction. If the complaint is against a person licensed by another board, the executive director will forward the complaint to that board not later than the 15th day after the date the agency determines that the information should be referred to the appropriate agency as provided in Government Code, Chapter 774.

(g) If the allegations do not fall within the board's jurisdiction, the executive director shall refer the complaint to the Ethics Committee. Based on its review of the complaint, the Ethics Committee may instruct the executive director to:

  (1) close the complaint with a letter to the complainant explaining why the complaint is not within the board's jurisdiction; or

  (2) advise the complainant of the additional information necessary to initiate an investigation.

(h) If the allegations in the complaint are within the board's jurisdiction and sufficient for investigation, the executive director shall:

  (1) evaluate the threat to public health and safety documented by the complaint;

  (2) establish an appropriate plan and schedule for its investigation to be noted in the complaint log;

  (3) notify all parties, as appropriate, to the circumstances of the complaint, that an investigation has been initiated, and provide a copy of the

board's policy regarding the time frame for conducting an investigation; and

(4) report the status of all continuing investigations to the complainant and the licensee or applicant every 90 days.

(i) The executive director will initiate the investigation of a complaint by requesting statements and evidence from all parties; by requesting that the complaint investigation be conducted by a department investigator; or may enlist the service of a private investigator.

(j) If an investigation is assigned to an investigator, the executive director will request a written report of the progress of the investigation at least two weeks before each meeting of the ethics committee until the investigation is complete and will provide a copy of the report to the committee.

(k) If an investigation uncovers evidence of a criminal act, the appropriate law enforcement officials will be notified only with approval of the executive director or the Ethics Committee. In any case, the complaint process will continue to its completion unless a written request is received from a law enforcement agency requesting that action on the complaint be delayed, stating the reason for requesting the delay, and stating an anticipated date by which that agency plans to take action on the case.

(l) If a law enforcement agency has requested a delay in the complaint process in writing, the executive director will request timely updates on that agency's progress in bringing the matter to a close.

(m) The executive director will inform the board if the services of a private investigator are needed for the timely completion of a complaint investigation or for any other reason.

(n) The subject of the complaint will be notified of the allegations either in writing, by phone or in person by the executive director or the investigator assigned to the case and will be required to provide a sworn response to the allegations within two weeks of that notice. Failure to respond to the allegations within the two-week period is evidence of failure to cooperate with the investigation and subject to disciplinary action.

(o) The ethics committee will review the complaint log to ensure that:

(1) complaint investigations are being handled in a timely manner;

(2) complaints are not dismissed without appropriate consideration;

(3) a person who files a complaint has an opportunity to explain the allegations made in the complaint; and

(4) any issues related to complaints which arise under the Act, or this chapter, are resolved.

(p) The ethics committee shall determine whether a violation exists and whether to dismiss the complaint as unsubstantiated or to consider appropriate disciplinary action.

(q) If a violation is found but it does not seriously affect the health and safety of clients or other persons, the committee may resolve the complaint by informal methods such as a cease and desist order or an informal agreement with the violator to correct the violation.

(r) If the complaint is not resolved by the committee, the committee may recommend that disciplinary action be taken or that other appropriate action as authorized by law be taken, including injunctive relief or civil penalties. Action may be taken based on the allegations in the complaint or any violations found during investigation.

(s) If no violation exists or the complaint is dismissed as unsubstantiated, the complainant and the licensee or applicant shall be notified in writing of the finding. The committee may include in that notice a statement of issues and recommendations that the committee wishes to bring to the attention of the subject of the complaint.

(t) If the executive director receives credible evidence that a licensee is engaging in acts that pose an immediate and significant threat of physical or emotional harm to the public, the executive director shall consult with the members of the ethics committee for authorization for an emergency suspension of the license.

§781.604. Ethics Committee Meetings and Policy

(a) The Ethics Committee will meet on a regular basis to review and recommend action on complaints filed against social workers. Additionally, the committee will hold informal hearings to review previous committee actions at the request of a party to a complaint.

(b) An agenda and completed reports of complaint investigations will be sent to committee members approximately two weeks prior to each meeting. The agenda will list all items to be considered by the committee. Complaints will be listed on the agenda by the assigned complaint tracking number.

(c) Persons who are not members of the committee are permitted to observe committee work unless the committee enters into executive session for legal consultation. Committee members, staff, consultants and licensees against whom the complaint is filed and the person filing the complaint may participate in the discussion of a complaint pending action before the committee. The committee chair or committee by vote may impose time limitations on discussion.

(d) A report on all completed investigations will be provided to committee members. The report will include copies of information obtained in the investigation and a summary sheet with a staff recommendation for the disposition for each case. Cases will be grouped on the agenda according to their recommended disposition. Cases that are recommended for closure will be listed together as a consent agenda item. Any committee member, consultant, or staff person may remove cases from the consent agenda for individual review upon request. All cases left on the consent agenda will be voted on as a group for closure. All other cases will be considered on an individual basis.

(e) The committee will base its decision regarding the validity of a complaint on the evidence documented in the report of the investigation. The committee may find that there is or is not evidence of a violation of licensing law or rules or the committee may request additional information of a case for later review. If the committee finds that a social worker has violated licensing law or rules, the committee will consider the established policy guidelines and other relevant factors in their recommendation of disciplinary action.

(f) All parties to a complaint will be notified of the findings and recommendations of the committee. Any party to the complaint who disagrees with the action of the committee may submit a written statement of the reasons for his or her disagreement, and may request an informal hearing before the committee. Request for an informal hearing must be made within 10 days of the date of the letter stating the disposition of the case.

§781.605. Informal Hearing Meetings

(a) Informal hearings will be scheduled for the next meeting of the complaints committee meeting consistent with public notice requirements. All parties to the complaint will be notified of the date and location of the informal hearing and of their right to be heard at that meeting or to submit relevant material to the committee for their review.

(b) All parties to the complaint will be given an opportunity to make a statement to the committee. Based on the evidence, the committee may revise its findings and recommendation as appropriate or reaffirm its original action. All parties to the complaint will be notified of the committee's decision.

(c) The board's legal counsel or an attorney from the department's Office of General Counsel shall attend each settlement conference.

§781.606. Licensing of Persons with Criminal Backgrounds

(a) The board may take action against a licensee or deny a license pursuant to Texas Occupations Code, Chapter 53, concerning felony or misdemeanor convictions, or the Act, §505.451(12), concerning felony convictions.

(b) The following felonies and misdemeanors relate to licensure as a social worker because these criminal offenses indicate an inability or a tendency to be unable to perform as a social worker:

   (1) a violation of the Act;

   (2) failure to report child abuse or neglect;

   (3) a misdemeanor involving deceptive business practices;

   (4) the offense of assault or sexual assault;

   (5) the felony offense of theft; or

   (6) any other misdemeanor or felony which would indicate an inability or a tendency to be unable to perform as a social worker.

(c) An applicant or licensee with a criminal background may provide or be requested to provide documentation of rehabilitation for consideration by the appropriate committee of the board.

(d) Documentation of rehabilitation may include the following:

(1) court records related to the conviction;

(2) documents related to the sentence imposed by the court;

(3) documents of completion of the sentence;

(4) documents of satisfactory completion of probation or parole;

(5) information about subsequent good conduct;

(6) letters of support from employers or others who have knowledge of the applicant's accomplishments following the conviction; and

(7) any other information that supports the applicant's qualifications for a license.

(8) summary of the arresting event and conditions which lead to the event.

(e) The licensee may be referred to the appropriate board committee for review and determination of eligibility or monitoring requirements. Licensees referred to the board are afforded due process under the APA.

§781.607. Suspension, Revocation, or Non-renewal

(a) If the board suspends a license or recognition, the suspension shall remain in effect for the period of time stated in the order or until the board determines that the reason for the suspension no longer exists.

(b) While on suspension, the licensee shall comply with the renewal requirements in this chapter including payment of fees and completion of continuing education; however, the suspension shall remain in effect pursuant to subsection (a) of this section.

(c) Upon revocation, suspension or non-renewal of a license, a licensee shall return his or her license to the board.

(d) The board may refuse to renew the license of a person who fails to pay an administrative penalty imposed in accordance with the Act unless the enforcement of the penalty is stayed or a court has ordered that the administrative penalty is not owed.

§781.608. Informal Disposition

(a) If a licensee agrees to the disciplinary action proposed by the ethics committee, an agreed order shall be prepared by the board office or the board's legal counsel and forwarded to the licensee or applicant. The order shall contain agreed findings of fact and conclusions of law.

(1) The licensee or applicant shall execute the order and return the signed order to the board office within 10 days of his or her receipt of the order.

(2) If the licensee or applicant signs and accepts the recommendations, the agreed order shall be submitted to the entire board for its approval. Placement of the agreed order on the board agenda shall constitute only a recommendation for approval by the board.

(3) If the licensee or applicant fails to return the signed order within the stated time period, the inaction shall constitute rejection of the settlement recommendations.

(4) If the licensee or applicant rejects the proposed settlement, the matter shall be referred to the executive director for appropriate action.

(b) The licensee or applicant shall be notified of the date, time, and place of the board meeting at which the proposed agreed order will be considered. Attendance by the licensee or applicant is voluntary.

(c) Upon an affirmative majority vote, the board shall enter an agreed order approving the accepted settlement recommendations. The board may not change the terms of a proposed order but may only approve or disapprove an agreed order unless the licensee or applicant is present at the board meeting and agrees to other terms proposed by the board.

(d) If the board does not approve a proposed agreed order, the licensee or applicant and the complainant shall be so informed. The matter shall be referred to the executive director for other appropriate action.

(e) A proposed agreed order is not effective until the full board has approved the agreed order. The order shall then be effective in accordance with the APA.

(f) A licensee's opportunity for an informal conference under this section shall satisfy the requirement of the APA, §2001.054(c).

(g) The board may order a license holder to pay a refund to a consumer as provided in an agreement resulting from an informal settlement conference instead of or in addition to imposing an administrative penalty. The amount of a refund ordered as provided in an agreement resulting from an informal settlement conference may not exceed the amount the consumer paid to the license holder for a service regulated by the Act and this title. The board may not require payment of other damages or estimate harm in a refund order.

§781.609. Default Orders

(a) If a right to a hearing is waived under §781.602(c) of this title (relating to Disciplinary Action; Notices) or §781.703(b) of this title (relating to Notice), the board shall consider an order taking disciplinary action as described in the written notice to the licensee or applicant.

(b) The licensee or applicant and the complainant shall be notified of the date, time, and place of the board meeting at which the default order will be considered. Attendance is voluntary.

(c) The board's legal counsel or any attorney from the department's Office of General Counsel shall attend the board meeting.

(d) Upon an affirmative majority vote, the board shall enter an order imposing appropriate disciplinary action.

§781.610. Monitoring of Licensees

(a) The executive director shall maintain a disciplinary action tracking system.

(b) Each licensee that has had disciplinary action taken against his or her license or recognition shall be required to submit regularly scheduled reports at intervals appropriate to each individual situation.

(c) The executive director shall review the reports regarding licensees on monitoring as a result of formal disciplinary action and notify the ethics committee if the requirements of the disciplinary action are not met.

(d) The ethics committee may consider more severe disciplinary proceedings if noncompliance occurs.

(e) The board may require monitoring of a licensee who may pose a potential threat to public health or safety, regardless of whether a formal complaint has been received by the board. The board may require a licensee on monitoring status to comply with specified conditions set forth by the board. A licensee placed on this type of monitoring is not considered to have formal disciplinary action taken against their license, but must comply fully with the order of the board or face possible formal disciplinary action levied by the board. Factors that may constitute a potential threat to public health or safety may include, but are not limited to, reports of chemical abuse by a licensee, mental and/or physical health concerns, and/or criminal activity or allegations, whether pending or in final disposition by a court of law.

(f) Participants of the AMEC program in accordance with §781.311 of this title (relating to Temporary License) shall be considered to be on monitoring status until released by the board and issued a regular license.

SUBCHAPTER G. FORMAL HEARINGS

§781.701. Purpose

These rules cover the hearing procedures and practices that are available to persons or parties who request formal hearings from the board. The intended effect of these rules is to supplement the contested case provisions of the Texas Government Code, Chapter 2001, Administrative Procedure Act (APA), the hearing procedures of the State Office of Administrative Hearings (Texas Government Code, Chapter 2003, and Rules of Procedure, 1 Texas Administrative Code, Chapter 155), and to make the public aware of these procedures and practices.

§781.702. Notice

(a) For purposes contested case proceedings before the State Office of Administrative Hearings, proper notice means notice sufficient to meet the provisions of the Texas Government Code, Chapter 2001 and the State Office of Administrative Hearings Rules of Procedure, 1 Texas Administrative Code, Chapter 155.

(b) For purposes of informal conferences, proper notice shall include the name and style of the case, the date, time, and place of the informal conference, and a short statement of the purpose of the conference.

(c) The following statement shall be attached to the notice of hearing or notice of informal conference, in bold letters of at least 10 point type:

FAILURE TO APPEAR

YOUR FAILURE TO APPEAR, IN PERSON OR BY REPRESENTATIVE, ON THE ABOVE DATE, TIME, AND PLACE, WILL BE CONSIDERED A WAIVER OF YOUR RIGHT TO A HEARING. THE FACTUAL ALLEGATIONS IN THIS NOTICE WILL BE DEEMED ADMITTED AS TRUE AND THE PROPOSED DISCIPLINARY ACTION WILL BE GRANTED BY DEFAULT.

§781.703. Default

(a) For purposes of this section, default means the failure of the respondent to appear in person or by legal representative on the day and at the time set for hearing in a contested case or informal conference, or the failure to appear by telephone, in accordance with the notice of hearing or notice of informal conference.

(b) *Remedies available upon default in a contested case before the State Office of Administrative Hearings (SOAH).* The Administrative Law Judge (ALJ) shall proceed in the party's absence and such failure to appear shall entitle the department to seek informal disposition as provided by the Texas Government Code, Chapter 2001. The ALJ shall grant any motion by the department to remove the case from the contested hearing docket and allow for informal disposition by the board.

(c) *Remedies available upon default in an informal conference.* The board may proceed to make such informal disposition of the case as it deems proper, as if no request for hearing had been received.

(d) The board may enter a default judgment by issuing an order against the defaulting party in which the factual allegations in the notice of violation or notice of hearing are deemed admitted as true without the requirement of submitting additional proof, upon the offer of proof that proper notice was provided to the defaulting party.

(e) *Motion to set aside and reopen.* A timely motion by the respondent to set aside the default order and reopen the record may be granted if the respondent establishes that the failure to attend the hearing was neither intentional nor the result of conscious indifference, and that such failure was due to mistake, accident, or circumstances beyond the respondent's control.

(1) A motion to set aside the default order and reopen the record shall be filed with the board prior to the time that the order of the board becomes final pursuant to the provisions of the Texas Government Code.

(2) A motion to set aside the default order and reopen the record is not a motion for rehearing and is not to be considered a substitute for a motion for rehearing. The filing of a motion to set aside the default order and reopen has no effect on either the statutory time periods for the filing of a motion for rehearing or on the time period for ruling on a motion for rehearing, as provided in the Texas Government Code.

(f) This subsection also applies to cases where service of the notice of hearing on a defaulting party is shown only by proof that the notice was sent to the party's last known address as shown on the department's records, with no showing of actual receipt by the defaulting party or the defaulting party's agent. In that situation, the default procedures described in subsection (c) of this section may be used if there is credible evidence that the notice of hearing was sent by certified or registered mail, return receipt requested, to the defaulting party's last known address.

§781.704. Action After Hearing

(a) *Reopening of hearing for new evidence.*

(1) The board may reopen a hearing where new evidence is offered which was unobtainable or unavailable at the time of the hearing.

(2) The department shall reopen a hearing to include such new evidence as part of the record if the board deems such evidence necessary for a proper and fair determination of the case. The reopened hearing will be limited to only such new evidence.

(3) Notice of any reopened hearing shall be provided to all previously designated parties, by certified mail, return receipt requested.

(b) *Final orders or decisions.*

(1) The final order or decision of the department will be rendered by the board or its designee.

(2) All final orders or decisions shall be in writing and shall set forth the findings of fact and conclusions required by law, either in the body of the order, by attachment, or by reference to an ALJ's proposal for decision.

(3) Unless otherwise permitted by statute or by these sections, all final orders shall be signed by the board chair, or her designee.

(c) *Motion for rehearing.* A motion for rehearing shall be governed by the APA or other pertinent statute and shall be filed with the board.

(d) *Appeals.* All appeals from final department orders or decisions shall be governed by the APA or other pertinent statute and shall be addressed to the board.

Subchapter H. Sanction Guidelines

§781.801. Purpose

The schedule of sanctions is adopted by rule pursuant to the Act, §505.254. The schedule is intended to be used by the ethics committee as a guide in assessing sanctions for violations of the Act or this chapter. The schedule is also intended to serve as a guide to administrative law judges, and as a written statement of applicable rules or policies of the Board pursuant to the Government Code. The failure of an administrative law judge to follow the schedule may serve as a basis to vacate or modify an order pursuant to the Government Code. No two disciplinary cases are the same. This schedule is not intended as a substitute for thoughtful consideration of each individual disciplinary matter.

§781.802. Relevant Factors

(a) When a licensee has violated the Act or this chapter, three general factors combine to determine the appropriate sanction:

  (1) the degree of culpability of the licensee;

  (2) the harm caused or posed; and

  (3) appropriate deterrence.

(b) Special factors are to be considered as set forth below. It is the responsibility of the licensee to bring exonerating factors to the attention of the board or ALJ.

  (1) *Seriousness of Violation.* The following factors are identified:

    (A) the nature of the harm caused, or the risk posed, to the health, safety or welfare of the public, such as emotional, physical, or financial;

    (B) the extent of the harm caused, or the risk posed, to the health, safety or welfare of the public, such as whether the harm is low, moderate or severe, and the number of persons harmed or exposed to risk; and

    (C) the frequency and time-periods covered by the violations, such as whether there were multiple violations and the period of time over which the violations occurred.

  (2) *Nature of the Violation.* The following factors are identified:

    (A) the relationship between the licensee and the person harmed, or exposed to harm;

    (B) the vulnerability of the person harmed, or exposed to harm;

    (C) the degree of culpability of the licensee, such as whether the violation was:

(i) intentional or premeditated;

(ii) due to blatant disregard or gross neglect; or

(iii) resulted from simple error or inadvertence; and

(iv) the extent to which the violation evidences lack of character, such as lack of integrity, trustworthiness, or honesty of the licensee.

(3) *Personal Accountability.* The following factors are identified:

(A) admission of wrong or error, and acceptance of responsibility;

(B) appropriate degree of remorse or concern;

(C) efforts to ameliorate the harm or make restitution;

(D) efforts to ensure future violations do not occur; and

(E) cooperation with any investigation or request for information.

(4) *Prevention of Violations.* The following factors are identified:

(A) the sanction required to deter future similar violations by the licensee;

(B) sanctions necessary to ensure compliance by the licensee of other provisions of the Act or this chapter; and

(C) sanctions necessary to deter other licensees from such violations.

(5) *Miscellaneous Factors.* The following factors are identified:

(A) professional experience at time of violation;

(B) presence or absence of prior or subsequent violations;

(C) conduct and work activity prior to and following the violation;

(D) character references; and

(E) any other factors justice may require.

§781.803. Severity Level and Sanction Guide

The following severity levels and sanction guides are based on the relevant factors in §781.802 of this title (relating to Relevant Factors):

(1) *Level One*—Revocation of license. These violations evidence intentional or gross misconduct on the part of the licensee and/or cause or pose a high degree of harm to the public and/or require severe punishment as a deterrent to the licensee, or other licensees. The fact that a license is ordered revoked does not necessarily mean the licensee can never regain licensure. The board may also impose an administrative penalty of not less than $250 or more than $5,000 for each Level One violation. Each day a violation continues or occurs is a separate violation for the purpose of imposing a penalty.

(2) *Level Two*—Extended suspension of license. These violations involve less misconduct, harm, or need for deterrence than Level One violations, but require termination of licensure for a period of not less than one year. The board may also impose an administrative penalty of not less than $250 or more than $4,000 for each Level Two violation. Each day a violation continues or occurs is a separate violation for the purpose of imposing a penalty.

(3) *Level Three*—Moderate suspension of license. These violations involve less misconduct, harm, or need for deterrence than Level Two violations, but require termination of licensure for some period of time. The board may also impose an administrative penalty of not less than $250 or more than $3,000 for each Level Three violation. Each day a violation continues or occurs is a separate violation for the purpose of imposing a penalty.

(4) *Level Four*—Probated suspension of license. These violations do not involve enough harm, misconduct, or need for deterrence to warrant termination of licensure, yet are severe enough to warrant monitoring of the licensee to ensure future compliance. Possible probationary terms are set out as in §781.806 of this title (relating to Probation) and may be ordered as appropriate. The board may also impose an administrative penalty of not less than $250 or more than $2,000 for each Level Four violation. Each day a violation continues or occurs is a separate violation for the purpose of imposing a penalty.

(5) *Level Five*—Reprimand. These violations involve minor misconduct not directly involving the health, safety or welfare of the particular member of the public at issue. The board may also impose an administrative penalty of not less than $250 or more than $1,000 for each Level Five violation. Each day a violation continues or occurs is a separate violation for the purpose of imposing a penalty.

§781.804. Other Disciplinary Actions

The ethics committee or executive director, as appropriate, may resolve pending complaints by issuance of formal advisory letters informing licensees of their duties under the Act or this chapter, and whether the conduct or omission complained of appears to violate such duties. Such advisory letters may be introduced as evidence in any subsequent disciplinary action involving acts or omissions after receipt of the advisory letters. The ethics committee or executive director, as appropriate, may also issue informal reminders to licensees regarding other licensing matters. The licensee is not entitled to a hearing on the matters set forth in the formal advisory letter or informal reminders, but may make a written response to be included with such letters in the social worker's licensing records.

§781.805. State Office of Administrative Hearings

In those cases requiring a hearing, the ethics committee, through the executive director, will issue a notice of violation letter to the licensee, and state the severity level and the recommended sanction. The recommended sanction reflects the judgment of the ethics committee based on the information available at that time. It is recognized that the evidence presented at a hearing could indicate a greater or lesser sanction. However, an administrative law judge may not impose a sanction more than one severity level higher or lower than proposed by the ethics committee.

§781.806. Probation

If probation is ordered or agreed to, the following terms may be required.

(1) *General Conditions.* There are 12 general conditions of probation. They appear in all disciplinary orders of the social work board that place licensee's on probation and they are presented below:

(A) *Obey all laws.* The licensee shall obey all federal, state and local laws and rules governing the practice of social work in this state.

(B) *Periodic reports.* Under penalty of perjury, the licensee shall submit periodic reports as requested by the board on forms provided by the board, stating whether there has been compliance with all the conditions of probation.

(C) *Surveillance program.* The licensee shall comply with the board's probation surveillance program.

(D) *Interview with the board or its designee.* The licensee shall appear in person for interviews with the board or its designee at various intervals and with reasonable notice.

(E) *Out-of-state practice or residence.* In the event the licensee should leave this state to reside or to practice outside the state, the licensee must notify the board in writing of the dates of departure and return. Periods of residency or practice outside this state will not count toward the time of this probationary period. The social work licensing authorities of the jurisdiction to which the licensee is moving or has moved must be promptly notified of the licensee's probationary status in this state. The probationary period will resume when the licensee returns to the state to reside or practice.

(F) *Completion of probation.* Upon successful completion of probation, the licensee's license will be fully restored by the executive director. The executive director will report this information to the full board at their next scheduled meeting.

(G) *Violation of probation.* If the licensee violates probation in any respect, the board, after giving formal notice and the opportunity to be heard, may revoke the licensee's license and order of recognition or take other appropriate disciplinary action. The period of probation shall be extended until the matter is final.

(H) *Notification of practice settings.* The licensee shall promptly notify all settings in which the licensee practices social work in writing of his or her probationary status.

(I) *Supervision Restrictions.* While on probation, the licensee shall not act as a supervisor or gain any hours of supervised practice required for any license issued by the board.

(J) *Costs of Compliance.* The licensee is responsible for all costs of compliance with all conditions of probation.

(K) *Renewal Requirements.* The licensee shall comply with the renewal requirements in the Act and the rules of the board.

(L) *General Compliance.* The licensee shall follow the Act and the rules of the board.

(2) *Special Conditions.* There are 13 special conditions of probation. At the discretion of the board, one or more of these conditions may appear in a disciplinary order of the board that places a licensee on probation. The following conditions presented below are suggested wording for disciplinary orders.

(A) *Actual Suspension.* As part of probation, the license is suspended for a period of (example: one) year beginning the effective day of this order.

(B) *Drug/Medication Use.* The licensee shall abstain completely from the personal use or possession of controlled substances and dangerous drugs as defined by law, or any drugs requiring a prescription. Orders forbidding the licensee from personal use or possession of controlled substances or dangerous drugs do not apply to medications lawfully prescribed to the licensee for a bona fide illness or condition by a licensed physician.

(C) *Alcohol.* Abstain from Use. The licensee shall abstain completely from the use of alcoholic beverages.

(D) *Body Fluid Testing.* The licensee shall immediately submit to body fluid testing, at the licensee's cost, upon the written request of the board or its designee.

(E) *Rehabilitation Program.* Within (example: 30) days of the effective date of the order, the licensee shall submit to the board for its prior approval a rehabilitation program in which the licensee shall participate at least weekly for at least (example: 50) weeks of the calendar year for the duration of probation. In the periodic reports to the board, the licensee shall provide documented evidence of continuing participation in this program including the dates of the weekly meetings attended and the address of each meeting. At the end of the required period, the director of the program shall provide the board with documented evidence concerning the licensee's completion of the program and arrangements for appropriate follow-up.

(F) *Community Service.* Within (example: 60) days of the effective date of the order, licensee shall submit to the board for its prior approval a community service program in which the licensee shall provide free social work services on a regular basis to a community or charitable facility or agency for at least (example: 20) hours a month for the first (example: 24) months of probation.

(G) *Medical Evaluation Treatment.* Within (example: 30) days of the effective date of the order, and on a periodic basis thereafter as may be required by the board or its designee, the licensee shall undergo a medical evaluation by a board approved physician who shall furnish a medical report to the board or its designee. If the licensee is required by the board or its designee to undergo medical treatment, the licensee shall, within (example: 30) days of the requirement notice, submit to the board for its prior approval the name and qualifications of a physician of the licensee's choice. Upon approval of the treating physician, the licensee shall undergo and continue medical treatment until further notice from the board. The licensee shall have the treating physician submit periodic reports to the board as the board directs. In cases where the evidence demonstrates that medical illness or disability was a contributing cause of the violations, the licensee shall not engage in the practice of social work until notified by the board of its determination that the licensee is medically fit to practice safely.

(H) *Psychosocial/Psychological/Psychiatric Evaluation.* Within (example: 30) days of the effective date of the decision, and on a periodic basis thereafter as may be required by the board or its designee, the licensee shall undergo evaluation by a licensed professional (social worker, psychologist, or psychiatrist) selected by the board. The evaluator shall furnish a written report to the board or its designee regarding the licensee's judgment and ability to function independently and safely as a social worker and any other information as the board may require. The cost of an evaluation shall be borne by the licensee. The licensee shall execute a release of information authorizing the evaluator to release all information to the board. The evaluation shall be treated as confidential by the board. In cases where the evidence demonstrates that mental illness or disability was a contributing cause of the violations, the licensee shall not engage in the practice of social work until notified by the board of its determination that the licensee is medically fit to practice safely.

(I) *Ethics Course.* Within (example: 60) days of the effective date of the order, the licensee shall select and submit to the board or its designee for prior approval a course in ethics, which the licensee shall take and successfully complete as directed by the board.

(J) *Supervision of the Licensee's Practice.* Within (example: 30) days of the effective date of this order, the licensee shall submit to the board for its prior approval the name and qualifications of one or more proposed supervisors and a plan by each such supervisor by which the licensee's practice would be supervised. Each proposed supervisor shall be licensed as an LCSW who is a board approved supervisor with expertise in the licensee's field of practice. The supervisor shall submit written reports to the board on a quarterly basis verifying that supervision has taken place as required and including an evaluation of the licensee's performance. It shall be the licensee's responsibility to assure that the required reports are filed in a timely fashion. The licensee shall give the supervisor access to the licensee's fiscal and client records. The supervisor shall be independent, with no current or prior business, professional or personal relationship with the licensee. The licensee shall not practice until the licensee has received notification that the board has approved the licensee's choice as a supervisor. If the supervisor quits or is otherwise no longer available, the licensee shall not practice until the board has approved a new supervisor. All costs of supervision shall be borne by the licensee. Supervision shall consist of at least one hour per week in individual face-to-face meetings.

(K) *Psychotherapy.* Within (example: 60) days of the effective date of the order, the licensee shall submit to the board for its prior approval the name and qualifications of one or more therapists of the licensee's choice. The therapist shall possess a valid license and shall have had no current or prior business, professional or personal relationship with the licensee. Upon approval by the board, the licensee shall undergo and continue treatment until the board determines that no further psychotherapy is necessary. The licensee shall have the treating psychotherapist submit periodic reports as determined by the board, and notify the board immediately if the therapist believes the licensee cannot safely continue to render services. All cost of therapy shall be the responsibility of the licensee. The licensee shall execute a release of information authorizing the therapist to divulge information to the board.

(L) *Education.* The licensee shall take and successfully complete such remedial education as the board may require.

(M) *Take and Pass Licensure Examinations.* The licensee shall take and pass the licensure exam currently required of new applicants for the license possessed by the licensee. The exam shall be taken on a regularly scheduled date. The licensee shall pay the established examination fee.

(N) *Other Conditions.* The board may order other terms of probation as may be appropriate.

§781.807. Release from Probation

On completion of the terms of board order, the licensee shall petition the executive director or board for an unrestricted license. The petition shall be in writing and shall include documentation and statements from the supervisor, if one was appointed, and any other parties designated in the terms of the board order that the terms of the board order have been fulfilled and that the licensee is qualified for unrestricted practice under the terms of the license.

(1) If the executive director is satisfied that the terms of the probation have been fulfilled, the executive director shall notify the licensee that the restrictions for the license have been removed and make a report to the board at their next scheduled meeting.

(2) If the executive director is not satisfied that the terms of the probation have been fulfilled, the executive director shall notify the licensee and shall bring the petition before the ethics committee for their review and recommendations.

ALERT: Rules guiding the social work profession can be changed at any time. It is the licensee's responsibility to visit the Texas State Board of Social Worker Examiners website on a regular basis to check for any changes to the rules. Inclusion of the most recent approved set of rules in this book (5/26/06) in no way guarantees that they are the most current rules. http://www.dshs.state.tx.us/socialwork/default.shtm

---

Family Code

Court Ordered Counseling in Divorce—§6

§6.505. Counseling

(a) While a divorce suit is pending, the court may direct the parties to counsel with a person named by the court.

(b) The person named by the court to counsel the parties shall submit a written report to the court and to the parties before the final hearing. In the report, the counselor shall give only an opinion as to whether there exists a reasonable expectation of reconciliation of the parties and, if so, whether further counseling would be beneficial. The sole purpose of the report is to aid the court in determining whether the suit for divorce should be continued pending further counseling.

(c) A copy of the report shall be furnished to each party.

(d) If the court believes that there is a reasonable expectation of the parties' reconciliation, the court may by written order continue the proceedings and direct the parties to a person named by the court for further counseling for a period fixed by the court not to exceed 60 days, subject to any terms, conditions, and limitations the court considers desirable. In ordering counseling, the court shall consider the circumstances of the parties, including the needs of the parties' family and the availability of counseling services. At the expiration of the period specified by the court, the counselor to whom the parties were directed shall report to the court whether the parties have complied with the court's order. Thereafter, the court shall proceed as in a divorce suit generally.

(e) If the court orders counseling under this section and the parties to the marriage are the parents of a child under 18 years of age born or adopted during the marriage, the counseling shall include counseling on issues that confront children who are the subject of a suit affecting the parent-child relationship.

Consent to Treatment of Child by non-Parent or Child—§32

§32.001. Consent by Non-Parent

(a) The following persons may consent to medical, dental, psychological, and surgical treatment of a child when the person having the right to consent as otherwise provided by law cannot be contacted and that person has not given actual notice to the contrary:

   (1) a grandparent of the child;

   (2) an adult brother or sister of the child;

(3) an adult aunt or uncle of the child;

(4) an educational institution in which the child is enrolled that has received written authorization to consent from a person having the right to consent;

(5) an adult who has actual care, control, and possession of the child and has written authorization to consent from a person having the right to consent;

(6) a court having jurisdiction over a suit affecting the parent-child relationship of which the child is the subject;

(7) an adult responsible for the actual care, control, and possession of a child under the jurisdiction of a juvenile court or committed by a juvenile court to the care of an agency of the state or county; or

(8) a peace officer who has lawfully taken custody of a minor, if the peace officer has reasonable grounds to believe the minor is in need of immediate medical treatment.

(b) The Texas Youth Commission may consent to the medical, dental, psychological, and surgical treatment of a child committed to it under Title 3 when the person having the right to consent has been contacted and that person has not given actual notice to the contrary.

(c) This section does not apply to consent for the immunization of a child.

(d) A person who consents to the medical treatment of a minor under Subsection (a)(7) or (8) is immune from liability for damages resulting from the examination or treatment of the minor, except to the extent of the person's own acts of negligence. A physician or dentist licensed to practice in this state, or a hospital or medical facility at which a minor is treated is immune from liability for damages resulting from the examination or treatment of a minor under this section, except to the extent of the person's own acts of negligence.

§32.002. Consent Form

(a) Consent to medical treatment under this subchapter must be in writing, signed by the person giving consent, and given to the doctor, hospital, or other medical facility that administers the treatment.

(b) The consent must include:

(1) the name of the child;

(2) the name of one or both parents, if known, and the name of any managing conservator or guardian of the child;

(3) the name of the person giving consent and the person's relationship to the child;

(4) a statement of the nature of the medical treatment to be given; and

(5) the date the treatment is to begin.

Section 4 of Acts 1995, 74th Leg., ch. 123, eff. Sept. 1, 1995, amends subsec. (a) of V.T.C.A., Family Code §35.02 [now this section] without reference to the repeal of said section by Acts 1995, 74th Leg., ch. 20, §2(1). As so amended, subsec. (a) reads:

"Consent to medical treatment under Sections 35.01 and 35.011 of this code shall be in writing, signed by the person giving consent, and given to the doctor, hospital, or other medical facility that administers the treatment."

§32.003. Consent to Treatment by Child

(a) A child may consent to medical, dental, psychological, and surgical treatment for the child by a licensed physician or dentist if the child:

(1) is on active duty with the armed services of the United States of America;

(2) is:

(A) 16 years of age or older and resides separate and apart from the child's parents, managing conservator, or guardian, with or without the consent of the parents, managing conservator, or guardian and regardless of the duration of the residence; and

(B) managing the child's own financial affairs, regardless of the source of the income;

(3) consents to the diagnosis and treatment of an infectious, contagious, or communicable disease that is required by law or a rule to be reported by the licensed physician or dentist to a local health officer or the Texas Department of Health, including all diseases within the scope of Section 81.041, Health and Safety Code;

(4) is unmarried and pregnant and consents to hospital, medical, or surgical treatment, other than abortion, related to the pregnancy;

(5) consents to examination and treatment for drug or chemical addiction, drug or chemical dependency, or any other condition directly related to drug or chemical use; or

(6) is unmarried and has actual custody of the child's biological child and consents to medical, dental, psychological, or surgical treatment for the child.

(b) Consent by a child to medical, dental, psychological, and surgical treatment under this section is not subject to disaffirmance because of minority.

(c) Consent of the parents, managing conservator, or guardian of a child is not necessary in order to authorize hospital, medical, surgical, or dental care under this section.

(d) A licensed physician, dentist, or psychologist may, with or without the consent of a child who is a patient, advise the parents, managing conservator, or guardian of the child of the treatment given to or needed by the child.

(e) A physician, dentist, psychologist, hospital, or medical facility is not liable for the examination and treatment of a child under this section except for the provider's or the facility's own acts of negligence.

(f) A physician, dentist, psychologist, hospital, or medical facility may rely on the written statement of the child containing the grounds on which the child has capacity to consent to the child's medical treatment.

§32.004. Consent to Counseling

(a) A child may consent to counseling for:

  (1) suicide prevention;

  (2) chemical addiction or dependency; or

  (3) sexual, physical, or emotional abuse.

(b) A licensed or certified physician, psychologist, counselor, or social worker having reasonable grounds to believe that a child has been sexually, physically, or emotionally abused, is contemplating suicide, or is suffering from a chemical or drug addiction or dependency may:

  (1) counsel the child without the consent of the child's parents or, if applicable, managing conservator or guardian;

  (2) with or without the consent of the child who is a client, advise the child's parents or, if applicable, managing conservator or guardian of the treatment given to or needed by the child; and

  (3) rely on the written statement of the child containing the grounds on which the child has capacity to consent to the child's own treatment under this section.

(c) Unless consent is obtained as otherwise allowed by law, a physician, psychologist, counselor, or social worker may not counsel a child if consent is prohibited by a court order.

(d) A physician, psychologist, counselor, or social worker counseling a child under this section is not liable for damages except for damages resulting from the person's negligence or willful misconduct.

(e) A parent, or, if applicable, managing conservator or guardian, who has not consented to counseling treatment of the child is not obligated to compensate a physician, psychologist, counselor, or social worker for counseling services rendered under this section.

§32.005. Examination Without Consent of Abuse or Neglect of Child

(a) Except as provided by Subsection (c), a physician, dentist, or psychologist having reasonable grounds to believe that a child's physical or mental condition has been adversely affected by abuse or neglect may examine the child without the consent of the child, the child's parents, or other person authorized to consent to treatment under this subchapter.

(b) An examination under this section may include X-rays, blood tests, photographs, and penetration of tissue necessary to accomplish those tests.

(c) Unless consent is obtained as otherwise allowed by law, a physician, dentist, or psychologist may not examine a child:

(1) 16 years of age or older who refuses to consent; or

(2) for whom consent is prohibited by a court order.

(d) A physician, dentist, or psychologist examining a child under this section is not liable for damages except for damages resulting from the physician's or dentist's negligence.

WAIVER OF JURISDICTION AND DISCRETIONARY TRANSFER—§54.02

§54.02. Waiver of Jurisdiction and Discretionary Transfer to Criminal Court

(a) The juvenile court may waive its exclusive original jurisdiction and transfer a child to the appropriate district court or criminal district court for criminal proceedings if:

(1) the child is alleged to have violated a penal law of the grade of felony;

(2) the child was:

(A) 14 years of age or older at the time he is alleged to have committed the offense, if the offense is a capital felony, an aggravated controlled substance felony, or a felony of the first degree, and no adjudication hearing has been conducted concerning that offense; or

(B) 15 years of age or older at the time the child is alleged to have committed the offense, if the offense is a felony of the second or third degree or a state jail felony, and no adjudication hearing has been conducted concerning that offense; and

(3) after a full investigation and a hearing, the juvenile court determines that there is probable cause to believe that the child before the court committed the offense alleged and that because of the seriousness of the offense alleged or the background of the child the welfare of the community requires criminal proceedings.

(b) The petition and notice requirements of Sections 53.04, 53.05, 53.06, and 53.07 of this code must be satisfied, and the summons must state that the hearing is for the purpose of considering discretionary transfer to criminal court.

(c) The juvenile court shall conduct a hearing without a jury to consider transfer of the child for criminal proceedings.

(d) Prior to the hearing, the juvenile court shall order and obtain a complete diagnostic study, social evaluation, and full investigation of the child, his circumstances, and the circumstances of the alleged offense.

(e) At the transfer hearing the court may consider written reports from probation officers, professional court employees, or professional consultants in addition to the testimony of witnesses. At least one day prior to the transfer hearing, the court shall provide the attorney for the child with access to all written matter to be considered by the court in making the transfer decision. The court may order counsel not to reveal items to the child or his parent, guardian, or guardian ad litem if such disclosure would materially harm the treatment and rehabilitation of the child or would substantially decrease the likelihood of receiving information from the same or similar sources in the future.

(f) In making the determination required by Subsection (a) of this section, the court shall consider, among other matters:

(1) whether the alleged offense was against person or property, with greater weight in favor of transfer given to offenses against the person;

(2) the sophistication and maturity of the child;

(3) the record and previous history of the child; and

(4) the prospects of adequate protection of the public and the likelihood of the rehabilitation of the child by use of procedures, services, and facilities currently available to the juvenile court.

(g) If the petition alleges multiple offenses that constitute more than one criminal transaction, the juvenile court shall either retain or transfer all offenses relating to a single transaction. A child is not subject to criminal prosecution at any time for any offense arising out of a criminal transaction for which the juvenile court retains jurisdiction.

(h) If the juvenile court waives jurisdiction, it shall state specifically in the order its reasons for waiver and certify its action, including the written order and findings of the court, and shall transfer the person to the appropriate court for criminal proceedings and cause the results of the diagnostic study of the person ordered under Subsection (d), including psychological information, to be transferred to the appropriate criminal prosecutor. On transfer of the person for criminal proceedings, the person shall be dealt with as an adult and in accordance with the Code of Criminal Procedure. The transfer of custody is an arrest.

(i) A waiver under this section is a waiver of jurisdiction over the child and the criminal court may not remand the child to the jurisdiction of the juvenile court.

(j) The juvenile court may waive its exclusive original jurisdiction and transfer a person to the appropriate district court or criminal district court for criminal proceedings if:

(1) the person is 18 years of age or older;

(2) the person was:

(A) 10 years of age or older and under 17 years of age at the time the person is alleged to have committed a capital felony or an offense under Section 19.02, Penal Code;

(B) 14 years of age or older and under 17 years of age at the time the person is alleged to have committed an aggravated controlled substance felony or a felony of the first degree other than an offense under Section 19.02, Penal Code; or

(C) 15 years of age or older and under 17 years of age at the time the person is alleged to have committed a felony of the second or third degree or a state jail felony;

(3) no adjudication concerning the alleged offense has been made or no adjudication hearing concerning the offense has been conducted;

(4) the juvenile court finds from a preponderance of the evidence that:

(A) for a reason beyond the control of the state it was not practicable to proceed in juvenile court before the 18th birthday of the person; or

(B) after due diligence of the state it was not practicable to proceed in juvenile court before the 18th birthday of the person because:

(i) the state did not have probable cause to proceed in juvenile court and new evidence has been found since the 18th birthday of the person;

(ii) the person could not be found; or

(iii) a previous transfer order was reversed by an appellate court or set aside by a district court; and

(5) the juvenile court determines that there is probable cause to believe that the child before the court committed the offense alleged.

(k) The petition and notice requirements of Sections 53.04, 53.05, 53.06, and 53.07 of this code must be satisfied, and the summons must state that the hearing is for the purpose of considering waiver of jurisdiction under Subsection (j) of this section.

(l) The juvenile court shall conduct a hearing without a jury to consider waiver of jurisdiction under Subsection (j) of this section.

(m) Notwithstanding any other provision of this section, the juvenile court shall waive its exclusive original jurisdiction and transfer a child to the appropriate district court or criminal court for criminal proceedings if:

(1) the child has previously been transferred to a district court or criminal district court for criminal proceedings under this section, unless:

(A) the child was not indicted in the matter transferred by the grand jury;

(B) the child was found not guilty in the matter transferred;

(C) the matter transferred was dismissed with prejudice; or

(D) the child was convicted in the matter transferred, the conviction was reversed on appeal, and the appeal is final; and

(2) the child is alleged to have violated a penal law of the grade of felony.

(n) A mandatory transfer under Subsection (m) may be made without conducting the study required in discretionary transfer proceedings by Subsection (d). The requirements of Subsection (b) that the summons state that the purpose of the hearing is to consider discretionary transfer to criminal court does not apply to a transfer proceeding under Subsection (m). In a proceeding under Subsection (m), it is sufficient that the summons provide fair notice that the purpose of the hearing is to consider mandatory transfer to criminal court.

(o) If a respondent is taken into custody for possible discretionary transfer proceedings under Subsection (j), the juvenile court shall hold a detention hearing in the same manner as provided by Section 54.01, except that the court shall order the respondent released unless it finds that the respondent:

 (1) is likely to abscond or be removed from the jurisdiction of the court;

 (2) may be dangerous to himself or herself or may threaten the safety of the public if released; or

 (3) has previously been found to be a delinquent child or has previously been convicted of a penal offense punishable by a term of jail or prison and is likely to commit an offense if released.

(p) If the juvenile court does not order a respondent released under Subsection (o), the court shall, pending the conclusion of the discretionary transfer hearing, order that the respondent be detained in:

 (1) a certified juvenile detention facility as provided by Subsection (q); or

 (2) an appropriate county facility for the detention of adults accused of criminal offenses.

(q) The detention of a respondent in a certified juvenile detention facility must comply with the detention requirements under this title, except that, to the extent practicable, the person shall be kept separate from children detained in the same facility.

(r) If the juvenile court orders a respondent detained in a county facility under Subsection (p), the county sheriff shall take custody of the respondent under the juvenile court's order. The juvenile court shall set or deny bond for the respondent as required by the Code of Criminal Procedure and other law applicable to the pretrial detention of adults accused of criminal offenses.

FAMILY VIOLENCE—§71

§71.0021. Dating Violence

(a) *"Dating violence"* means an act by an individual that is against another individual with whom that person has or has had a dating relationship and that is intended to result in physical harm, bodily injury, assault, or sexual assault or that is a threat that reasonably places the individual in fear of imminent physical harm, bodily injury, assault, or sexual assault, but does not include defensive measures to protect oneself.

(b) For purposes of this title, "dating relationship" means a relationship between individuals who have or have had a continuing relationship of a romantic or intimate nature. The existence of such a relationship shall be determined based on consideration of:

(1) the length of the relationship;

(2) the nature of the relationship; and

(3) the frequency and type of interaction between the persons involved in the relationship.

(c) A casual acquaintanceship or ordinary fraternization in a business or social context does not constitute a "dating relationship" under Subsection (b).

§71.003. Family

"Family" includes individuals related by consanguinity or affinity, as determined under Sections 573.022 and 573.024, Government Code, individuals who are former spouses of each other, individuals who are the biological parents of the same child, without regard to marriage, and a foster child and foster parent, without regard to whether those individuals reside together.

§71.004. Family Violence

"Family violence" means:

(1) an act by a member of a family or household against another member of the family or household that is intended to result in physical harm, bodily injury, assault, or sexual assault or that is a threat that reasonably places the member in fear of imminent physical harm, bodily injury, assault, or sexual assault, but does not include defensive measures to protect oneself; or

(2) abuse, as that term is defined by Sections 261.001(1)(C), (E), and (G) by a member of a family or household toward a child of the family or household.

PROTECTIVE ORDERS—§81

§81.001. Entitlement to Protective Order

A court shall render a protective order as provided by Section 85.001(b) if the court finds that family violence has occurred and is likely to occur in the future.

§81.002. No Fee for Applicant

An applicant for a protective order or an attorney representing an applicant may not be assessed a fee, cost, charge, or expense by a district or county clerk of the court or a sheriff, constable, or other public official or employee in connection with the filing, serving, or entering of a protective order or for any other service described by this subsection, including:

(1) a fee to dismiss, modify, or withdraw a protective order;

(2) a fee for certifying copies;

(3) a fee for comparing copies to originals;

(4) a court reporter fee;

(5) a judicial fund fee;

(6) a fee for any other service related to a protective order; or

(7) a fee to transfer a protective order.

§81.003. Fees and Costs Paid by Party Found to Have Committed Family Violence

(a) Except on a showing of good cause or of the indigence of a party found to have committed family violence, the court shall require in a protective order that the party against whom the order is rendered pay the $16 protective order fee, the standard fees charged by the clerk of the court in a general civil proceeding for the cost of serving the order, the costs of court, and all other fees, charges, or expenses incurred in connection with the protective order.

(b) The court may order a party against whom an agreed protective order is rendered under Section 85.005 to pay the fees required in Subsection (a).

REPORTING FAMILY VIOLENCE—§91

§91.001. Definitions

In this subtitle:

(1) *"Family violence"* has the meaning assigned by Section 71.004.

(2) *"Medical professional"* means a licensed doctor, nurse, physician assistant, or emergency medical technician.

§91.002. Reporting by Witnesses Encouraged

A person who witnesses family violence is encouraged to report the family violence to a local law enforcement agency.

§91.003. Information Provided by Medical Professionals

A medical professional who treats a person for injuries that the medical professional has reason to believe were caused by family violence shall:

(1) immediately provide the person with information regarding the nearest family violence shelter center;

(2) document in the person's medical file:

(A) the fact that the person has received the information provided under Subdivision (1); and

(B) the reasons for the medical professional's belief that the person's injuries were caused by family violence; and

(3) give the person a written notice in substantially the following form, completed with the required information, in both English and Spanish:

"It is a crime for any person to cause you any physical injury or harm even if that person is a member or former member of your family or household.

"Notice To Adult Victims Of Family Violence"

"You may report family violence to a law enforcement officer by calling the following telephone numbers: ______________________.

"If you, your child, or any other household resident has been injured or if you feel you are going to be in danger after a law enforcement officer investigating family violence leaves your residence or at a later time, you have the right to:

"Ask the local prosecutor to file a criminal complaint against the person committing family violence; and

"Apply to a court for an order to protect you. You may want to consult with a legal aid office, a prosecuting attorney, or a private attorney. A court can enter an order that:

"(1) prohibits the abuser from committing further acts of violence;

"(2) prohibits the abuser from threatening, harassing, or contacting you at home;

"(3) directs the abuser to leave your household; and

"(4) establishes temporary custody of the children or any property.

"A Violation Of Certain Provisions Of Court-ordered Protection May Be A Felony."

"Call The Following Violence Shelters Or Social Organizations If You Need Protection: ____________."

Special Appointments And Social Studies—§107

Subchapter D. Social Study

§107.051. Order for Social Study

(a) The court may order the preparation of a social study into the circumstances and condition of the child and of the home of any person requesting managing conservatorship or possession of the child.

(b) The social study may be made by a private entity, a person appointed by the court, or a state agency, including the Department of Protective and Regulatory Services if the department is a party to the suit.

(c) In a suit in which adoption is requested or possession of or access to the child is an issue and in which the Department of Protective and Regulatory Services is not a party, the court shall appoint a private agency or another person, including a domestic relations office, to conduct the social study.

§107.0511. Pre-Adoptive Home Screening

(a) In this section, "*department*" means the Department of Protective and Regulatory Services.

(b) A pre-adoptive home screening shall be conducted as provided by this section to evaluate each party in a proceeding described by Subsection (c) who requests termination of the parent-child relationship or an adoption.

(c) Except for a suit brought by a licensed child-placing agency or the department, the home screening under this section shall be filed in any suit for:

(1) termination of the parent-child relationship in which a person other than a parent may be appointed managing conservator of a child; or

(2) an adoption.

(d) Other than in a suit in which a licensed child-placing agency or the department is appointed managing conservator of the child, the home screening under this section must be filed with the court before the court may sign the final order for termination of the parent-child relationship.

(e) The costs of a home screening in a suit for adoption under this section shall be paid by the prospective adoptive parent.

(f) Unless otherwise agreed to by the court, the home screening under this section must comply with the minimum requirements for the screening under rules adopted by the Board of Protective and Regulatory Services.

(g) In a stepparent adoption, the pre-adoptive home screening under this section and the post-placement adoptive report under Section 107.052 may be combined.

§107.052. Post-Placement Adoptive Report

(a) In a proceeding in which a pre-adoptive home screening is required by Section 107.0511 for an adoption, a post-placement adoptive report must be conducted and filed with the court before the court may render a final order in the adoption.

(b) Unless otherwise agreed to by the court, the post-placement adoptive report must comply with the minimum requirements for the report under rules adopted by the Board of Protective and Regulatory Services.

§107.053. Prospective Adoptive Parents to Receive Copy

In all adoptions a copy of the report shall be made available to the prospective adoptive parents prior to a final order of adoption.

§107.054. Report Filed with Court

The agency or person making the social study shall file with the court on a date set by the court a report containing its findings and conclusions. The report shall be made a part of the record of the suit.

§107.055. Introduction of Report at Trial

(a) Disclosure to the jury of the contents of a report to the court of a social study is subject to the rules of evidence.

(b) In a contested case, the agency or person making the social study shall furnish copies of the report to the attorneys for the parties before the earlier of:

(1) the seventh day after the date the social study is completed; or

(2) the fifth day before the date of commencement of the trial.

(c) The court may compel the attendance of witnesses necessary for the proper disposition of the suit, including a representative of the agency making the social study, who may be compelled to testify.

§107.056. Preparation Fee

If the court orders a social study to be conducted and a report to be prepared, the court shall award the agency or other person a reasonable fee for the preparation of the study that shall be taxed as costs and paid directly to the agency or other person. The person or agency may enforce the order for the fee.

Conservatorship, Possession, and Access—§153

§153.001. Public Policy

(a) The public policy of this state is to:

(1) assure that children will have frequent and continuing contact with parents who have shown the ability to act in the best interest of the child;

(2) provide a safe, stable, and nonviolent environment for the child; and

(3) encourage parents to share in the rights and duties of raising their child after the parents have separated or dissolved their marriage.

(b) A court may not render an order that conditions the right of a conservator to possession of or access to a child on the payment of child support.

§153.002. Best Interest of Child

The best interest of the child shall always be the primary consideration of the court in determining the issues of conservatorship and possession of and access to the child.

§153.0072. Collaborative Law

(a) On a written agreement of the parties and their attorneys, a suit affecting the parent-child relationship may be conducted under collaborative law procedures.

(b) Collaborative law is a procedure in which the parties and their counsel agree in writing to use their best efforts and make a good faith attempt to resolve the suit affecting the parent-child relationship on an agreed basis without resorting to judicial intervention except to have the court approve the settlement agreement, make the legal pronouncements, and sign the orders required by law to effectuate the agreement of the parties as the court determines appropriate. The parties' counsel may not serve as litigation counsel except to ask the court to approve the settlement agreement.

(c) A collaborative law agreement must include provisions for:

(1) full and candid exchange of information between the parties and their attorneys as necessary to make a proper evaluation of the case;

(2) suspending court intervention in the dispute while the parties are using collaborative law procedures;

(3) hiring experts, as jointly agreed, to be used in the procedure;

(4) withdrawal of all counsel involved in the collaborative law procedure if the collaborative law procedure does not result in settlement of the dispute; and

(5) other provisions as agreed to by the parties consistent with a good faith effort to collaboratively settle the matter.

§153.073. Rights of Parent at All Times

(a) Unless limited by court order, a parent appointed as a conservator of a child has at all times the right:

(1) to receive information from any other conservator of the child concerning the health, education, and welfare of the child;

(2) to confer with the other parent to the extent possible before making a decision concerning the health, education, and welfare of the child;

(3) of access to medical, dental, psychological, and educational records of the child;

(4) to consult with a physician, dentist, or psychologist of the child;

(5) to consult with school officials concerning the child's welfare and educational status, including school activities;

(6) to attend school activities;

(7) to be designated on the child's records as a person to be notified in case of an emergency;

(8) to consent to medical, dental, and surgical treatment during an emergency involving an immediate danger to the health and safety of the child; and

(9) to manage the estate of the child to the extent the estate has been created by the parent or the parent's family.

(b) The court shall specify in the order the rights that a parent retains at all times.

§153.074. Rights and Duties During Period of Possession

Unless limited by court order, a parent appointed as a conservator of a child has the following rights and duties during the period that the parent has possession of the child:

(1) the duty of care, control, protection, and reasonable discipline of the child;

(2) the duty to support the child, including providing the child with clothing, food, shelter, and medical and dental care not involving an invasive procedure;

(3) the right to consent for the child to medical and dental care not involving an invasive procedure; and

(4) the right to direct the moral and religious training of the child.

§153.075. Duties of Parent not Appointed Conservator

The court may order a parent not appointed as a managing or a possessory conservator to perform other parental duties, including paying child support.

§153.010. Order for Family Counseling

(a) If the court finds at the time of a hearing that the parties have a history of conflict in resolving an issue of conservatorship or possession of or access to the child, the court may order a party to:

(1) participate in counseling with a mental health professional who:

(A) has a background in family therapy;

(B) has a mental health license that requires as a minimum a master's degree; and

(C) has training in domestic violence if the court determines that the training is relevant to the type of counseling needed; and

(2) pay the cost of counseling.

(b) If a person possessing the requirements of Subsection (a)(1) is not available in the county in which the court presides, the court may appoint a person the court believes is qualified to conduct the counseling ordered under Subsection (a).

§153.132. Rights and Duties of Parent Appointed Sole Managing Conservator

Unless limited by court order, a parent appointed as sole managing conservator of a child has the rights and duties provided by Subchapter B and the following exclusive rights:

(1) the right to designate the primary residence of the child;

(2) the right to consent to medical, dental, and surgical treatment involving invasive procedures, and to consent to psychiatric and psychological treatment;

(3) the right to receive and give receipt for periodic payments for the support of the child and to hold or disburse these funds for the benefit of the child;

(4) the right to represent the child in legal action and to make other decisions of substantial legal significance concerning the child;

(5) the right to consent to marriage and to enlistment in the armed forces of the United States;

(6) the right to make decisions concerning the child's education;

(7) the right to the services and earnings of the child; and

(8) except when a guardian of the child's estate or a guardian or attorney *ad litem* has been appointed for the child, the right to act as an agent of the child in relation to the child's estate if the child's action is required by a state, the United States, or a foreign government.

§153.133. Agreement for Joint Managing Conservatorship

(a) If a written agreement of the parents is filed with the court, the court shall render an order appointing the parents as joint managing conservators only if the agreement:

(1) designates the conservator who has the exclusive right to designate the primary residence of the child and:

(A) establishes, until modified by further order, the geographic area within which the conservator shall maintain the child's primary residence; or

(B) specifies that the conservator may designate the child's primary residence without regard to geographic location;

(2) specifies the rights and duties of each parent regarding the child's physical care, support, and education;

(3) includes provisions to minimize disruption of the child's education, daily routine, and association with friends;

(4) allocates between the parents, independently, jointly, or exclusively, all of the remaining rights and duties of a parent provided by Chapter 151;

(5) is voluntarily and knowingly made by each parent and has not been repudiated by either parent at the time the order is rendered; and

(6) is in the best interest of the child.

(b) The agreement may contain an alternative dispute resolution procedure that the parties agree to use before requesting enforcement or modification of the terms and conditions of the joint conservatorship through litigation, except in an emergency.

§153.192. Right and Duties of Parent Appointed Possessory Conservator

(a) Unless limited by court order, a parent appointed as possessory conservator of a child has the rights and duties provided by Subchapter B and any other right or duty expressly granted to the possessory conservator in the order.

(b) In ordering the terms and conditions for possession of a child by a parent appointed possessory conservator, the court shall be guided by the guidelines in Subchapter E.

Adoption—§162

§162.413. Counseling

The applicant must participate in counseling for not less than one hour with a social worker or mental health professional with expertise in postadoption counseling after the administrator has accepted the application for registration and before the release of confidential information.

Child Abuse or Neglect—§261

§261.001. Definitions

In this chapter:

(1) "*Abuse*" includes the following acts or omissions by a person:

(A) mental or emotional injury to a child that results in an observable and material impairment in the child's growth, development, or psychological functioning;

(B) causing or permitting the child to be in a situation in which the child sustains a mental or emotional injury that results in an observable and material impairment in the child's growth, development, or psychological functioning;

(C) physical injury that results in substantial harm to the child, or the genuine threat of substantial harm from physical injury to the child, including an injury that is at variance with the history or explanation given and excluding an accident or reasonable discipline by a parent, guardian, or managing or possessory conservator that does not expose the child to a substantial risk of harm;

(D) failure to make a reasonable effort to prevent an action by another person that results in physical injury that results in substantial harm to the child;

(E) sexual conduct harmful to a child's mental, emotional, or physical welfare;

(F) failure to make a reasonable effort to prevent sexual conduct harmful to a child;

(G) compelling or encouraging the child to engage in sexual conduct as defined by Section 43.01, Penal Code;

(H) causing, permitting, encouraging, engaging in, or allowing the photographing, filming, or depicting of the child if the person knew or should have known that the resulting photograph, film, or depiction of the child is obscene as defined by Section 43.21, Penal Code, or pornographic;

(I) the current use by a person of a controlled substance as defined by Chapter 481, Health and Safety Code, in a manner or to the extent that the use results in physical, mental, or emotional injury to a child; or

(J) causing, expressly permitting, or encouraging a child to use a controlled substance as defined by Chapter 481, Health and Safety Code.

(2) "*Department*" means the Department of Protective and Regulatory Services.

(3) "*Designated agency*" means the agency designated by the court as responsible for the protection of children.

(4) "*Neglect*" includes:

(A) the leaving of a child in a situation where the child would be exposed to a substantial risk of physical or mental harm, without arranging for necessary care for the child, and the demonstration of an intent not to return by a parent, guardian, or managing or possessory conservator of the child;

(B) the following acts or omissions by a person:

(i) placing a child in or failing to remove a child from a situation that a reasonable person would realize requires judgment or actions beyond the child's level of maturity, physical condition, or mental abilities and that results in bodily injury or a substantial risk of immediate harm to the child;

(ii) failing to seek, obtain, or follow through with medical care for a child, with the failure resulting in or presenting a substantial risk of death, disfigurement, or bodily injury or with the failure resulting in an observable and material impairment to the growth, development, or functioning of the child;

(iii) the failure to provide a child with food, clothing, or shelter necessary to sustain the life or health of the child, excluding failure caused primarily by financial inability unless relief services had been offered and refused; or

(iv) placing a child in or failing to remove the child from a situation in which the child would be exposed to a substantial risk of sexual conduct harmful to the child; or

(C) the failure by the person responsible for a child's care, custody, or welfare to permit the child to return to the child's home without arranging for the necessary care for the child after the child has been absent from the home for any reason, including having been in residential placement or having run away.

(5) *"Person responsible for a child's care, custody, or welfare"* means a person who traditionally is responsible for a child's care, custody, or welfare, including:

(A) a parent, guardian, managing or possessory conservator, or foster parent of the child;

(B) a member of the child's family or household as defined by Chapter 71;

(C) a person with whom the child's parent cohabits;

(D) school personnel or a volunteer at the child's school; or

(E) personnel or a volunteer at a public or private child-care facility that provides services for the child or at a public or private residential institution or facility where the child resides.

(6) " *Report"* means a report that alleged or suspected abuse or neglect of a child has occurred or may occur.

(7) *"Board"* means the Board of Protective and Regulatory Services.

(8) "*Born addicted to alcohol or a controlled substance*" means a child:

(A) who is born to a mother who during the pregnancy used a controlled substance, as defined by Chapter 481, Health and Safety Code, other than a controlled substance legally obtained by prescription, or alcohol; and

(B) who, after birth as a result of the mother's use of the controlled substance or alcohol:

(i) experiences observable withdrawal from the alcohol or controlled substance;

(ii) exhibits observable or harmful effects in the child's physical appearance or functioning; or

(iii) exhibits the demonstrable presence of alcohol or a controlled substance in the child's bodily fluids.

§261.101. Persons Required to Report; Time to Report

(a) A person having cause to believe that a child's physical or mental health or welfare has been adversely affected by abuse or neglect by any person shall immediately make a report as provided by this subchapter.

(b) If a professional has cause to believe that a child has been abused or neglected or may be abused or neglected or that a child is a victim of an offense under Section 21.11, Penal Code, the professional shall make a report not later than the 48th hour after the hour the professional first suspects that the child has been or may be abused or neglected or is a victim of an offense under Section 21.11, Penal Code. A professional may not delegate to or rely on another person to make the report. In this subsection, "professional" means an individual who is licensed or certified by the state or who is an employee of a facility licensed, certified, or operated by the state and who, in the normal course of official duties or duties for which a license or certification is required, has direct contact with children. The term includes teachers, nurses, doctors, day-care employees, employees of a clinic or health care facility that provides reproductive services, juvenile probation officers, and juvenile detention or correctional officers.

(c) The requirement to report under this section applies without exception to an individual whose personal communications may otherwise be privileged, including an attorney, a member of the clergy, a medical practitioner, a social worker, a mental health professional, and an employee of a clinic or health care facility that provides reproductive services.

(d) Unless waived in writing by the person making the report, the identity of an individual making a report under this chapter is confidential and may be disclosed only:

 (1) as provided by Section 261.201; or

 (2) to a law enforcement officer for the purposes of conducting a criminal investigation of the report.

§261.102. Matters to be Reported

A report should reflect the reporter's belief that a child has been or may be abused or neglected or has died of abuse or neglect.

§261.103. Report Made to Appropriate Agency

(a) Except as provided by Subsection (b), a report shall be made to:

 (1) any local or state law enforcement agency;

 (2) the department if the alleged or suspected abuse involves a person responsible for the care, custody, or welfare of the child;

 (3) the state agency that operates, licenses, certifies, or registers the facility in which the alleged abuse or neglect occurred; or

 (4) the agency designated by the court to be responsible for the protection of children.

(b) A report may be made to the Texas Youth Commission instead of the entities listed under Subsection (a) if the report is based on information provided by a child while under the supervision of the commission concerning the child's alleged abuse of another child.

§261.104. Contents of Report

The person making a report shall identify, if known:

(1) the name and address of the child;

(2) the name and address of the person responsible for the care, custody, or welfare of the child; and

(3) any other pertinent information concerning the alleged or suspected abuse or neglect.

§261.106. Immunities

(a) A person acting in good faith who reports or assists in the investigation of a report of alleged child abuse or neglect or who testifies or otherwise participates in a judicial proceeding arising from a report, petition, or investigation of alleged child abuse or neglect is immune from civil or criminal liability that might otherwise be incurred or imposed.

(b) Immunity from civil and criminal liability extends to an authorized volunteer of the department or a law enforcement officer who participates at the request of the department in an investigation of alleged or suspected abuse or neglect or in an action arising from an investigation if the person was acting in good faith and in the scope of the person's responsibilities.

(c) A person who reports the person's own abuse or neglect of a child or who acts in bad faith or with malicious purpose in reporting alleged child abuse or neglect is not immune from civil or criminal liability.

§261.107. False Report; Penalty

(a) A person commits an offense if the person knowingly or intentionally makes a report as provided in this chapter that the person knows is false or lacks factual foundation. An offense under this section is a Class A misdemeanor unless it is shown on the trial of the offense that the person has previously been convicted under this section, in which case the offense is a state jail felony.

(b) A finding by a court in a suit affecting the parent-child relationship that a report made under this chapter before or during the suit was false or lacking factual foundation may be grounds for the court to modify an order providing for possession of or access to the child who was the subject of the report by restricting further access to the child by the person who made the report.

(c) The appropriate county prosecuting attorney shall be responsible for the prosecution of an offense under this section.

§261.108. Frivolous Claims Against Person Reporting

(a) In this section:

(1) "Claim" means an action or claim by a party, including a plaintiff, counterclaimant, cross-claimant, or third-party plaintiff, requesting recovery of damages.

(2) " Defendant" means a party against whom a claim is made.

(b) A court shall award a defendant reasonable attorney's fees and other expenses related to the defense of a claim filed against the defendant for damages or other relief arising from reporting or assisting in the investigation of a report under this chapter or participating in a judicial proceeding resulting from the report if:

(1) the court finds that the claim is frivolous, unreasonable, or without foundation because the defendant is immune from liability under Section 261.106; and

(2) the claim is dismissed or judgment is rendered for the defendant.

(c) To recover under this section, the defendant must, at any time after the filing of a claim, file a written motion stating that:

(1) the claim is frivolous, unreasonable, or without foundation because the defendant is immune from liability under Section 261.106; and

(2) the defendant requests the court to award reasonable attorney's fees and other expenses related to the defense of the claim.

§261.109. Failure to Report; Penalty

(a) A person commits an offense if the person has cause to believe that a child's physical or mental health or welfare has been or may be adversely affected by abuse or neglect and knowingly fails to report as provided in this chapter.

(b) An offense under this section is a Class B misdemeanor.

§261.201. Confidentiality and Disclosure of Information

(a) The following information is confidential, is not subject to public release under Chapter 552, Government Code, and may be disclosed only for purposes consistent with this code and applicable federal or state law or under rules adopted by an investigating agency:

(1) a report of alleged or suspected abuse or neglect made under this chapter and the identity of the person making the report; and

(2) except as otherwise provided in this section, the files, reports, records, communications, audiotapes, videotapes, and working papers used or developed in an investigation under this chapter or in providing services as a result of an investigation.

(b) A court may order the disclosure of information that is confidential under this section if:

(1) a motion has been filed with the court requesting the release of the information;

(2) a notice of hearing has been served on the investigating agency and all other interested parties; and

(3) after hearing and an in camera review of the requested information, the court determines that the disclosure of the requested information is:

(A) essential to the administration of justice; and

(B) not likely to endanger the life or safety of:

(i) a child who is the subject of the report of alleged or suspected abuse or neglect;

(ii) a person who makes a report of alleged or suspected abuse or neglect; or

(iii) any other person who participates in an investigation of reported abuse or neglect or who provides care for the child.

(c) In addition to Subsection (b), a court, on its own motion, may order disclosure of information that is confidential under this section if:

(1) the order is rendered at a hearing for which all parties have been given notice;

(2) the court finds that disclosure of the information is:

(A) essential to the administration of justice; and

(B) not likely to endanger the life or safety of:

(i) a child who is the subject of the report of alleged or suspected abuse or neglect;

(ii) a person who makes a report of alleged or suspected abuse or neglect; or

(iii) any other person who participates in an investigation of reported abuse or neglect or who provides care for the child; and

(3) the order is reduced to writing or made on the record in open court.

(d) The adoptive parents of a child who was the subject of an investigation and an adult who was the subject of an investigation as a child are entitled to examine and make copies of any report, record, working paper, or other information in the possession, custody, or control of the state that pertains to the history of the child. The department may edit the documents to protect the identity of the biological parents and any other person whose identity is confidential.

(e) Before placing a child who was the subject of an investigation, the department shall notify the prospective adoptive parents of their right to examine any report, record, working paper, or other information in the possession, custody, or control of the state that pertains to the history of the child.

(f) The department shall provide prospective adoptive parents an opportunity to examine information under this section as early as practicable before placing a child.

(g) Notwithstanding Subsection (b), the department, on request and subject to department rule, shall provide to the parent, managing conservator, or other legal representative of a child who is the subject of reported abuse or neglect information concerning the reported abuse or neglect that would otherwise be confidential under this section if the department has edited the information to protect the confidentiality of the identity of the person who made the report and any other person whose life or safety may be endangered by the disclosure.

(h) This section does not apply to an investigation of child abuse or neglect in a home or facility regulated under Chapter 42, Human Resources Code.

§261.202. Privileged Communication

In a proceeding regarding the abuse or neglect of a child, evidence may not be excluded on the ground of privileged communication except in the case of communications between an attorney and client.

§261.301. Investigation of Report

(a) With assistance from the appropriate state or local law enforcement agency, the department or designated agency shall make a prompt and thorough investigation of a report of child abuse or neglect allegedly committed by a person responsible for a child's care, custody, or welfare. The investigation shall be conducted without regard to any pending suit affecting the parent-child relationship.

(b) A state agency shall investigate a report that alleges abuse or neglect occurred in a facility operated, licensed, certified, or registered by that agency as provided by Subchapter E. In conducting an investigation for a facility operated, licensed, certified, registered, or listed by the department, the department shall perform the investigation as provided by:

  (1) Subchapter E; and

  (2) the Human Resources Code.

(c) The department is not required to investigate a report that alleges child abuse or neglect by a person other than a person responsible for a child's care, custody, or welfare. The appropriate state or local law enforcement agency shall investigate that report if the agency determines an investigation should be conducted.

(d) The department may by rule assign priorities and prescribe investigative procedures for investigations based on the severity and immediacy of the alleged harm to the child. The primary purpose of the investigation shall be the protection of the child.

(e) As necessary to provide for the protection of the child, the department or designated agency shall determine:

(1) the nature, extent, and cause of the abuse or neglect;

(2) the identity of the person responsible for the abuse or neglect;

(3) the names and conditions of the other children in the home;

(4) an evaluation of the parents or persons responsible for the care of the child;

(5) the adequacy of the home environment;

(6) the relationship of the child to the persons responsible for the care, custody, or welfare of the child; and

(7) all other pertinent data.

(f) An investigation of a report to the department of serious physical or sexual abuse of a child shall be conducted jointly by an investigator from the appropriate local law enforcement agency and the department or agency responsible for conducting an investigation under Subchapter E.

(g) The inability or unwillingness of a local law enforcement agency to conduct a joint investigation under Subsection (f) does not constitute grounds to prevent or prohibit the department from performing its duties under this subtitle. The department shall document any instance in which a law enforcement agency is unable or unwilling to conduct a joint investigation under Subsection (f).

§261.303. Interference With Investigation; Court Order

(a) A person may not interfere with an investigation of a report of child abuse or neglect conducted by the department or designated agency.

(b) If admission to the home, school, or any place where the child may be cannot be obtained, then for good cause shown the court having family law jurisdiction shall order the parent, the person responsible for the care of the children, or the person in charge of any place where the child may be to allow entrance for the interview, examination, and investigation.

(c) If a parent or person responsible for the child's care does not consent to release of the child's prior medical, psychological, or psychiatric records or to a medical, psychological, or psychiatric examination of the child that is requested by the department or designated agency, the court having family law jurisdiction shall, for good cause shown, order the records to be released or the examination to be made at the times and places designated by the court.

(d) A person, including a medical facility, that makes a report under Subchapter B1 shall release to the department or designated agency, as part of the required report under Section 261.103, records that directly relate to the suspected abuse or neglect without requiring parental consent or a court order.

§261.305. Access to Mental Health Records

(a) An investigation may include an inquiry into the possibility that a parent or a person responsible for the care of a child who is the subject of a report under Subchapter B1 has a history of medical or mental illness.

(b) If the parent or person does not consent to an examination or allow the department or designated agency to have access to medical or mental health records requested by the department or agency, the court having family law jurisdiction, for good cause shown, shall order the examination to be made or that the department or agency be permitted to have access to the records under terms and conditions prescribed by the court.

(c) If the court determines that the parent or person is indigent, the court shall appoint an attorney to represent the parent or person at the hearing. The fees for the appointed attorney shall be paid as provided by Chapter 107.

(d) A parent or person responsible for the child's care is entitled to notice and a hearing when the department or designated agency seeks a court order to allow a medical, psychological, or psychiatric examination or access to medical or mental health records.

(e) This access does not constitute a waiver of confidentiality.

§261.316. Exemption From Fees for Medical Records

The department is exempt from the payment of a fee otherwise required or authorized by law to obtain a medical record from a hospital or health care provider if the request for a record is made in the course of an investigation by the department.

Health and Safety Code

HIV Testing, Confidentiality, and Consent—§81

§81.103. Confidentiality; Criminal Penalty

(a) A test result is confidential. A person that possesses or has knowledge of a test result may not release or disclose the test result or allow the test result to become known except as provided by this section.

(b) A test result may be released to:

(1) the department under this chapter;

(2) a local health authority if reporting is required under this chapter;

(3) the Centers for Disease Control of the United States Public Health Service if reporting is required by federal law or regulation;

(4) the physician or other person authorized by law who ordered the test;

(5) a physician, nurse, or other health care personnel who have a legitimate need to know the test result in order to provide for their protection and to provide for the patient's health and welfare;

(6) the person tested or a person legally authorized to consent to the test on the person's behalf;

(7) the spouse of the person tested if the person tests positive for AIDS or HIV infection, antibodies to HIV, or infection with any other probable causative agent of AIDS;

(8) a person authorized to receive test results under Article 21.31, Code of Criminal Procedure, concerning a person who is tested as required or authorized under that article; and

(9) a person exposed to HIV infection as provided by Section 81.050.

(c) The court shall notify persons receiving test results under Subsection (b)(8) of the requirements of this section.

(d) A person tested or a person legally authorized to consent to the test on the person's behalf may voluntarily release or disclose that person's test results to any other person, and may authorize the release or disclosure of the test results. An authorization under this subsection must be in writing and signed by the person tested or the person legally authorized to consent to the test on the person's behalf. The authorization must state the person or class of persons to whom the test results may be released or disclosed.

(e) A person may release or disclose a test result for statistical summary purposes only without the written consent of the person tested if information that could identify the person is removed from the report.

(j) A person commits an offense if, with criminal negligence and in violation of this section, the person releases or discloses a test result or other information or allows a test result or other information to become known. An offense under this subsection is a Class A misdemeanor.

§81.104. Injunction; Civil Liability

(a) A person may bring an action to restrain a violation or threatened violation of Section 81.102 or 81.103.

(b) A person who violates Section 81.102 or who is found in a civil action to have negligently released or disclosed a test result or allowed a test result to become known in violation of Section 81.103 is liable for:

(1) actual damages;

(2) a civil penalty of not more than $5,000; and

(3) court costs and reasonable attorney's fees incurred by the person bringing the action.

(c) A person who is found in a civil action to have willfully released or disclosed a test result or allowed a test result to become known in violation of Section 81.103 is liable for:

(1) actual damages;

(2) a civil penalty of not less than $5,000 nor more than $10,000; and

(3) court costs and reasonable attorney's fees incurred by the person bringing the action.

(d) Each release or disclosure made, or allowance of a test result to become known, in violation of this subchapter constitutes a separate offense.

(e) A defendant in a civil action brought under this section is not entitled to claim any privilege as a defense to the action.

§81.105. Informed Consent

(a) Except as otherwise provided by law, a person may not perform a test designed to identify HIV or its antigen or antibody without first obtaining the informed consent of the person to be tested.

(b) Consent need not be written if there is documentation in the medical record that the test has been explained and the consent has been obtained.

§81.106. General Consent

(a) A person who has signed a general consent form for the performance of medical tests or procedures is not required to also sign or be presented with a specific consent form relating to medical tests or procedures to determine HIV infection, antibodies to HIV, or infection with any other probable causative agent of AIDS that will be performed on the person during the time in which the general consent form is in effect.

(b) Except as otherwise provided by this chapter, the result of a test or procedure to determine HIV infection, antibodies to HIV, or infection with any probable causative agent of AIDS performed under the authorization of a general consent form in accordance with this section may be used only for diagnostic or other purposes directly related to medical treatment.

§81.107. Consent to Test for Accidental Exposures

(a) In a case of accidental exposure to blood or other body fluids under Section 81.102(a)(4)(D), the health care agency or facility may test a person who may have exposed the health care worker to HIV without the person's specific consent to the test.

§81.109. Counseling Required for Positive Test Results

(a) A positive test result may not be revealed to the person tested without giving that person the immediate opportunity for individual, face-to-face post-test counseling about:

- (1) the meaning of the test result;
- (2) the possible need for additional testing;
- (3) measures to prevent the transmission of HIV;
- (4) the availability of appropriate health care services, including mental health care, and appropriate social and support services in the geographic area of the person's residence;
- (5) the benefits of partner notification; and
- (6) the availability of partner notification programs.

(b) Post-test counseling should:

- (1) increase a person's understanding of HIV infection;
- (2) explain the potential need for confirmatory testing;
- (3) explain ways to change behavior conducive to HIV transmission;
- (4) encourage the person to seek appropriate medical care; and
- (5) encourage the person to notify persons with whom there has been contact capable of transmitting HIV.

(c) Subsection (a) does not apply if:

- (1) a report of a test result is used for statistical or research purposes only and any information that could identify the person is removed from the report; or
- (2) the test is conducted for the sole purpose of screening blood, blood products, bodily fluids, organs, or tissues to determine suitability for donation.

(d) A person who is injured by an intentional violation of this section may bring a civil action for damages and may recover for each violation from a person who violates this section:

- (1) $1,000 or actual damages, whichever is greater; and
- (2) reasonable attorney fees.

(e) This section does not prohibit disciplinary proceedings from being conducted by the appropriate licensing authorities for a health care provider's violation of this section.

(f) A person performing a test to show HIV infection, antibodies to HIV, or infection with any other probable causative agent of AIDS is not liable under Subsection (d) for failing to provide post-test counseling if the person tested does not appear for the counseling.

TREATMENT FACILITIES MARKETING PRACTICES ACT—§164

§164.002. Legislative Purpose

The purpose of this chapter is to safeguard the public against fraud, deceit, and misleading marketing practices and to foster and encourage competition and fair dealing by mental health facilities and chemical dependency treatment facilities by prohibiting or restricting practices by which the public has been injured in connection with the marketing and advertising of mental health services and the admission of patients. Nothing in this chapter should be construed to prohibit a mental health facility from advertising its services in a general way or promoting its specialized services. However, the public should be able to distinguish between the marketing activities of the facility and its clinical functions.

§164.003. Definitions

In this chapter:

(1) "*Advertising*" or "advertise" means a solicitation or inducement, through print or electronic media, including radio, television, or direct mail, to purchase the services provided by a treatment facility.

(2) "*Chemical dependency*" has the meaning assigned by Section 462.001.

(3) "*Chemical dependency facility*" means a treatment facility as that term is defined by Section 462.001.

(4) "*Intervention and assessment service*" means a service that offers assessment, counseling, evaluation, intervention, or referral services or makes treatment recommendations to an individual with respect to mental illness or chemical dependency.

(5) "*Mental health facility*" means:

(A) a "*mental health facility*" as defined by Section 571.003;

(B) a residential treatment facility, other than a mental health facility, in which persons are treated for emotional problems or disorders in a 24-hour supervised living environment; and

(C) an adult day-care facility or adult day health care facility as defined by Section 103.003, Human Resources Code.

(6) "*Mental health professional*" means a:

(A) *"physician"* as defined by Section 571.003;

(B) *"licensed professional counselor"* as defined by Section 503.002, Occupations Code;

(C) *"chemical dependency counselor"* as defined by Section 504.001, Occupations Code;

(D) *"psychologist" offering "psychological services"* as defined by Section 501.003, Occupations Code;

(E) *"registered nurse"* licensed under Chapter 301, Occupations Code;

(F) *"vocational nurse"* licensed under Chapter 301, Occupations Code;

(G) *"licensed marriage and family therapist"* as defined by Section 502.002, Occupations Code; and

(H) *"social worker"* as defined by Section 505.002, Occupations Code.

(7) *"Mental health services"* has the meaning assigned by Section 531.002.

(8) *"Mental illness"* has the meaning assigned by Section 571.003.

(9) *"Referral source"* means a person who is in a position to refer or who refers a person to a treatment facility. "Referral source" does not include a physician, an insurer, a health maintenance organization (HMO), a preferred provider arrangement (PPA), or other third party payor or discount provider organization (DPO) where the insurer, HMO, PPA, third party payor, or DPO pays in whole or in part for the treatment of mental illness or chemical dependency.

(10) *"Treatment facility"* means a chemical dependency facility and a mental health facility.

§164.004. Exemptions

This chapter does not apply to:

(1) a treatment facility

(A) operated by the Texas Department of Mental Health and Mental Retardation, a federal agency, or a political subdivision;

(B) funded by the Texas Commission on Alcohol and Drug Abuse;

(2) a community center established under Subchapter A, Chapter 534, or a facility operated by a community center; or

(3) a facility owned and operated by a nonprofit or not-for-profit organization offering counseling concerning family violence, help for runaway children, or rape.

§164.005. Conditioning Employee or Agent Relationships on Patient Revenue

A treatment facility may not permit or provide compensation or anything of value to its employees or agents, condition employment or continued employment of its employees or agents, set its employee or agent performance standards, or condition its employee or agent evaluations, based on:

(1) the number of patient admissions resulting from an employee's or agent's efforts;

(2) the number or frequency of telephone calls or other contacts with referral sources or patients if the purpose of the telephone calls or contacts is to solicit patients for the treatment facility; or

(3) the existence of or volume of determinations made respecting the length of patient stay.

§164.006. Soliciting and Contracting with Certain Referral Sources

A treatment facility or a person employed or under contract with a treatment facility, if acting on behalf of the treatment facility, may not:

(1) contact a referral source or potential client for the purpose of soliciting, directly or indirectly, a referral of a patient to the treatment facility without disclosing its soliciting agent's, employee's, or contractor's affiliation with the treatment facility;

(2) offer to provide or actually provide mental health or chemical dependency services to a public or private school in this state, on a part-time or full-time basis, the services of any of its employees or agents who make, or are in a position to make, a referral, if the services are provided on an individual basis to individual students or their families. Nothing herein prohibits a treatment facility from:

(A) offering or providing educational programs in group settings to public schools in this state if the affiliation between the educational program and the treatment facility is disclosed;

(B) providing counseling services to a public school in this state in an emergency or crisis situation if the services are provided in response to a specific request by a school; provided that, under no circumstances may a student be referred to the treatment facility offering the services; or

(C) entering into a contract with the board of trustees of a school district with an alternative education program under Section 464.020, or with the board's designee, for the provision of chemical dependency treatment services;

(3) provide to an entity of state or local government, on a part-time or full-time basis, the mental health or chemical dependency services of any of its employees, agents, or contractors who make or are in a position to make referrals unless:

(A) the treatment facility discloses to the governing authority of the entity:

(i) the employee's, agent's, or contractor's relationship to the facility; and

(ii) the fact that the employee, agent, or contractor might make a referral, if permitted, to the facility; and

(B) the employee, agent, or contractor makes a referral only if:

(i) the treatment facility obtains the governing authority's authorization in writing for the employee, agent, or contractor to make the referrals; and

(ii) the employee, agent, or contractor discloses to the prospective patient the employee's, agent's, or contractor's relationship to the facility at initial contact; or

(4) in relation to intervention and assessment services, contract with, offer to remunerate, or remunerate a person who operates an intervention and assessment service that makes referrals to a treatment facility for inpatient treatment of mental illness or chemical dependency unless the intervention and assessment service is:

(A) operated by a community mental health and mental retardation center funded by the Texas Department of Mental Health and Mental Retardation;

(B) operated by a county or regional medical society;

(C) a qualified mental health referral service as defined by Section 164.007; or

(D) owned and operated by a nonprofit or not-for-profit organization offering counseling concerning family violence, help for runaway children, or rape.

§164.007. Qualified Mental Health Referral Service: Definition and Standards

(a) A qualified mental health referral service means a service that conforms to all of the following standards:

(1) the referral service does not exclude as a participant in the referral service an individual who meets the qualifications for participation and qualifications for participation cannot be based in whole or in part on an individual's or entity's affiliation or nonaffiliation with other participants in the referral service;

(2) a payment the participant makes to the referral service is assessed equally against and collected equally from all participants, and is only based on the cost of operating the referral service and not on the volume or value of any referrals to or business otherwise generated by the participants of the referral service;

(3) the referral service imposes no requirements on the manner in which the participant provides services to a referred person, except that the referral service may require that the participant charge the person

referred at the same rate as it charges other persons not referred by the referral service, or that these services be furnished free of charge or at a reduced charge;

(4) a referral made to a mental health professional or chemical dependency treatment facility is made only in accordance with Subdivision (1) and the referral service does not make referrals to mental health facilities other than facilities maintained or operated by the Texas Department of Mental Health and Mental Retardation, community mental health and mental retardation centers, or other political subdivisions, provided that a physician may make a referral directly to any mental health facility;

(5) the referral service is staffed by appropriately licensed and trained mental health professionals and a person who makes assessments for the need for treatment of mental illness or chemical dependency is a mental health professional as defined by this chapter;

(6) in response to each inquiry or after personal assessment, the referral service makes referrals, on a clinically appropriate, rotational basis, to at least three mental health professionals or chemical dependency treatment facilities whose practice addresses or facilities are located in the county of residence of the person seeking the referral or assessment, but if there are not three providers in the inquirer's county of residence, the referral service may include additional providers from other counties nearest the inquirer's county of residence;

(7) no information that identifies the person seeking a referral, such as name, address, or telephone number, is used, maintained, distributed, or provided for a purpose other than making the requested referral or for administrative functions necessary to operating the referral service;

(8) the referral service makes the following disclosures to each person seeking a referral:

(A) the manner in which the referral service selects the group of providers participating in the referral service;

(B) whether the provider participant has paid a fee to the referral service;

(C) the manner in which the referral service selects a particular provider from its list of provider participants to which to make a referral;

(D) the nature of the relationship or any affiliation between the referral service and the group of provider participants to whom it could make a referral; and

(E) the nature of any restriction that would exclude a provider from continuing as a provider participant;

(9) the referral service maintains each disclosure in a written record certifying that the disclosure has been made and the record certifying that the disclosure has been made is signed by either the person seeking a referral or by the person making the disclosure on behalf of the referral service; and

(10) if the referral service refers callers to a 1-900 telephone number or another telephone number that requires the payment of a toll or fee payable to or collected by the referral service, the referral service discloses the per minute charge.

(b) A qualified mental health referral service may not limit participation by a person for a reason other than:

(1) failure to have a current, valid license without limitation to practice in this state;

(2) failure to maintain professional liability insurance while participating in the service;

(3) a decision by a peer review committee that the person has failed to meet prescribed standards or has not acted in a professional or ethical manner;

(4) termination of the contract between the participant and the qualified mental health referral service by either party under the terms of the contract; or

(5) significant dissatisfaction of consumers that is documented and verifiable.

§164.010. Prohibited Acts

It is a violation of this chapter, in connection with the marketing of mental health services, for a person to:

(1) advertise, expressly or impliedly, the services of a treatment facility through the use of:

(A) promises of cure or guarantees of treatment results that cannot be substantiated; or

(B) any unsubstantiated claims;

(2) advertise, expressly or impliedly, the availability of intervention and assessment services unless and until the services are available and are provided by mental health professionals licensed or certified to provide the particular service;

(3) fail to disclose before soliciting a referral source or prospective patient to induce a person to use the services of the treatment facility an affiliation between a treatment facility and its soliciting agents, employees, or contractors;

(4) obtain information considered confidential by state or federal law regarding a person for the purpose of soliciting that person to use the

services of a treatment facility unless and until consent is obtained from the person or, in the case of a minor, the person's parent, managing conservator, or legal guardian or another person with authority to give that authorization; or

(5) represent that a referral service is a qualified mental health referral service unless and until the referral service complies with Section 164.007.

MEDICAL RECORDS PRIVACY—§181

§181.001. Definitions

(a) Unless otherwise defined in this chapter, each term that is used in this chapter has the meaning assigned by the Health Insurance Portability and Accountability Act and Privacy Standards.

(b) In this chapter:

(1) "*Covered entity*" means any person who:

(A) for commercial, financial, or professional gain, monetary fees, or dues, or on a cooperative, nonprofit, or pro bono basis, engages, in whole or in part, and with real or constructive knowledge, in the practice of assembling, collecting, analyzing, using, evaluating, storing, or transmitting protected health information. The term includes a business associate, health care payer, governmental unit, information or computer management entity, school, health researcher, health care facility, clinic, health care provider, or person who maintains an Internet site;

(B) comes into possession of protected health information;

(C) obtains or stores protected health information under this chapter; or

(D) is an employee, agent, or contractor of a person described by Paragraph (A), (B), or (C) insofar as the employee, agent, or contractor creates, receives, obtains, maintains, uses, or transmits protected health information.

(2) "*Health care operations*" has the meaning assigned by the Health Insurance Portability and Accountability Act and Privacy Standards. The term does not include marketing as described in 45 C.F.R. Section 164.514(e) and any subsequent amendments.

(3) "*Health Insurance Portability and Accountability Act and Privacy Standards*" means the privacy requirements of the Administrative Simplification subtitle of the Health Insurance Portability and Accountability Act of 1996 (Pub. L. No. 104-191) and the final rules adopted on December 28, 2000, and published at 65 Fed. Reg. 82798 et seq., and any subsequent amendments.

(5) *"Protected health information"* means individually identifiable health information, including demographic information collected from an individual, that:

(A) relates to:

(i) the past, present, or future physical or mental health or condition of an individual;

(ii) the provision of health care to an individual; or

(iii) the past, present, or future payment for the provision of health care to an individual; and

(B) identifies the individual or with respect to which there is a reasonable basis to believe the information can be used to identify the individual.

§181.002. Applicability

(a)This chapter does not affect the validity of another statute of this state that provides greater confidentiality for information made confidential by this chapter.

(b) To the extent that this chapter conflicts with another law with respect to protected health information collected by a governmental body or unit, this chapter controls.

§181.004. Rules

A state agency that licenses or regulates a covered entity may adopt rules as necessary to carry out the purposes of this chapter.

§181.057. Information Relating to Offenders with Mental Impairments

This chapter does not apply to an agency described by Section 614.017 with respect to the disclosure, receipt, transfer, or exchange of medical and health information and records relating to individuals in the custody of an agency or in community supervision.

§181.058. Educational Records

In this chapter, protected health information does not include:

(1) education records covered by the Family Educational Rights and Privacy Act of 1974 (20 U.S.C. Section 1232g) and its subsequent amendments; or

(2) records described by 20 U.S.C. Section 1232g(a)(4)(B)(iv) and its subsequent amendments.

§181.101. Compliance with Federal Regulations

A covered entity shall comply with the Health Insurance Portability and Accountability Act and Privacy Standards relating to:

(1) an individual's access to the individual's protected health information;

(2) amendment of protected health information;

(3) uses and disclosures of protected health information, including requirements relating to consent; and

(3) notice of privacy practices for protected health information.

§181.102. Information for Research

(a) A covered entity may disclose protected health information to a person performing health research, regardless of the source of funding of the research, for the purpose of conducting health research, only if the person performing health research has obtained:

(1) individual consent or authorization for use or disclosure of protected health information for research required by federal law;

(2) the express written authorization of the individual required by this chapter;

(3) documentation that a waiver of individual consent or authorization required for use or disclosure of protected health information has been granted by an institutional review board or privacy board as required under federal law; or

(4) documentation that a waiver of the individual's express written authorization required by this chapter has been granted by a privacy board established under this section.

(b) A privacy board:

(1) must consist of members with varying backgrounds and appropriate professional competency as necessary to review the effect of the research protocol for the project or projects on the privacy rights and related interests of the individuals whose protected health information would be used or disclosed;

(2) must include at least one member who is not affiliated with the covered entity or an entity conducting or sponsoring the research and not related to any person who is affiliated with an entity described by this subsection; and

(3) may not have any member participating in the review of any project in which the member has a conflict of interest.

(c) A privacy board may grant a waiver of the express written authorization for the use of protected health information if the privacy board obtains the following documentation:

(1) a statement identifying the privacy board and the date on which the waiver of the express written authorization was approved by the privacy board;

(2) a statement that the privacy board has determined that the waiver satisfies the following criteria:

(A) the use or disclosure of protected health information involves no more than minimal risk to the affected individuals;

(B) the waiver will not adversely affect the privacy rights and welfare of those individuals;

(C) the research could not practicably be conducted without the waiver;

(D) the research could not practicably be conducted without access to and use of the protected health information;

(E) the privacy risks to individuals whose protected health information is to be used or disclosed are reasonable in relation to the anticipated benefits, if any, to the individuals and the importance of the knowledge that may reasonably be expected to result from the research;

(F) there is an adequate plan to protect the identifiers from improper use and disclosure;

(G) there is an adequate plan to destroy the identifiers at the earliest opportunity consistent with conduct of the research, unless there is a health or research justification for retaining the identifiers or the retention is otherwise required by law; and

(H) there are adequate written assurances that the protected health information will not be reused or disclosed to another person or entity, except:

(i) as required by law;

(ii) for authorized oversight of the research project; or

(iii) for other research for which the use or disclosure of protected health information would be permitted by state or federal law;

(3) a brief description of the protected health information for which use or access has been determined to be necessary by the privacy board under Subdivision (2)(D); and

(4) a statement that the waiver of express written authorization has been approved by the privacy board following the procedures under Subsection (e).

(d) A waiver must be signed by the presiding officer of the privacy board or the presiding officer's designee.

(e) The privacy board must review the proposed research at a convened meeting at which a majority of the privacy board members are present, including at least one member who satisfies the requirements of Subsection (b)(2). The waiver of express written authorization must be approved by the majority of the privacy board members present at the meeting, unless the privacy board elects to use an expedited review procedure. The privacy board may use an expedited review procedure only if the research involves no more than minimal risk to the privacy of the individual who is the subject of the protected health information of which use or disclosure is being sought. If the privacy board elects to use an expedited review procedure, the review and approval of the waiver of express written authorization may be made by the presiding officer of the privacy board or by one or more members of the privacy board as designated by the presiding officer.

(f) A covered entity may disclose protected health information to a person performing health research if the covered entity obtains from the person performing the health research representations that:

(1) use or disclosure is sought solely to review protected health information as necessary to prepare a research protocol or for similar purposes preparatory to research;

(2) no protected health information is to be removed from the covered entity by the person performing the health research in the course of the review; and

(3) the protected health information for which use or access is sought is necessary for the research purposes.

(g) A person who is the subject of protected health information collected or created in the course of a clinical research trial may access the information at the conclusion of the research trial.

§181.103. Disclosure of Information to Public Health Authority

A covered entity may use or disclose protected health information without the express written authorization of the individual for public health activities or to comply with the requirements of any federal or state health benefit program or any federal or state law. A covered entity may disclose protected health information:

(1) to a public health authority that is authorized by law to collect or receive such information for the purpose of preventing or controlling disease, injury, or disability, including the reporting of disease, injury, vital events such as birth or death, and the conduct of public health surveillance, public health investigations, and public interventions;

(2) to a public health authority or other appropriate government authority authorized by law to receive reports of child or adult abuse, neglect, or exploitation; and

(3) to any state agency in conjunction with a federal or state health benefit program.

§181.151. Reidentified Information

A person may not reidentify or attempt to reidentify an individual who is the subject of any protected health information without obtaining the individual's consent or authorization if required under this chapter or other state or federal law.

§181.201. Injunctive Relief; Civil Penalty

(a) The attorney general may institute an action for injunctive relief to restrain a violation of this chapter.

(b) In addition to the injunctive relief provided by Subsection (a), the attorney general may institute an action for civil penalties against a covered entity for a violation of this chapter. A civil penalty assessed under this section may not exceed $3,000 for each violation.

(c) If the court in which an action under Subsection (b) is pending finds that the violations have occurred with a frequency as to constitute a pattern or practice, the court may assess a civil penalty not to exceed $250,000.

§181.202. Disciplinary Action

In addition to the penalties prescribed by this chapter, a violation of this chapter by an individual or facility that is licensed by an agency of this state is subject to investigation and disciplinary proceedings, including probation or suspension by the licensing agency. If there is evidence that the violations of this chapter constitute a pattern or practice, the agency may revoke the individual's or facility's license.

§181.203. Exclusion from State Programs

In addition to the penalties prescribed by this chapter, a covered entity shall be excluded from participating in any state-funded health care program if a court finds the covered entity engaged in a pattern or practice of violating this chapter.

§181.204. Availability of Other Remedies

This chapter does not affect any right of a person under other law to bring a cause of action or otherwise seek relief with respect to conduct that is a violation of this chapter.

NURSING HOME RESIDENTS REQUIRING MH OR MR SERVICES—§242.158

§242.158 Identification of Certain Nursing Home Residents Requiring Mental Health or Mental Retardation Services

(a) Each resident of a nursing home who is considering making a transition to a community-based care setting shall be identified to determine the presence of a mental illness or mental retardation, regardless of whether the resident is receiving treatment or services for a mental illness or mental retardation.

(b) In identifying residents having a mental illness or mental retardation, the department shall use an identification process that is at least as effective as the mental health and mental retardation identification process established by federal law. The results of the identification process may not be used to prevent a resident from remaining in the nursing home unless the nursing home is unable to provide adequate care for the resident.

(c) The department shall compile and provide to the Texas Department of Mental Health and Mental Retardation information regarding each resident identified as having a mental illness or mental retardation before the resident makes a transition from the nursing home to a community-based care setting.

(d) The Texas Department of Mental Health and Mental Retardation shall use the information provided under Subsection (c) solely for the purposes of:

(1) determining the need for and funding levels of mental health and mental retardation services for residents making a transition from a nursing home to a community-based care setting;

(2) providing mental health or mental retardation services to an identified resident after the resident makes that transition; and

(3) referring an identified resident to a local mental health or mental retardation authority or private provider for additional mental health or mental retardation services.

(e) This section does not authorize the department to decide for a resident of a nursing home that the resident will make a transition from the nursing home to a community-based care setting.

REPORTS OF ABUSE OR NEGLECT OF PATIENTS—§464

§464.010. Reports of Abuse or Neglect

(a) A person, including treatment facility personnel, who believes that a client's physical or mental health or welfare has been, is, or will be adversely affected by abuse or neglect caused by any person shall report the facts underlying that belief to the commission. This requirement is in addition to the requirements prescribed by Chapter 261, Family Code, and Chapter 48, Human Resources Code.

(b) The commission shall prescribe procedures for the investigation of reports under Subsection (a) and for coordination with law enforcement agencies or other agencies.

(c) An individual who in good faith reports to the commission under this section is immune from civil or criminal liability based on the report. That immunity extends to participation in a judicial proceeding resulting from the report but does not extend to an individual who caused the abuse or neglect.

(d) The commission may request the attorney general's office to file a petition for temporary care and protection of a client of a residential treatment facility if it appears that immediate removal of the client is necessary to prevent further abuse.

(e) All records made by the commission during its investigation of alleged abuse or neglect are confidential and may not be released except that the release may be made:

(1) on court order;

(2) on written request and consent of the person under investigation or that person's authorized attorney; or

(3) as provided by Section 464.011.

Voluntary Mental Health Services—§571 and 572

§571.019. Limitation of Liability

(a) A person who participates in the examination, certification, apprehension, custody, transportation, detention, treatment, or discharge of any person or in the performance of any other act required or authorized by this subtitle and who acts in good faith, reasonably, and without negligence is not criminally or civilly liable for that action.

(b) A physician performing a medical examination and providing information to the court in a court proceeding held under this subtitle or providing information to a peace officer to demonstrate the necessity to apprehend a person under Chapter 573 is considered an officer of the court and is not liable for the examination or testimony when acting without malice.

(c) A physician or inpatient mental health facility that discharges a voluntary patient is not liable for the discharge if:

(1) a written request for the patient's release was filed and not withdrawn; and

(2) the person who filed the written request for discharge is notified that the person assumes all responsibility for the patient on discharge.

§572.001. Request for Admission

(a) A person 16 years of age or older or a person younger than 16 years of age who is or has been married may request admission to an inpatient mental health facility by filing a request with the administrator of the facility to which admission is requested. The parent, managing conservator, or guardian of a person younger than 16 years of age who is not and has not been married may request the admission of the person to an inpatient mental health facility by filing a request with the administrator of the facility to which admission is requested.

(b) An admission request must be in writing and signed by the person requesting the admission.

(c) A person or agency appointed as the guardian or a managing conservator of a minor younger than 16 years of age and acting as an employee or agent of the state or a political subdivision of the state may request admission of the minor only with the minor's consent.

(d) The administrator of an inpatient mental health facility may admit a minor who is 16 years of age or older or a person younger than 16 years of age who is or has been married to an inpatient mental health facility as a voluntary patient without the consent of the parent, managing conservator, or guardian.

(e) A request for admission as a voluntary patient must state that the person for whom admission is requested agrees to voluntarily remain in the facility until the person's discharge and that the person consents to the diagnosis, observation, care, and treatment provided until the earlier of:

(1) the person's discharge; or

(2) the period prescribed by Section 572.004.

§572.002. Admission

The facility administrator or the administrator's authorized, qualified designee may admit a person for whom a proper request for voluntary inpatient services is filed if the administrator or the designee determines:

(1) from a preliminary examination that the person has symptoms of mental illness and will benefit from the inpatient services;

(2) that the person has been informed of the person's rights as a voluntary patient; and

(3) that the admission was voluntarily agreed to:

(A) by the person, if the person is:

(i) 16 years of age or older; or

(ii) younger than 16 years of age and is or has been married; or

(B) by the person's parent, managing conservator, or guardian, if the person is younger than 16 years of age and is not and has not been married.

§572.0022. Information on Medications

(a) A mental health facility shall provide to a patient in the patient's primary language, if possible, and in accordance with board rules information relating to prescription medication ordered by the patient's treating physician.

(b) The facility shall also provide the information to the patient's family on request, but only to the extent not otherwise prohibited by state or federal confidentiality laws.

§572.0025. Intake, Assessment, and Admission

(a) The board shall adopt rules governing the voluntary admission of a patient to an inpatient mental health facility, including rules governing the intake and assessment procedures of the admission process.

(b) The rules governing the intake process shall establish minimum standards for:

(1) reviewing a prospective patient's finances and insurance benefits;

(2) explaining to a prospective patient the patient's rights; and

(3) explaining to a prospective patient the facility's services and treatment process.

(c) The assessment provided for by the rules may be conducted only by a professional who meets the qualifications prescribed by board rules.

(d) The rules governing the assessment process shall prescribe:

(1) the types of professionals who may conduct an assessment;

(2) the minimum credentials each type of professional must have to conduct an assessment; and

(3) the type of assessment that professional may conduct.

(e) In accordance with board rule, a facility shall provide annually a minimum of eight hours of inservice training regarding intake and assessment for persons who will be conducting an intake or assessment for the facility. A person may not conduct intake or assessments without having completed the initial and applicable annual inservice training.

(f) A prospective voluntary patient may not be formally accepted for treatment in a facility unless:

(1) the facility has a physician's order admitting the prospective patient, which order may be issued orally, electronically, or in writing, signed by the physician, provided that, in the case of an oral order or an electronically transmitted unsigned order, a signed original is presented to the mental health facility within 24 hours of the initial order; the order must be from:

(A) an admitting physician who has conducted an in-person physical and psychiatric examination within 72 hours of the admission; or

(B) an admitting physician who has consulted with a physician who has conducted an in-person examination within 72 hours of the admission; and

(2) the facility administrator or a person designated by the administrator has agreed to accept the prospective patient and has signed a statement to that effect.

(g) An assessment conducted as required by rules adopted under this section does not satisfy a statutory or regulatory requirement for a personal evaluation of a patient or a prospective patient by a physician before admission.

(h) In this section:

(1) "*Admission*" means the formal acceptance of a prospective patient to a facility.

(2) "*Assessment*" means the administrative process a facility uses to gather information from a prospective patient, including a medical

history and the problem for which the patient is seeking treatment, to determine whether a prospective patient should be examined by a physician to determine if admission is clinically justified.

(3) "*Intake*" means the administrative process for gathering information about a prospective patient and giving a prospective patient information about the facility and the facility's treatment and services.

§572.003. Rights of Patients

(a) A person's voluntary admission to an inpatient mental health facility under this chapter does not affect the person's civil rights or legal capacity or affect the person's right to obtain a writ of habeas corpus.

(b) In addition to the rights provided by this subtitle, a person voluntarily admitted to an inpatient mental health facility under this chapter has the right:

(1) to be reviewed periodically to determine the person's need for continued inpatient treatment; and

(2) to have an application for court-ordered mental health services filed only as provided by Section 572.005.

(c) A person admitted to an inpatient mental health facility under this chapter shall be informed of the rights provided under this section and Section 572.004:

(1) orally in simple, nontechnical terms, within 24 hours after the time the person is admitted, and in writing in the person's primary language, if possible; or

(2) through the use of a means reasonably calculated to communicate with a hearing impaired or visually impaired person, if applicable.

(d) The patient's parent, managing conservator, or guardian shall also be informed of the patient's rights as required by this section if the patient is a minor.

§572.004. Discharge

(a) A voluntary patient is entitled to leave an inpatient mental health facility in accordance with this section after a written request for discharge is filed with the facility administrator or the administrator's designee. The request must be signed, timed, and dated by the patient or a person legally responsible for the patient and must be made a part of the patient's clinical record. If a patient informs an employee of or person associated with the facility of the patient's desire to leave the facility, the employee or person shall, as soon as possible, assist the patient in creating the written request and present it to the patient for the patient's signature.

(b) The facility shall, within four hours after a request for discharge is filed, notify the physician responsible for the patient's treatment. If that physician is not available during that period, the facility shall notify any available physician of the request.

(c) The notified physician shall discharge the patient before the end of the four-hour period unless the physician has reasonable cause to believe that the patient might meet the criteria for court-ordered mental health services or emergency detention.

(d) A physician who has reasonable cause to believe that a patient might meet the criteria for court-ordered mental health services or emergency detention shall examine the patient as soon as possible within 24 hours after the time the request for discharge is filed. The physician shall discharge the patient on completion of the examination unless the physician determines that the person meets the criteria for court-ordered mental health services or emergency detention. If the physician makes a determination that the patient meets the criteria for court-ordered mental health services or emergency detention, the physician shall, not later than 4 p.m. on the next succeeding business day after the date on which the examination occurs, either discharge the patient or file an application for court-ordered mental health services or emergency detention and obtain a written order for further detention. The physician shall notify the patient if the physician intends to detain the patient under this subsection or intends to file an application for court-ordered mental health services or emergency detention. A decision to detain a patient under this subsection and the reasons for the decision shall be made a part of the patient's clinical record.

(e) If extremely hazardous weather conditions exist or a disaster occurs, the physician may request the judge of a court that has jurisdiction over proceedings brought under Chapter 574 to extend the period during which the patient may be detained. The judge or a magistrate appointed by the judge may by written order made each day extend the period during which the patient may be detained until 4 p.m. on the first succeeding business day. The written order must declare that an emergency exists because of the weather or the occurrence of a disaster.

(f) The patient is not entitled to leave the facility if before the end of the period prescribed by this section:

(1) a written withdrawal of the request for discharge is filed; or

(2) an application for court-ordered mental health services or emergency detention is filed and the patient is detained in accordance with this subtitle.

(g) A plan for continuing care shall be prepared in accordance with Section 574.081 for each patient discharged. If sufficient time to prepare a continuing care plan before discharge is not available, the plan may be prepared and mailed to the appropriate person within 24 hours after the patient is discharged.

(h) The patient or other person who files a request for discharge of a patient shall be notified that the person filing the request assumes all responsibility for the patient on discharge.

§572.005. Application for Court-Ordered Treatment

(a) An application for court-ordered mental health services may not be filed against a patient receiving voluntary inpatient services unless:

  (1) a request for release of the patient has been filed with the facility administrator; or

  (2) in the opinion of the physician responsible for the patient's treatment, the patient meets the criteria for court-ordered mental health services and:

    (A) is absent from the facility without authorization;

    (B) is unable to consent to appropriate and necessary psychiatric treatment; or

    (C) refuses to consent to necessary and appropriate treatment recommended by the physician responsible for the patient's treatment and that physician completes a certificate of medical examination for mental illness that, in addition to the information required by Section 574.011, includes the opinion of the physician that:

      (i) there is no reasonable alternative to the treatment recommended by the physician; and

      (ii) the patient will not benefit from continued inpatient care without the recommended treatment.

(b) The physician responsible for the patient's treatment shall notify the patient if the physician intends to file an application for court-ordered mental health services.

COURT ORDERED EMERGENCY SERVICES—§573

§573.001. Apprehension by Peace Officer Without Warrant

(a) A peace officer, without a warrant, may take a person into custody if the officer:

  (1) has reason to believe and does believe that:

    (A) the person is mentally ill; and

    (B) because of that mental illness there is a substantial risk of serious harm to the person or to others unless the person is immediately restrained; and

  (2) believes that there is not sufficient time to obtain a warrant before taking the person into custody.

(b) A substantial risk of serious harm to the person or others under Subsection (a)(1)(B) may be demonstrated by:

  (1) the person's behavior; or

(2) evidence of severe emotional distress and deterioration in the person's mental condition to the extent that the person cannot remain at liberty.

(c) The peace officer may form the belief that the person meets the criteria for apprehension:

(1) from a representation of a credible person; or

(2) on the basis of the conduct of the apprehended person or the circumstances under which the apprehended person is found.

(d) A peace officer who takes a person into custody under Subsection (a) shall immediately transport the apprehended person to:

(1) the nearest appropriate inpatient mental health facility; or

(2) a facility deemed suitable by the county's mental health authority, if an appropriate inpatient mental health facility is not available.

(e) A jail or similar detention facility may not be deemed suitable except in an extreme emergency.

(f) A person detained in a jail or a nonmedical facility shall be kept separate from any person who is charged with or convicted of a crime.

§573.011. Application for Emergency Detention

(a) An adult may file a written application for the emergency detention of another person.

(b) The application must state:

(1) that the applicant has reason to believe and does believe that the person evidences mental illness;

(2) that the applicant has reason to believe and does believe that the person evidences a substantial risk of serious harm to himself or others;

(3) a specific description of the risk of harm;

(4) that the applicant has reason to believe and does believe that the risk of harm is imminent unless the person is immediately restrained;

(5) that the applicant's beliefs are derived from specific recent behavior, overt acts, attempts, or threats;

(6) a detailed description of the specific behavior, acts, attempts, or threats; and

(7) a detailed description of the applicant's relationship to the person whose detention is sought.

(c) The application may be accompanied by any relevant information.

§573.021. Preliminary Examination

(a) A facility shall temporarily accept a person for whom an application for detention is filed.

(b) A person accepted for a preliminary examination may be detained in custody for not longer than 24 hours after the time the person is presented to the facility unless a written order for further detention is obtained. If the 24-hour period ends on a Saturday, Sunday, legal holiday, or before 4 p.m. on the first succeeding business day, the person may be detained until 4 p.m. on the first succeeding business day. If extremely hazardous weather conditions exist or a disaster occurs, the presiding judge or magistrate may, by written order made each day, extend by an additional 24 hours the period during which the person may be detained. The written order must declare that an emergency exists because of the weather or the occurrence of a disaster.

(c) A physician shall examine the person as soon as possible within 24 hours after the time the person is apprehended.

(d) A facility must comply with this section only to the extent that the commissioner determines that a facility has sufficient resources to perform the necessary services under this section.

(e) A person may not be detained in a private mental health facility without the consent of the facility administrator.

§573.022. Emergency Admission and Detention

(a) A person may be admitted to a facility for emergency detention only if the physician who conducted the preliminary examination of the person makes a written statement that:

  (1) is acceptable to the facility;

  (2) states that after a preliminary examination it is the physician's opinion that:

    (A) the person is mentally ill;

    (B) the person evidences a substantial risk of serious harm to himself or others;

    (C) the described risk of harm is imminent unless the person is immediately restrained; and

    (D) emergency detention is the least restrictive means by which the necessary restraint may be accomplished; and

  (3) includes:

    (A) a description of the nature of the person's mental illness;

    (B) a specific description of the risk of harm the person evidences that may be demonstrated either by the person's behavior or by evidence of severe emotional distress and deterioration in the person's mental condition to the extent that the person cannot remain at liberty; and

    (C) the specific detailed information from which the physician formed the opinion in Subdivision (2).

(b) A county mental health facility that has admitted a person for emergency detention under this section may transport the person to:

(1) a facility of the single portal authority for the area;

(2) an appropriate inpatient mental health facility, if no single portal authority serves the area; or

(3) a facility deemed suitable by the county's mental health authority, if no single portal authority serves the area and an appropriate inpatient mental health facility is not available.

§573.023. Release from Emergency Detention

(a) A person apprehended under Subchapter A or detained under Subchapter B shall be released on completion of the preliminary examination unless the person is admitted to a facility under Section 573.022.

(b) A person admitted to a facility under Section 573.022 shall be released if the facility administrator determines at any time during the emergency detention period that one of the criteria prescribed by Section 573.022(2) no longer applies.

§573.025. Rights of Persons Apprehended or Detained

(a) A person apprehended or detained under this chapter has the right:

(1) to be advised of the location of detention, the reasons for the detention, and the fact that the detention could result in a longer period of involuntary commitment;

(2) to a reasonable opportunity to communicate with and retain an attorney;

(3) to be transported to a location as provided by Section 573.024 if the person is not admitted for emergency detention, unless the person is arrested or objects;

(4) to be released from a facility as provided by Section 573.023;

(5) to be advised that communications with a mental health professional may be used in proceedings for further detention; and

(6) to be transported in accordance with Sections 573.026 and 574.045, if the person is detained under Section 573.022 or transported under an order of protective custody under Section 574.023.

(b) A person apprehended or detained under this subtitle shall be informed of the rights provided by this section:

(1) orally in simple, nontechnical terms, within 24 hours after the time the person is admitted to a facility, and in writing in the person's primary language if possible; or

(2) through the use of a means reasonably calculated to communicate with a hearing or visually impaired person, if applicable.

TEMPORARY AND EXTENDED MENTAL HEALTH SERVICES—§574

§574.010. Independent Psychiatric Evaluation and Expert Testimony

(a) The court may order an independent evaluation of the proposed patient by a psychiatrist chosen by the proposed patient if the court determines that the evaluation will assist the finder of fact. The psychiatrist may testify on behalf of the proposed patient.

(b) If the court determines that the proposed patient is indigent, the court may authorize reimbursement to the attorney ad litem for court-approved expenses incurred in obtaining expert testimony and may order the proposed patient's county of residence to pay the expenses.

§574.034. Order for Temporary Mental Health Services

(a) The judge may order a proposed patient to receive court-ordered temporary inpatient mental health services only if the judge or jury finds, from clear and convincing evidence, that:

  (1) the proposed patient is mentally ill; and

  (2) as a result of that mental illness the proposed patient:

    (A) is likely to cause serious harm to himself;

    (B) is likely to cause serious harm to others; or

    (C) is:

      (i) suffering severe and abnormal mental, emotional, or physical distress;

      (ii) experiencing substantial mental or physical deterioration of the proposed patient's ability to function independently, which is exhibited by the proposed patient's inability, except for reasons of indigence, to provide for the proposed patient's basic needs, including food, clothing, health, or safety; and

      (iii) unable to make a rational and informed decision as to whether or not to submit to treatment.

(b) The judge may order a proposed patient to receive court-ordered temporary outpatient mental health services only if:

  (1) the judge finds that appropriate mental health services are available to the patient; and

  (2) the judge or jury finds, from clear and convincing evidence, that:

    (A) the proposed patient is mentally ill;

    (B) the nature of the mental illness is severe and persistent;

    (C) as a result of the mental illness, the proposed patient will, if not treated, continue to:

      (i) suffer severe and abnormal mental, emotional, or physical distress; and

(ii) experience deterioration of the ability to function independently to the extent that the proposed patient will be unable to live safely in the community without court-ordered outpatient mental health services; and

(D) the proposed patient has an inability to participate in outpatient treatment services effectively and voluntarily, demonstrated by:

(i) any of the proposed patient's actions occurring within the two-year period which immediately precedes the hearing; or

(ii) specific characteristics of the proposed patient's clinical condition that make impossible a rational and informed decision whether to submit to voluntary outpatient treatment.

(c) If the judge or jury finds that the proposed patient meets the commitment criteria prescribed by Subsection (a), the judge or jury must specify which criterion listed in Subsection (a)(2) forms the basis for the decision.

(d) To be clear and convincing under Subsection (a), the evidence must include expert testimony and, unless waived, evidence of a recent overt act or a continuing pattern of behavior that tends to confirm:

(1) the likelihood of serious harm to the proposed patient or others; or

(2) the proposed patient's distress and the deterioration of the proposed patient's ability to function.

(e) To be clear and convincing under Subdivision (b)(2), the evidence must include expert testimony and, unless waived, evidence of a recent overt act or a continuing pattern of behavior that tends to confirm:

(1) the proposed patient's distress;

(2) the deterioration of ability to function independently to the extent that the proposed patient will be unable to live safely in the community; and

(3) the proposed patient's inability to participate in outpatient treatment services effectively and voluntarily.

(f) The proposed patient and the proposed patient's attorney, by a written document filed with the court, may waive the right to cross-examine witnesses, and, if that right is waived, the court may admit, as evidence, the certificates of medical examination for mental illness. The certificates admitted under this subsection constitute competent medical or psychiatric testimony, and the court may make its findings solely from the certificates. If the proposed patient and the proposed patient's attorney do not waive in writing the right to cross-examine witnesses, the court shall proceed to hear testimony. The testimony must include competent medical or psychiatric testimony. In addition, the court may consider the testimony of a nonphysician mental health professional as provided by Section 574.031(f).

(g) An order for temporary inpatient or outpatient mental health services shall state that treatment is authorized for not longer than 90 days. The order may not specify a shorter period.

(h) A judge may not issue an order for temporary inpatient or outpatient mental health services for a proposed patient who is charged with a criminal offense that involves an act, attempt, or threat of serious bodily injury to another person.

(i) A judge may advise, but may not compel, the proposed patient to:

   (1) receive treatment with psychoactive medication as specified by the outpatient mental health services treatment plan;

   (2) participate in counseling; and

   (3) refrain from the use of alcohol or illicit drugs.

§574.035. Order for Extended Mental Health Services

(a) The judge may order a proposed patient to receive court-ordered extended inpatient mental health services only if the jury, or the judge if the right to a jury is waived, finds, from clear and convincing evidence, that:

   (1) the proposed patient is mentally ill;

   (2) as a result of that mental illness the proposed patient:

      (A) is likely to cause serious harm to himself;

      (B) is likely to cause serious harm to others; or

      (C) is:

         (i) suffering severe and abnormal mental, emotional, or physical distress;

         (ii) experiencing substantial mental or physical deterioration of the proposed patient's ability to function independently, which is exhibited by the proposed patient's inability, except for reasons of indigence, to provide for the proposed patient's basic needs, including food, clothing, health, or safety; and

         (iii) unable to make a rational and informed decision as to whether or not to submit to treatment;

   (3) the proposed patient's condition is expected to continue for more than 90 days; and

   (4) the proposed patient has received court-ordered inpatient mental health services under this subtitle or under Article 46.02, Code of Criminal Procedure, for at least 60 consecutive days during the preceding 12 months.

(b) The judge may order a proposed patient to receive court-ordered extended outpatient mental health services only if:

   (1) the judge finds that appropriate mental health services are available to the patient; and

(2) the jury, or the judge if the right to a jury is waived, finds from clear and convincing evidence that:

(A) the proposed patient is mentally ill;

(B) the nature of the mental illness is severe and persistent;

(C) as a result of the mental illness, the proposed patient will, if not treated, continue to:

(i) suffer severe and abnormal mental, emotional, or physical distress; and

(ii) experience deterioration of the ability to function independently to the extent that the proposed patient will be unable to live safely in the community without court-ordered outpatient mental health services;

(D) the proposed patient has an inability to participate in outpatient treatment services effectively and voluntarily, demonstrated by:

(i) any of the proposed patient's actions occurring within the two-year period which immediately precedes the hearing; or

(ii) specific characteristics of the proposed patient's clinical condition that make impossible a rational and informed decision whether to submit to voluntary outpatient treatment;

(E) the proposed patient's condition is expected to continue for more than 90 days; and

(F) the proposed patient has received court-ordered inpatient mental health services under this subtitle or under Section 5, Article 46.02, Code of Criminal Procedure, for at least 60 consecutive days during the preceding 12 months.

(c) If the jury or judge finds that the proposed patient meets the commitment criteria prescribed by Subsection (a), the jury or judge must specify which criterion listed in Subsection (a)(2) forms the basis for the decision.

(d) The jury or judge is not required to make the finding under Subsection (a)(4) or (b)(2)(F) if the proposed patient has already been subject to an order for extended mental health services.

(e) To be clear and convincing under Subsection (a), the evidence must include expert testimony and evidence of a recent overt act or a continuing pattern of behavior that tends to confirm:

(1) the likelihood of serious harm to the proposed patient or others; or

(2) the proposed patient's distress and the deterioration of the proposed patient's ability to function.

(f) To be clear and convincing under Subdivision (b)(2), the evidence must include expert testimony and evidence of a recent overt act or a continuing pattern of behavior that tends to confirm:

(1) the proposed patient's distress;

(2) the deterioration of ability to function independently to the extent that the proposed patient will be unable to live safely in the community; and

(3) the proposed patient's inability to participate in outpatient treatment services effectively and voluntarily.

(g) The court may not make its findings solely from the certificates of medical examination for mental illness but shall hear testimony. The court may not enter an order for extended mental health services unless appropriate findings are made and are supported by testimony taken at the hearing. The testimony must include competent medical or psychiatric testimony.

(h) An order for extended inpatient or outpatient mental health services shall state that treatment is authorized for not longer than 12 months. The order may not specify a shorter period.

(i) A judge may not issue an order for extended inpatient or outpatient mental health services for a proposed patient who is charged with a criminal offense that involves an act, attempt, or threat of serious bodily injury to another person.

(j) A judge may advise, but may not compel, the proposed patient to:

(1) receive treatment with psychoactive medication as specified by the outpatient mental health services treatment plan;

(2) participate in counseling; and

(3) refrain from the use of alcohol or illicit drugs.

§574.036. Order of Care or Commitment

(a) The judge shall dismiss the jury, if any, after a hearing in which a person is found to be mentally ill and to meet the criteria for court-ordered temporary or extended mental health services.

(b) The judge may hear additional evidence relating to alternative settings for care before entering an order relating to the setting for the care the person will receive.

(c) The judge shall consider in determining the setting for care the recommendation for the most appropriate treatment alternative filed under Section 574.012.

(d) The judge shall order the mental health services provided in the least restrictive appropriate setting available.

(e) The judge may enter an order:

(1) committing the person to a mental health facility for inpatient care if the trier of fact finds that the person meets the commitment criteria prescribed by Section 574.034(a) or 574.035(a); or

(2) committing the person to outpatient mental health services if the trier of fact finds that the person meets the commitment criteria prescribed by Section 574.034(b) or 574.035(b).

§574.037. Court-Ordered Outpatient Services

(a) The court, in an order that directs a patient to participate in outpatient mental health services, shall identify a person who is responsible for those services. The person identified must be the facility administrator or an individual involved in providing court-ordered outpatient services. A person may not be designated as responsible for the ordered services without the person's consent unless the person is the facility administrator of a department facility or the facility administrator of a community center that provides mental health services in the region in which the committing court is located.

(b) The person responsible for the services shall submit to the court within two weeks after the court enters the order a general program of the treatment to be provided. The program must be incorporated into the court order.

(c) The person responsible for the services shall inform the court of:

(1) the patient's failure to comply with the court order; and

(2) any substantial change in the general program of treatment that occurs before the order expires.

(d) A facility must comply with this section to the extent that the commissioner determines that the designated mental health facility has sufficient resources to perform the necessary services.

(e) A patient may not be detained in a private mental health facility without the consent of the facility administrator.

§574.0415. Information on Medications

(a) A mental health facility shall provide to a patient in the patient's primary language, if possible, and in accordance with board rules information relating to prescription medication ordered by the patient's treating physician.

(b) The facility shall also provide the information to the patient's family on request, but only to the extent not otherwise prohibited by state or federal confidentiality laws.

§574.042. Commitment to Private Facility

The court may order a patient committed to a private mental hospital at no expense to the state if the court receives:

(1) an application signed by the patient or the patient's guardian or next friend requesting that the patient be placed in a designated private mental hospital at the patient's or applicant's expense; and

(2) written agreement from the hospital administrator of the private mental hospital to admit the patient and to accept responsibility for the patient in accordance with this subtitle.

RIGHTS OF PATIENTS—§574.105

§574.105. Rights of Patient

A patient for whom an application for an order to authorize the administration of a psychoactive medication is filed is entitled to:

(1) representation by a court-appointed attorney who is knowledgeable about issues to be adjudicated at the hearing;

(2) meet with that attorney as soon as is practicable to prepare for the hearing and to discuss any of the patient's questions or concerns;

(3) receive, immediately after the time of the hearing is set, a copy of the application and written notice of the time, place, and date of the hearing;

(4) be told, at the time personal notice of the hearing is given, of the patient's right to a hearing and right to the assistance of an attorney to prepare for the hearing and to answer any questions or concerns;

(5) be present at the hearing;

(6) request from the court an independent expert; and

(7) oral notification, at the conclusion of the hearing, of the court's determinations of the patient's capacity and best interests.

§574.106. Hearing on Patient's Capacity and Order Authorizing Psychoactive Medication

(a) The court may issue an order authorizing the administration of one or more classes of psychoactive medication only if the court finds by clear and convincing evidence after the hearing that:

(1) the patient is under an order for temporary or extended mental health services under Section 574.034 or 574.035;

(2) the patient lacks the capacity to make a decision regarding the administration of the proposed medication; and

(3) treatment with the proposed medication is in the best interest of the patient.

(b) In making its findings, the court shall consider:

(1) the patient's expressed preferences regarding treatment with psychoactive medication;

(2) the patient's religious beliefs;

(3) the risks and benefits, from the perspective of the patient, of taking psychoactive medication;

(4) the consequences to the patient if the psychoactive medication is not administered;

(5) the prognosis for the patient if the patient is treated with psychoactive medication; and

(6) alternatives to treatment with psychoactive medication.

(c) A hearing under this subchapter shall be conducted on the record by the probate judge or judge with probate jurisdiction, except as provided by Subsection (d).

(d) A judge may refer a hearing to a magistrate or court-appointed master who has training regarding psychoactive medications. The magistrate or master may effectuate the notice, set hearing dates, and appoint attorneys as required in this subchapter. A record is not required if the hearing is held by a magistrate or court-appointed master.

(e) A party is entitled to a hearing de novo by the judge if an appeal of the magistrate's or master's report is filed with the court within three days after the report is issued. The hearing de novo shall be held within 30 days of the filing of the application for an order to authorize psychoactive medication.

(f) If a hearing or an appeal of a master's or magistrate's report is to be held in a county court in which the judge is not a licensed attorney, the proposed patient or the proposed patient's attorney may request that the proceeding be transferred to a court with a judge who is licensed to practice law in this state. The county judge shall transfer the case after receiving the request, and the receiving court shall hear the case as if it had been originally filed in that court.

(g) As soon as practicable after the conclusion of the hearing, the patient is entitled to have provided to the patient and the patient's attorney written notification of the court's determinations under this section. The notification shall include a statement of the evidence on which the court relied and the reasons for the court's determinations.

(h) An order entered under this section shall authorize the administration to a patient, regardless of the patient's refusal, of one or more classes of psychoactive medications specified in the application and consistent with the patient's diagnosis. The order shall permit an increase or decrease in a medication's dosage, restitution of medication authorized but discontinued during the period the order is valid, or the substitution of a medication within the same class.

(i) The classes of psychoactive medications in the order must conform to classes determined by the department.

(j) An order issued under this section may be reauthorized or modified on the petition of a party. The order remains in effect pending action on a petition for reauthorization or modification. For the purpose of this subsection, "modification" means a change of a class of medication authorized in the order.

§574.109. Effect of Order

(a) A person's consent to take a psychoactive medication is not valid and may not be relied on if the person is subject to an order issued under Section 574.106.

(b) The issuance of an order under Section 574.106 is not a determination or adjudication of mental incompetency and does not limit in any other respect that person's rights as a citizen or the person's property rights or legal capacity.

VOLUNTARY ADMISSION FOR COURT-ORDERED SERVICES—§574.151

Voluntary Admission for Certain Persons for Whom Motion for Court-Ordered Services Has Been Filed

§574.151. Applicability

This subchapter applies only to a person for whom a motion for court-ordered mental health services is filed under Section 574.001, for whom a final order on that motion has not been entered under Section 574.034 or 574.035, and who requests voluntary admission to an inpatient mental health facility:

(1) while the person is receiving at that facility involuntary inpatient services under Subchapter B or under Chapter 573; or

(2) before the 31st day after the date the person was released from that facility under Section 573.023 or 574.028.

§574.152. Capacity to Consent to Voluntary Admission

A person described by Section 574.151 is rebuttably presumed to have the capacity to consent to admission to the inpatient mental health facility for voluntary inpatient mental health services.

§574.153. Rights of Person Admitted to Voluntary Inpatient Treatment

(a) A person described by Section 574.151 who is admitted to the inpatient mental health facility for voluntary inpatient mental health services has all of the rights provided by Chapter 576 for a person receiving voluntary or involuntary inpatient mental health services.

(b) A right assured by Section 576.021 may not be waived by the patient, the patient's attorney or guardian, or any other person acting on behalf of the patient.

§574.154. Participation in Research Program

Notwithstanding any other law, a person described by Section 574.151 may not participate in a research program in the inpatient mental health facility unless:

(1) the patient provides written consent to participate in the research program under a protocol that has been approved by the facility's institutional review board; and

(2) the institutional review board specifically reviews the patient's consent under the approved protocol.

§576.001. Rights Under Constitution and Law

(a) A person with mental illness in this state has the rights, benefits, responsibilities, and privileges guaranteed by the constitution and laws of the United States and this state.

(b) Unless a specific law limits a right under a special procedure, a patient has:

(1) the right to register and vote at an election;

(2) the right to acquire, use, and dispose of property, including contractual rights;

(3) the right to sue and be sued;

(4) all rights relating to the grant, use, and revocation of a license, permit, privilege, or benefit under law;

(5) the right to religious freedom; and

(6) all rights relating to domestic relations.

§576.002. Presumption of Competency

(a) The provision of court-ordered, emergency, or voluntary mental health services to a person is not a determination or adjudication of mental incompetency and does not limit the person's rights as a citizen, or the person's property rights or legal capacity.

(b) There is a rebuttable presumption that a person is mentally competent unless a judicial finding to the contrary is made under the Texas Probate Code.

§576.005. Confidentiality of Records

Records of a mental health facility that directly or indirectly identify a present, former, or proposed patient are confidential unless disclosure is permitted by other state law.

§576.006. Rights Subject to Limitation

(a) A patient in an inpatient mental health facility has the right to:

(1) receive visitors;

(2) communicate with a person outside the facility by telephone and by uncensored and sealed mail; and

(3) communicate by telephone and by uncensored and sealed mail with legal counsel, the department, the courts, and the state attorney general.

(b) The rights provided in Subsection (a) are subject to the general rules of the facility. The physician ultimately responsible for the patient's treatment may also restrict a right only to the extent that the restriction is necessary to the patient's welfare or to protect another person but may not restrict the right to communicate with legal counsel, the department, the courts, or the state attorney general.

(c) If a restriction is imposed under this section, the physician ultimately responsible for the patient's treatment shall document the clinical reasons for the restriction and the duration of the restriction in the patient's clinical record. That physician shall inform the patient and, if appropriate, the patient's parent, managing conservator, or guardian of the clinical reasons for the restriction and the duration of the restriction.

§576.007. Notification of Release

(a) The department or facility shall make a reasonable effort to notify an adult patient's family before the patient is discharged or released from a facility providing voluntary or involuntary mental health services if the patient grants permission for the notification.

(b) The department shall notify each adult patient of the patient's right to have his family notified under this section.

§576.008. Notification of Protection / Advocacy System

A patient shall be informed in writing, at the time of admission and discharge, of the existence, purpose, telephone number, and address of the protection and advocacy system established in this state under the federal Protection and Advocacy for Mentally Ill Individuals Act of 1986 (42 U.S.C. Sec. 10801, et seq.).

§576.009. Notification of Rights

A patient receiving involuntary inpatient mental health services shall be informed of the rights provided by this subtitle:

(1) orally, in simple, nontechnical terms, and in writing that, if possible, is in the person's primary language; or

(2) through the use of a means reasonably calculated to communicate with a hearing impaired or visually impaired person, if applicable.

§576.021. General Rights Relating to Treatment

(a) A patient receiving mental health services under this subtitle has the right to:

(1) appropriate treatment for the patient's mental illness in the least restrictive appropriate setting available;

(2) not receive unnecessary or excessive medication;

(3) refuse to participate in a research program;

(4) an individualized treatment plan and to participate in developing the plan; and

(5) a humane treatment environment that provides reasonable protection from harm and appropriate privacy for personal needs.

(b) participation in a research program does not affect a right provided by this chapter.

(c) A right provided by this section may not be waived by the patient, the patient's attorney or guardian, or any other person behalf of the patient.

§576.022. Adequacy of Treatment

(a) The facility administrator of an inpatient mental health facility shall provide adequate medical and psychiatric care and treatment to every patient in accordance with the highest standards accepted in medical practice.

(b) The facility administrator of an inpatient mental health facility may give the patient accepted psychiatric treatment and therapy.

§576.023. Periodic Examination

The facility administrator is responsible for the examination of each patient of the facility at least once every six months and more frequently as practicable.

§576.024. Use of Physical Restraint

(a) A physical restraint may not be applied to a patient unless a physician prescribes the restraint.

(b) A physical restraint shall be removed as soon as possible.

(c) Each use of a physical restraint and the reason for the use shall be made a part of the patient's clinical record. The physician who prescribed the restraint shall sign the record.

§576.025. Administration of Psychoactive Medication

(a) A person may not administer a psychoactive medication to a patient receiving voluntary or involuntary mental health services who refuses the administration unless:

  (1) the patient is having a medication-related emergency;

  (2) the patient is younger than 16 years of age and the patient's parent, managing conservator, or guardian consents to the administration on behalf of the patient;

  (3) the refusing patient's representative authorized by law to consent on behalf of the patient has consented to the administration;

  (4) the administration of the medication regardless of the patient's refusal is authorized by an order issued under Section 574.106; or

  (5) the patient is receiving court-ordered mental health services authorized by an order issued under:

    (A) Article 46.02 or 46.03, Code of Criminal Procedure; or

    (B) Chapter 55, Family Code.

(b) Consent to the administration of psychoactive medication given by a patient or by a person authorized by law to consent on behalf of the patient is valid only if:

(1) the consent is given voluntarily and without coercive or undue influence;

(2) the treating physician or a person designated by the physician provided the following information, in a standard format approved by the department, to the patient and, if applicable, to the patient's representative authorized by law to consent on behalf of the patient:

(A) the specific condition to be treated;

(B) the beneficial effects on that condition expected from the medication;

(C) the probable health and mental health consequences of not consenting to the medication;

(D) the probable clinically significant side effects and risks associated with the medication;

(E) the generally accepted alternatives to the medication, if any, and why the physician recommends that they be rejected; and

(F) the proposed course of the medication;

(3) the patient and, if appropriate, the patient's representative authorized by law to consent on behalf of the patient is informed in writing that consent may be revoked; and

(4) the consent is evidenced in the patient's clinical record by a signed form prescribed by the facility or by a statement of the treating physician or a person designated by the physician that documents that consent was given by the appropriate person and the circumstances under which the consent was obtained.

(c) If the treating physician designates another person to provide the information under Subsection (b), then, not later than two working days after that person provides the information, excluding weekends and legal holidays, the physician shall meet with the patient and, if appropriate, the patient's representative who provided the consent, to review the information and answer any questions.

(d) A patient's refusal or attempt to refuse to receive psychoactive medication, whether given verbally or by other indications or means, shall be documented in the patient's clinical record.

(e) In prescribing psychoactive medication, a treating physician shall:

(1) prescribe, consistent with clinically appropriate medical care, the medication that has the fewest side effects or the least potential for adverse side effects, unless the class of medication has been demonstrated or justified not to be effective clinically; and

(2) administer the smallest therapeutically acceptable dosages of medication for the patient's condition.

(f) If a physician issues an order to administer psychoactive medication to a patient without the patient's consent because the patient is having a medication-related emergency:

(1) the physician shall document in the patient's clinical record in specific medical or behavioral terms the necessity of the order and that the physician has evaluated but rejected other generally accepted, less intrusive forms of treatment, if any; and

(2) treatment of the patient with the psychoactive medication shall be provided in the manner, consistent with clinically appropriate medical care, least restrictive of the patient's personal liberty.

(g) In this section, "medication-related emergency" and "psychoactive medication" have the meanings assigned by Section 574.101.

§576.026. Independent Evaluation

(a) A patient receiving inpatient mental health services under this subtitle is entitled to obtain at the patient's cost an independent psychiatric, psychological, or medical examination or evaluation by a psychiatrist, physician, or nonphysician mental health professional chosen by the patient. The facility administrator shall allow the patient to obtain the examination or evaluation at any reasonable time.

(b) If the patient is a minor, the minor and the minor's parent, legal guardian, or managing or possessory conservator is entitled to obtain the examination or evaluation. The cost of the examination or evaluation shall be billed by the professional who performed the examination or evaluation to the person responsible for payment of the minor's treatment as a cost of treatment.

§576.027. List of Medications

(a) The facility administrator of an inpatient mental health facility shall provide to a patient, a person designated by the patient, and the patient's legal guardian or managing conservator, if any, a list of the medications prescribed for administration to the patient while the patient is in the facility. The list must include for each medication:

(1) the name of the medication;

(2) the dosage and schedule prescribed for the administration of the medication; and

(3) the name of the physician who prescribed the medication.

(b) The list must be provided within four hours after the facility administrator receives a written request for the list from the patient, a person designated by the patient, or the patient's legal guardian or managing conservator and on the discharge of the patient. If sufficient time to prepare the list before discharge is not available, the list may be mailed within 24 hours after discharge to the patient, a person designated by the patient, and the patient's legal guardian or managing conservator.

(c) A patient or the patient's legal guardian or managing conservator, if any, may waive the right of any person to receive the list of medications while the patient is participating in a research project if release of the list would jeopardize the results of the project.

LEGALLY ADEQUATE CONSENT—§591

§591.006. Consent

(a) Consent given by a person is legally adequate if the person:

  (1) is not a minor and has not been adjudicated incompetent to manage the person's personal affairs by an appropriate court of law;

  (2) understands the information; and

  (3) consents voluntarily, free from coercion or undue influence.

(b) The person giving the consent must be informed of and understand:

  (1) the nature, purpose, consequences, risks, and benefits of and alternatives to the procedure;

  (2) that the withdrawal or refusal of consent will not prejudice the future provision of care and services; and

  (3) the method used in the proposed procedure if the person is to receive unusual or hazardous treatment procedures, experimental research, organ transplantation, or nontherapeutic surgery.

MENTAL RETARDATION—§592

§592.001. Purpose

The purpose of this chapter is to recognize and protect the individual dignity and worth of each person with mental retardation.

§592.002. Rules

The board by rule shall ensure the implementation of the rights guaranteed in this chapter.

§592.011. Rights Guaranteed

(a) Each person with mental retardation in this state has the rights, benefits, and privileges guaranteed by the constitution and laws of the United States and this state.

(b) The rights specifically listed in this subtitle are in addition to all other rights that persons with mental retardation have and are not exclusive or intended to limit the rights guaranteed by the constitution and laws of the United States and this state.

§592.012. Protection from Exploitation and Abuse

Each person with mental retardation has the right to protection from exploitation and abuse because of the person's mental retardation.

§592.013. Least Restrictive Living Environment

Each person with mental retardation has the right to live in the least restrictive setting appropriate to the person's individual needs and abilities and in a variety of living situations, including living:

(1) alone;

(2) in a group home;

(3) with a family; or

(4) in a supervised, protective environment.

§592.014. Education

Each person with mental retardation has the right to receive publicly supported educational services, including those services provided under the Education Code, that are appropriate to the person's individual needs regardless of the person's:

(1) chronological age;

(2) degree of retardation;

(3) accompanying disabilities or handicaps; or

(4) admission or commitment to mental retardation services.

§592.015. Employment

An employer, employment agency, or labor organization may not deny a person equal opportunities in employment because of the person's mental retardation, unless:

(1) the person's mental retardation significantly impairs the person's ability to perform the duties and tasks of the position for which the person has applied; or

(2) the denial is based on a bona fide occupational qualification reasonably necessary to the normal operation of the particular business or enterprise.

§592.016. Housing

An owner, lessee, sublessee, assignee, or managing agent or other person having the right to sell, rent, or lease real property, or an agent or employee of any of these, may not refuse to sell, rent, or lease to any person or group of persons solely because the person is a person with mental retardation or a group that includes one or more persons with mental retardation.

§592.017. Treatment and Services

Each person with mental retardation has the right to receive for mental retardation adequate treatment and habilitative services that:

(1) are suited to the person's individual needs;

(2) maximize the person's capabilities;

(3) enhance the person's ability to cope with the person's environment; and

(4) are administered skillfully, safely, and humanely with full respect for the dignity and personal integrity of the person.

§592.018. Determination of Mental Retardation

A person thought to be a person with mental retardation has the right promptly to receive a determination of mental retardation using diagnostic techniques that are adapted to that person's cultural background, language, and ethnic origin to determine if the person is in need of mental retardation services as provided by Subchapter A, Chapter 593.

§592.019. Administrative Hearing

A person who files an application for a determination of mental retardation has the right to request and promptly receive an administrative hearing under Subchapter A, Chapter 593, to contest the findings of the determination of mental retardation.

§592.020. Independent Determination of Mental Retardation

A person for whom a determination of mental retardation is performed or a person who files an application for a determination of mental retardation under Section 593.004 and who questions the validity or results of the determination of mental retardation has the right to an additional, independent determination of mental retardation performed at the person's own expense.

§592.021. Additional Rights

Each person with mental retardation has the right to:

(1) presumption of competency;

(2) due process in guardianship proceedings; and

(3) fair compensation for the person's labor for the economic benefit of another, regardless of any direct or incidental therapeutic value to the person.

§592.031. Rights in General

(a) Each client has the same rights as other citizens of the United States and this state unless the client's rights have been lawfully restricted.

(b) Each client has the rights listed in this subchapter in addition to the rights guaranteed by Subchapter B.

§592.032. Least Restrictive Alternative

Each client has the right to live in the least restrictive habilitation setting and to be treated and served in the least intrusive manner appropriate to the client's individual needs.

§592.033. Individualized Plan

(a) Each client has the right to a written, individualized habilitation plan developed by appropriate specialists.

(b) The client, and the parent of a client who is a minor or the guardian of the person, shall participate in the development of the plan.

(c) The plan shall be implemented as soon as possible but not later than the 30th day after the date on which the client is admitted or committed to mental retardation services.

(d) The content of an individualized habilitation plan is as required by the department.

§592.034. Review and Reevaluation

(a) Each client has the right to have the individualized habilitation plan reviewed at least:

    (1) once a year if the client is in a residential care facility; or

    (2) quarterly if the client has been admitted for other services.

(b) The purpose of the review is to:

    (1) measure progress;

    (2) modify objectives and programs if necessary; and

    (3) provide guidance and remediation techniques.

(c) Each client has the right to a periodic reassessment.

§592.035. Participation in Planning

(a) Each client, and parent of a client who is a minor or the guardian of the person, have the right to:

    (1) participate in planning the client's treatment and habilitation; and

    (2) be informed in writing at reasonable intervals of the client's progress.

(b) If possible, the client, parent, or guardian of the person shall be given the opportunity to choose from several appropriate alternative services available to the client from a service provider.

§592.036. Withdrawal from Voluntary Services

(a) Except as provided by Section 593.030, a client, the parent if the client is a minor, or a guardian of the person may withdraw the client from mental retardation services.

(b) This section does not apply to a person who was committed to a residential care facility as provided by Subchapter C, Chapter 593.

§592.037. Freedom from Mistreatment

Each client has the right not to be mistreated, neglected, or abused by a service provider.

§592.038. Freedom from Unnecessary Medication

(a) Each client has the right to not receive unnecessary or excessive medication.

(b) Medication may not be used:

(1) as punishment;

(2) for the convenience of the staff;

(3) as a substitute for a habilitation program; or

(4) in quantities that interfere with the client's habilitation program.

(c) Medication for each client may be authorized only by prescription of a physician and a physician shall closely supervise its use.

§592.039. Grievances

A client, or a person acting on behalf of a person with mental retardation or a group of persons with mental retardation, has the right to submit complaints or grievances regarding the infringement of the rights of a person with mental retardation or the delivery of mental retardation services against a person, group of persons, organization, or business to the appropriate public responsibility committee for investigation and appropriate action.

§592.040. Information About Rights

(a) On admission for mental retardation services, each client, and the parent if the client is a minor or the guardian of the person of the client, shall be given written notice of the rights guaranteed by this subtitle. The notice shall be in plain and simple language.

(b) Each client shall be orally informed of these rights in plain and simple language.

(c) Notice given solely to the parent or guardian of the person is sufficient if the client is manifestly unable to comprehend the rights.

§592.051. General Rights of Residents

Each resident has the right to:

(1) a normal residential environment;

(2) a humane physical environment;

(3) communication and visits; and

(4) possess personal property.

§592.052. Medical and Dental Care and Treatment

Each resident has the right to prompt, adequate, and necessary medical and dental care and treatment for physical and mental ailments and to prevent an illness or disability.

§592.053. Standards of Care

Medical and dental care and treatment shall be performed under the appropriate supervision of a licensed physician or dentist and shall be consistent with accepted standards of medical and dental practice in the community.

§592.054. Duties of Superintendent or Director

(a) Except as limited by this subtitle, the superintendent or director shall provide without further consent necessary care and treatment to each court-committed resident and make available necessary care and treatment to each voluntary resident.

(b) Notwithstanding Subsection (a), consent is required for all surgical procedures.

§592.055. Unusual or Hazardous Treatment

This subtitle does not permit the department to perform unusual or hazardous treatment procedures, experimental research, organ transplantation, or nontherapeutic surgery for experimental research.

MENTAL RETARDATION RECORDS—§595

§595.001. Confidentiality of Records

Records of the identity, diagnosis, evaluation, or treatment of a person that are maintained in connection with the performance of a program or activity relating to mental retardation are confidential and may be disclosed only for the purposes and under the circumstances authorized under Sections 595.003 and 595.004.

§595.002. Rules

The board shall adopt rules to carry out this chapter that the department considers necessary or proper to:

(1) prevent circumvention or evasion of the chapter; or

(2) facilitate compliance with the chapter.

§595.003. Consent to Disclosure

(a) The content of a confidential record may be disclosed in accordance with the prior written consent of:

(1) the person about whom the record is maintained;

(2) the person's parent if the person is a minor;

(3) the guardian if the person has been adjudicated incompetent to manage the person's personal affairs; or

(4) if the person is dead:

(A) the executor or administrator of the deceased's estate; or

(B) if an executor or administrator has not been appointed, the deceased's spouse or, if the deceased was not married, an adult related to the deceased within the first degree of consanguinity.

(b) Disclosure is permitted only to the extent, under the circumstances, and for the purposes allowed under department rules.

§595.004. Right to Personal Record

(a) The content of a confidential record shall be made available on the request of the person about whom the record was made unless:

(1) the person is a client; and

(2) the qualified professional responsible for supervising the client's habilitation states in a signed written statement that having access to the record is not in the client's best interest.

(b) The parent of a minor or the guardian of the person shall be given access to the contents of any record about the minor or person.

§595.005. Exceptions

(a) The content of a confidential record may be disclosed without the consent required under Section 595.003 to:

(1) medical personnel to the extent necessary to meet a medical emergency;

(2) qualified personnel for management audits, financial audits, program evaluations, or research approved by the department; or

(3) personnel legally authorized to conduct investigations concerning complaints of abuse or denial of rights of persons with mental retardation.

(b) A person who receives confidential information under Subsection (a)(2) may not directly or indirectly identify a person receiving services in a report of the audit, evaluation, or research, or otherwise disclose any identities.

(c) The department may disclose without the consent required under Section 595.003 a person's educational records to a school district that provides or will provide educational services to the person.

(d) If authorized by an appropriate order of a court of competent jurisdiction granted after application showing good cause, the content of a record may be disclosed without the consent required under Section 595.003. In determining whether there is good cause, a court shall weigh the public interest and need for disclosure against the injury to the person receiving services. On granting the order, the court, in determining the extent to which any disclosure of all or any part of a record is necessary, shall impose appropriate safeguards against unauthorized disclosure.

§595.006. Use of Record in Criminal Proceedings

Except as authorized by a court order under Section 595.005, a confidential record may not be used to:

(1) initiate or substantiate a criminal charge against a person receiving services; or

(2) conduct an investigation of a person receiving services.

§595.007. Confidentiality of Past Services

The prohibition against disclosing information in a confidential record applies regardless of when the person received services.

§595.008. Exchange of Records

The prohibitions against disclosure apply to an exchange of records between government agencies or persons, except for exchanges of information necessary for:

(1) delivery of services to clients; or

(2) payment for mental retardation services as defined in this subtitle.

§595.009. Receipt of Information by Persons Other Than Client or Patient

(a) A person who receives information that is confidential under this chapter may not disclose the information except to the extent that disclosure is consistent with the authorized purposes for which the information was obtained.

(b) This section does not apply to the person about whom the record is made, or the parent, if the person is a minor, or the guardian of the person.

§595.010. Disclosure of Physical or Mental Condition

This chapter does not prohibit a qualified professional from disclosing the current physical and mental condition of a person with mental retardation to the person's parent, guardian, relative, or friend.

MENTAL HEALTH RECORDS—§611

§611.001. Definitions

In this chapter:

(1) *"Patient"* means a person who consults or is interviewed by a professional for diagnosis, evaluation, or treatment of any mental or emotional condition or disorder, including alcoholism or drug addiction.

(2) *"Professional"* means:

(A) a person authorized to practice medicine in any state or nation;

(B) a person licensed or certified by this state to diagnose, evaluate, or treat any mental or emotional condition or disorder; or

(C) a person the patient reasonably believes is authorized, licensed, or certified as provided by this subsection.

§611.002. Confidentiality of Information and Prohibition Against Disclosure

(a) Communications between a patient and a professional, and records of the identity, diagnosis, evaluation, or treatment of a patient that are created or maintained by a professional, are confidential.

(b) Confidential communications or records may not be disclosed except as provided by Section 611.004 or 611.0045.

(c) This section applies regardless of when the patient received services from a professional.

§611.003. Persons Who May Claim Privilege of Confidentiality

(a) The privilege of confidentiality may be claimed by:

(1) the patient;

(2) a person listed in Section 611.004(a)(4) or (a)(5) who is acting on the patient's behalf; or

(3) the professional, but only on behalf of the patient.

(b) The authority of a professional to claim the privilege of confidentiality on behalf of the patient is presumed in the absence of evidence to the contrary.

§611.004. Authorized Disclosure of Confidential Information Other than in Judicial or Administrative Proceeding

(a) A professional may disclose confidential information only:

(1) to a governmental agency if the disclosure is required or authorized by law;

(2) to medical or law enforcement personnel if the professional determines that there is a probability of imminent physical injury by the patient to the patient or others or there is a probability of immediate mental or emotional injury to the patient;

(3) to qualified personnel for management audits, financial audits, program evaluations, or research, in accordance with Subsection (b);

(4) to a person who has the written consent of the patient, or a parent if the patient is a minor, or a guardian if the patient has been adjudicated as incompetent to manage the patient's personal affairs;

(5) to the patient's personal representative if the patient is deceased;

(6) to individuals, corporations, or governmental agencies involved in paying or collecting fees for mental or emotional health services provided by a professional;

(7) to other professionals and personnel under the professionals' direction who participate in the diagnosis, evaluation, or treatment of the patient;

(8) in an official legislative inquiry relating to a state hospital or state school as provided by Subsection (c);

(9) to designated persons or personnel of a correctional facility in which a person is detained if the disclosure is for the sole purpose of providing treatment and health care to the person in custody;

(10) to an employee or agent of the professional who requires mental health care information to provide mental health care services or in complying with statutory, licensing, or accreditation requirements, if the professional has taken appropriate action to ensure that the employee or agent:

(A) will not use or disclose the information for any other purposes; and

(B) will take appropriate steps to protect the information; or

(11) to satisfy a request for medical records of a deceased or incompetent person pursuant to Section 4.01(e), Medical Liability and Insurance Improvement Act of Texas (Article 4590i, Vernon's Texas Civil Statutes).

(b) Personnel who receive confidential information under Subsection (a)(3) may not directly or indirectly identify or otherwise disclose the identity of a patient in a report or in any other manner.

(c) The exception in Subsection (a)(8) applies only to records created by the state hospital or state school or by the employees of the hospital or school. Information or records that identify a patient may be released only with the patient's proper consent.

(d) A person who receives information from confidential communications or records may not disclose the information except to the extent that disclosure is consistent with the authorized purposes for which the person first obtained the information. This subsection does not apply to a person listed in Subsection (a)(4) or (a)(5) who is acting on the patient's behalf.

§611.0045. Right to Mental Health Record

(a) Except as otherwise provided by this section, a patient is entitled to have access to the content of a confidential record made about the patient.

(b) The professional may deny access to any portion of a record if the professional determines that release of that portion would be harmful to the patient's physical, mental, or emotional health.

(c) If the professional denies access to any portion of a record, the professional shall give the patient a signed and dated written statement that having access to the record would be harmful to the patient's physical, mental, or emotional health and shall include a copy of the written statement in the patient's records. The statement must specify the portion of the record to which access is denied, the reason for denial, and the duration of the denial.

(d) The professional who denies access to a portion of a record under this section shall redetermine the necessity for the denial at each time a request for the denied portion is made. If the professional again denies access, the professional shall notify the patient of the denial and document the denial as prescribed by Subsection (c).

(e) If a professional denies access to a portion of a confidential record, the professional shall allow examination and copying of the record by another professional if the patient selects the professional to treat the patient for the same or a related condition as the professional denying access.

(f) The content of a confidential record shall be made available to a person listed by Section 611.004(a)(4) or (5) who is acting on the patient's behalf.

(g) A professional shall delete confidential information about another person who has not consented to the release, but may not delete information relating to the patient that another person has provided, the identity of the person responsible for that information, or the identity of any person who provided information that resulted in the patient's commitment.

(h) If a summary or narrative of a confidential record is requested by the patient or other person requesting release under this section, the professional shall prepare the summary or narrative.

(i) The professional or other entity that has possession or control of the record shall grant access to any portion of the record to which access is not specifically denied under this section within a reasonable time and may charge a reasonable fee.

(j) Notwithstanding Section 5.08, Medical Practice Act (Article 4495b, Vernon's Texas Civil Statutes), this section applies to the release of a confidential record created or maintained by a professional, including a physician, that relates to the diagnosis, evaluation, or treatment of a mental or emotional condition or disorder, including alcoholism or drug addiction.

(k) The denial of a patient's access to any portion of a record by the professional or other entity that has possession or control of the record suspends, until the release of that portion of the record, the running of an applicable statute of limitations on a cause of action in which evidence relevant to the cause of action is in that portion of the record.

§611.005. Legal Remedies for Improper Disclosure or Failure to Disclose

(a) A person aggrieved by the improper disclosure of or failure to disclose confidential communications or records in violation of this chapter may petition the district court of the county in which the person resides for appropriate relief, including injunctive relief. The person may petition a district court of Travis County if the person is not a resident of this state.

(b) In a suit contesting the denial of access under Section 611.0045, the burden of proving that the denial was proper is on the professional who denied the access.

(c) The aggrieved person also has a civil cause of action for damages.

§611.006. Authorized Disclosure of Confidential Information in Judicial or Administrative Proceeding

(a) A professional may disclose confidential information in:

(1) a judicial or administrative proceeding brought by the patient or the patient's legally authorized representative against a professional, including malpractice proceedings;

(2) a license revocation proceeding in which the patient is a complaining witness and in which disclosure is relevant to the claim or defense of a professional;

(3) a judicial or administrative proceeding in which the patient waives the patient's right in writing to the privilege of confidentiality of information or when a representative of the patient acting on the patient's behalf submits a written waiver to the confidentiality privilege;

(4) a judicial or administrative proceeding to substantiate and collect on a claim for mental or emotional health services rendered to the patient;

(5) a judicial proceeding if the judge finds that the patient, after having been informed that communications would not be privileged, has made communications to a professional in the course of a court-ordered examination relating to the patient's mental or emotional condition or disorder, except that those communications may be disclosed only with respect to issues involving the patient's mental or emotional health;

(6) a judicial proceeding affecting the parent-child relationship;

(7) any criminal proceeding, as otherwise provided by law;

(8) a judicial or administrative proceeding regarding the abuse or neglect, or the cause of abuse or neglect, of a resident of an institution, as that term is defined by Chapter 242;

(9) a judicial proceeding relating to a will if the patient's physical or mental condition is relevant to the execution of the will;

(10) an involuntary commitment proceeding for court-ordered treatment or for a probable cause hearing under:

(A) Chapter 462;

(B) Chapter 574; or

(C) Chapter 593; or

(11) a judicial or administrative proceeding where the court or agency has issued an order or subpoena.

(b) On granting an order under Subsection (a)(5), the court, in determining the extent to which disclosure of all or any part of a communication is necessary, shall impose appropriate safeguards against unauthorized disclosure.

§611.007. Revocation of Consent

(a) Except as provided by Subsection (b), a patient or a patient's legally authorized representative may revoke a disclosure consent to a professional at any time. A revocation is valid only if it is written, dated, and signed by the patient or legally authorized representative.

(b) A patient may not revoke a disclosure that is required for purposes of making payment to the professional for mental health care services provided to the patient.

(c) A patient may not maintain an action against a professional for a disclosure made by the professional in good faith reliance on an authorization if the professional did not have notice of the revocation of the consent.

§611.008. Request by Patient

(a) On receipt of a written request from a patient to examine or copy all or part of the patient's recorded mental health care information, a professional, as promptly as required under the circumstances but not later than the 15th day after the date of receiving the request, shall:

   (1) make the information available for examination during regular business hours and provide a copy to the patient, if requested; or

   (2) inform the patient if the information does not exist or cannot be found.

(b) Unless provided for by other state law, the professional may charge a reasonable fee for retrieving or copying mental health care information and is not required to permit examination or copying until the fee is paid unless there is a medical emergency.

(c) A professional may not charge a fee for copying mental health care information under Subsection (b) to the extent the fee is prohibited under Subchapter M, Chapter 161.

HUMAN RESOURCES CODE

ELDER ABUSE—§48

§48.001. Purpose

The purpose of this chapter is to provide for the authority to investigate the abuse, neglect, or exploitation of an elderly or disabled person and to provide protective services to that person.

§48.002. Definitions

(a) Except as otherwise provided under Section 48.251, in this chapter:

(1) *"Elderly person"* means a person 65 years of age or older.

(2) *"Abuse"* means:

(A) the negligent or willful infliction of injury, unreasonable confinement, intimidation, or cruel punishment with resulting physical or emotional harm or pain to an elderly or disabled person by the person's caretaker, family member, or other individual who has an ongoing relationship with the person; or

(B) sexual abuse of an elderly or disabled person, including any involuntary or nonconsensual sexual conduct that would constitute an offense under Section 21.08, Penal Code (indecent exposure) or Chapter 22, Penal Code (assaultive offenses), committed by the person's caretaker, family member, or other individual who has an ongoing relationship with the person.

(3) *"Exploitation"* means the illegal or improper act or process of a caretaker, family member, or other individual who has an ongoing relationship with the elderly or disabled person using the resources of an elderly or disabled person for monetary or personal benefit, profit, or gain without the informed consent of the elderly or disabled person.

(4) *"Neglect"* means the failure to provide for one's self the goods or services, including medical services, which are necessary to avoid physical or emotional harm or pain or the failure of a caretaker to provide such goods or services.

(5) *"Protective services"* means the services furnished by the department or by a protective services agency to an elderly or disabled person who has been determined to be in a state of abuse, neglect, or exploitation. These services may include social casework, case management, and arranging for psychiatric and health evaluation, home care, day care, social services, health care, and other services consistent with this chapter.

(6) "*Protective services agency*" means a public or private agency, corporation, board, or organization that provides protective services to elderly or disabled persons in the state of abuse, neglect, or exploitation.

(7) "*Department*" means the Department of Protective and Regulatory Services.

(8) "*Disabled person*" means a person with a mental, physical, or developmental disability that substantially impairs the person's ability to provide adequately for the person's care or protection and who is:

(A) 18 years of age or older; or

(B) under 18 years of age and who has had the disabilities of minority removed.

(9) "*Legal holiday*" means a state holiday listed in Subchapter B, Chapter 662, Government Code, or an officially declared county holiday.

(10) "*Volunteer*" means a person who:

(A) performs services for or on behalf of the department under the supervision of a department employee; and

(B) does not receive compensation that exceeds the authorized expenses the person incurs in performing those services.

(b) The definitions of "abuse," "neglect," and "exploitation" adopted by the department as prescribed by Section 48.251 apply to an investigation of abuse, neglect, or exploitation in a facility subject to Subchapters F and H.

§48.051. Report

(a) Except as prescribed by Subsection (b), a person having cause to believe that an elderly or disabled person is in the state of abuse, neglect, or exploitation shall report the information required by Subsection (d) immediately to the department.

(b) If a person has cause to believe that an elderly or disabled person has been abused, neglected, or exploited in a facility operated, licensed, certified, or registered by a state agency other than the Texas Department of Mental Health and Mental Retardation, the person shall report the information to the state agency that operates, licenses, certifies, or registers the facility for investigation by that agency.

(c) The duty imposed by Subsections (a) and (b) applies without exception to a person whose professional communications are generally confidential, including an attorney, clergy member, medical practitioner, social worker, and mental health professional.

(d) The report may be made orally or in writing. It shall include:

(1) the name, age, and address of the elderly or disabled person;

(2) the name and address of any person responsible for the elderly or disabled person's care;

(3) the nature and extent of the elderly or disabled person's condition;
(4) the basis of the reporter's knowledge; and
(5) any other relevant information.

§48.052. Failure to Report; Penalty

(a) A person commits an offense if the person has cause to believe that an elderly or disabled person has been abused, neglected, or exploited or is in the state of abuse, neglect, or exploitation and knowingly fails to report in accordance with this chapter. An offense under this subsection is a Class A misdemeanor.

(b) This section does not apply if the alleged abuse, neglect, or exploitation occurred in a facility licensed under Chapter 242, Health and Safety Code. Failure to report abuse, neglect, or exploitation that occurs in a facility licensed under that chapter is governed by that chapter.

§48.053. False Report; Penalty

A person commits an offense if the person knowingly or intentionally reports information as provided in this chapter that the person knows is false or lacks factual foundation. An offense under this section is a Class B misdemeanor.

§48.054. Immunity

(a) A person filing a report under this chapter or testifying or otherwise participating in any judicial proceeding arising from a petition, report, or investigation is immune from civil or criminal liability on account of his or her petition, report, testimony, or participation, unless the person acted in bad faith or with a malicious purpose.

(b) A person, including an authorized department volunteer, medical personnel, or law enforcement officer, who at the request of the department participates in an investigation required by this chapter or in an action that results from that investigation is immune from civil or criminal liability for any act or omission relating to that participation if the person acted in good faith and, if applicable, in the course and scope of the person's assigned responsibilities or duties.

(c) A person who reports the person's own abuse, neglect, or exploitation of another person or who acts in bad faith or with malicious purpose in reporting alleged abuse, neglect, or exploitation is not immune from civil or criminal liability.

§48.203. Voluntary Protective Services

(a) An elderly or disabled person may receive voluntary protective services if the person requests or consents to receive those services.

(b) The elderly or disabled person who receives protective services shall participate in all decisions regarding his or her welfare, if able to do so.

(c) The least restrictive alternatives should be made available to the elderly or disabled person who receives protective services.

(d) If an elderly or disabled person withdraws or refuses consent, the services may not be provided.

Insurance Code

Chapter 1305. Workers' Compensation Health Care Networks

Subchapter D. Contracting Provisions

§1305.151. Transfer of Risk

A contract under this subchapter may not involve a transfer of risk.

§ 1305.152. Network Contracts with Providers

(a) A network shall enter into a written contract with each provider or group of providers that participates in the network. A provider contract under this section is confidential and is not subject to disclosure as public information under Chapter 552, Government Code.

(b) A network is not required to accept an application for participation in the network from a health care provider who otherwise meets the requirements specified in this chapter for participation if the network determines that the network has contracted with a sufficient number of qualified health care providers.

(c) Provider contracts and subcontracts must include, at a minimum, the following provisions:

(1) a hold-harmless clause stating that the network and the network's contracted providers are prohibited from billing or attempting to collect any amounts from employees for health care services under any circumstances, including the insolvency of the insurance carrier or the network, except as provided by Section 1305.451(b)(6);

(2) a statement that the provider agrees to follow treatment guidelines adopted by the network under Section 1305.304, as applicable to an employee's injury;

(3) a continuity of treatment clause that states that if a provider leaves the network, the insurance carrier or network is obligated to continue to reimburse the provider for a period not to exceed 90 days at the contracted rate for care of an employee with a life-threatening condition or an acute condition for which disruption of care would harm the employee;

(4) a clause regarding appeal by the provider of termination of provider status and applicable written notification to employees regarding such a termination, including provisions determined by the commissioner; and

(5) any other provisions required by the commissioner by rule.

(d) Continued care as described by Subsection (c)(3) must be requested by a provider. A dispute involving continuity of care is subject to the dispute resolution process under Subchapter I.

(e) An insurance carrier and a network may not use any financial incentive or make a payment to a health care provider that acts directly or indirectly as an inducement to limit medically necessary services.

§ 1305.153. Provider Reimbursement

(a) The amount of reimbursement for services provided by a network provider is determined by the contract between the network and the provider or group of providers.

(b) If an insurance carrier or network has preauthorized a health care service, the insurance carrier or network or the network's agent or other representative may not deny payment to a provider except for reasons other than medical necessity.

(c) Out-of-network providers who provide care as described by Section 1305.006 shall be reimbursed as provided by the Texas Workers' Compensation Act and applicable rules of the commissioner of workers' compensation.

(d) Subject to Subsection (a), billing by, and reimbursement to, contracted and out-of-network providers is subject to the requirements of the Texas Workers' Compensation Act and applicable rules of the commissioner of workers' compensation, as consistent with this chapter. This subsection may not be construed to require application of rules of the commissioner of workers' compensation regarding reimbursement if application of those rules would negate reimbursement amounts negotiated by the network.

(e) An insurance carrier shall notify in writing a network provider if the carrier ontests the compensability of the injury for which the provider provides health care services. A carrier may not deny payment for health care services provided by a network provider before that notification on the grounds that the injury was not compensable. Payment for medically necessary health care services provided prior to written notification of a compensability denial is not subject to denial, recoupment, or refund from a network provider based on compensability. If the insurance carrier successfully contests compensability, the carrier is liable for health care provided before issuance of the notification required by this subsection, up to a maximum of $7,000.

§1305.154. Network-Carrier Contracts

(a) Except for emergencies and out-of-network referrals, a network may provide health care services to employees only through a written contract with an insurance carrier. A network-carrier contract under this section is confidential and is not subject to disclosure as public information under Chapter 552, Government Code.

(b) A carrier and a network may negotiate the functions to be provided by the network, except that the network shall contract with providers for the provision of health care, and shall perform functions related to the operation of a quality improvement program and credentialing in accordance with the requirements of this chapter.

(c) A network's contract with a carrier must include:

(1) a description of the functions that the carrier delegates to the network, consistent with the requirements of Subsection (b), and the reporting requirements for each function;

(2) a statement that the network and any management contractor or third party to which the network delegates a function will perform all delegated functions in full compliance with all requirements of this chapter, the Texas Workers' Compensation Act, and rules of the commissioner or the commissioner of workers' compensation;

(3) a provision that the contract:

(A) may not be terminated without cause by either party without 90 days' prior written notice; and

(B) must be terminated immediately if cause exists;

(4) a hold-harmless provision stating that the network, a management contractor, a third party to which the network delegates a function, and the network's contracted providers are prohibited from billing or attempting to collect any amounts from employees for health care services under any circumstances, including the insolvency of the carrier or the network, except as provided by Section 1305.451(b)(6);

(5) a statement that the carrier retains ultimate responsibility for ensuring that all delegated functions and all management contractor functions are performed in accordance with applicable statutes and rules and that the contract may not be construed to limit in any way the carrier's responsibility, including financial responsibility, to comply with all statutory and regulatory requirements;

(6) a statement that the network's role is to provide the services described under Subsection (b) as well as any other services or functions delegated by the carrier, including functions delegated to a management contractor, subject to the carrier's oversight and monitoring of the network's performance;

(7) a requirement that the network provide the carrier, at least monthly and in a form usable for audit purposes, the data necessary for the carrier to comply with reporting requirements of the department and the division of workers' compensation with respect to any services provided under the contract, as determined by commissioner rules;

(8) a requirement that the carrier, the network, any management contractor, and any third party to which the network delegates a function comply with the data reporting requirements of the Texas Workers' Compensation Act and rules of the commissioner of workers' compensation;

(9) a contingency plan under which the carrier would, in the event of termination of the contract or a failure to perform, reassume one or more functions of the network under the contract, including functions related to:

(A) payments to providers and notification to employees;

(B) quality of care;

(C) utilization review;

(D) retrospective review; and

(E) continuity of care, including a plan for identifying and transitioning employees to new providers;

(10) a provision that requires that any agreement by which the network delegates any function to a management contractor or any third party be in writing, and that such an agreement require the delegated third party or management contractor to be subject to all the requirements of this subchapter;

(11) a provision that requires the network to provide to the department the license number of a management contractor or any delegated third party who performs a function that requires a license as a utilization review agent under Article 21.58A or any other license under this code or another insurance law of this state;

(12) an acknowledgment that:

(A) any management contractor or third party to whom the network delegates a function must perform in compliance with this chapter and other applicable statutes and rules, and that the management contractor or third party is subject to the carrier's and the network's oversight and monitoring of its performance; and

(B) if the management contractor or the third party fails to meet monitoring standards established to ensure that functions delegated to the management contractor or the third party under the delegation contract are in full compliance with all statutory and regulatory requirements, the carrier or the network may cancel the delegation of one or more delegated functions;

(13) a requirement that the network and any management contractor or third party to which the network delegates a function provide all necessary information to allow the carrier to provide information to employees as required by Section 1305.451; and

(14) a provision that requires the network, in contracting with a third party directly or through another third party, to require the third party to permit the commissioner to examine at any time any information the commissioner believes is relevant to the third party's financial condition or the ability of the network to meet the network's responsibilities in

connection with any function the third party performs or has been delegated.

§1305.1545. Restrictions on Payment and Reimbursement

(a) An insurance carrier or third-party administrator may not reimburse a doctor or other health care provider, an institutional provider, or an organization of doctors and health care providers on a discounted fee basis for services that are provided to an injured employee unless:

(1) the carrier or third-party administrator has contracted with either:

(A) the doctor or other health care provider, institutional provider, or organization of doctors and health care providers; or

(B) a network that has contracted with the doctor or other health care provider, institutional provider, or organization of doctors and health care providers; and

(2) the doctor or other health care provider, institutional provider, or organization of doctors and health care providers has agreed to the contract and has agreed to provide health care services under the terms of the contract.

(b) A party to a carrier-network contract may not sell, lease, or otherwise transfer information regarding the payment or reimbursement terms of the contract without the express authority of and prior adequate notification to the other contracting parties. This subsection does not affect the authority of the commissioner under this code to request and obtain information.

(c) An insurance carrier or third-party administrator who violates this section:

(1) commits an unfair claim settlement practice in violation of Subchapter A, Chapter 542, Insurance Code; and

(2) is subject to administrative penalties under Chapters 82 and 84, Insurance Code.

Subtitle F. Physicians And Health Care Providers

Chapter 1451. Access To Certain Practitioners And Facilities

Subchapter A. General Provisions

§1451.001. Definitions; Health Care Practitioners

In this chapter:

(1) "*Acupuncturist*" means an individual licensed to practice acupuncture by the Texas State Board of Medical Examiners.

(2) *"Advanced practice nurse"* means an individual licensed by the Board of Nurse Examiners as a registered nurse and recognized by that board as an advanced practice nurse.

(3) *"Audiologist"* means an individual licensed to practice audiology by the State Board of Examiners for Speech-Language Pathology and Audiology.

(4) *"Chemical dependency counselor"* means an individual licensed by the Texas Commission on Alcohol and Drug Abuse.

(5) *"Chiropractor"* means an individual licensed by the Texas Board of Chiropractic Examiners.

(6) *"Dentist"* means an individual licensed to practice dentistry by the State Board of Dental Examiners.

(7) *"Dietitian"* means an individual licensed by the Texas State Board of Examiners of Dietitians.

(8) *"Hearing instrument fitter and dispenser"* means an individual licensed by the State Committee of Examiners in the Fitting and Dispensing of Hearing Instruments.

(9) *"Licensed clinical social worker"* means an individual licensed by the Texas State Board of Social Worker Examiners as a licensed clinical social worker.

(10) *"Licensed professional counselor"* means an individual licensed by the Texas State Board of Examiners of Professional Counselors.

(11) *"Marriage and family therapist"* means an individual licensed by the Texas State Board of Examiners of Marriage and Family Therapists.

(12) *"Occupational therapist"* means an individual licensed as an occupational therapist by the Texas Board of Occupational Therapy Examiners.

(13) *"Optometrist"* means an individual licensed to practice optometry by the Texas Optometry Board.

(14) *"Physical therapist"* means an individual licensed as a physical therapist by the Texas Board of Physical Therapy Examiners.

(15) *"Physician"* means an individual licensed to practice medicine by the Texas State Board of Medical Examiners. The term includes a doctor of osteopathic medicine.

(16) *"Physician assistant"* means an individual licensed by the Texas State Board of Physician Assistant Examiners.

(17) *"Podiatrist"* means an individual licensed to practice podiatry by the Texas State Board of Podiatric Medical Examiners.

(18) *"Psychological associate"* means an individual licensed as a psychological associate by the Texas State Board of Examiners of

Psychologists who practices solely under the supervision of a licensed psychologist.

(19) "*Psychologist*" means an individual licensed as a psychologist by the Texas State Board of Examiners of Psychologists.

(20) "*Speech-language pathologist*" means an individual licensed to practice speech-language pathology by the State Board of Examiners for Speech-Language Pathology and Audiology.

(21) "*Surgical assistant*" means an individual licensed as a surgical assistant by the Texas State Board of Medical Examiners.

SUBCHAPTER B. DESIGNATION OF PRACTITIONERS UNDER ACCIDENT AND HEALTH INSURANCE POLICY

§1451.051. Applicability of Subchapter

(a) This subchapter applies to an .accident and health insurance policy, including an individual, blanket, or group policy.

(b) This subchapter applies to an accident and health insurance policy issued by a stipulated premium company subject to Chapter 884.

§1451.052. Applicability of General Provisions of Other Law

The provisions of Chapter 1201, including provisions relating to the applicability, purpose, and enforcement of that chapter, the construction of policies under that chapter, rulemaking under that chapter, and definitions of terms applicable in that chapter, apply to this subchapter.

§1451.053. Practitioner Designation

(a) An accident and health insurance policy may not make a benefit contingent on treatment or examination by one or more particular health care practitioners listed in Section 1451.001 unless the policy contains a provision that designates the practitioners whom the insurer will and will not recognize.

(b) The insurer may include the provision anywhere in the policy or in an endorsement attached to the policy.

§1451.054. Terms Used to Designate Health Care Practitioners

A provision of an accident and health insurance policy that designates the health care practitioners whom the insurer will and will not recognize must use the terms defined by Section 1451.001 with the meanings assigned by that section.

SUBCHAPTER C. SELECTION OF PRACTITIONERS

§1451.101. Definitions

In this subchapter:

(1) *"Health insurance policy"* means a policy, contract, or agreement described by Section 1451.102.

(2) *"Insured"* means an individual who is issued, is a party to, or is a beneficiary under a health insurance policy.

(3) *"Insurer"* means an insurer, association, or organization described by Section 1451.102.

(4) *"Nurse first assistant"* has the meaning assigned by Section 301.1525, Occupations Code.

§1451.102. Applicability of Subchapter

Except as provided by this subchapter, this subchapter applies only to an individual, group, blanket, or franchise insurance policy, insurance agreement, or group hospital service contract that provides health benefits, accident benefits, or health and accident benefits for medical or surgical expenses incurred as a result of an accident or sickness and that is delivered, issued for delivery, or renewed in this state by any incorporated or unincorporated insurance company, association, or organization, including:

(1) a fraternal benefit society operating under Chapter 885;

(2) a general casualty company operating under Chapter 861;

(3) a life, health, and accident insurance company operating under Chapter 841 or 982;

(4) a Lloyd's plan operating under Chapter 941;

(5) a local mutual aid association operating under Chapter 886;

(6) a mutual insurance company writing insurance other than life insurance operating under Chapter 883;

(7) a mutual life insurance company operating under Chapter 882;

(8) a reciprocal exchange operating under Chapter 942;

(9) a statewide mutual assessment company, mutual assessment company, or mutual assessment life, health, and accident association operating under Chapter 881 or 887; and

(10) a stipulated premium company operating under Chapter 884.

§1451.103. Conflicting Provisions Void

(a) A provision of a health insurance policy that conflicts with this subchapter is void to the extent of the conflict.

(b) The presence in a health insurance policy of a provision void under Subsection (a) does not affect the validity of other policy provisions.

(c) An insurer shall bring each approved policy form that contains a provision that conflicts with this subchapter into compliance with this subchapter by use of:

 (1) a rider or endorsement approved by the commissioner; or

 (2) a new or revised policy form approved by the commissioner.

§1451.104. Nondiscriminatory Payment or Reimbursement; Exception

(a) An insurer may not classify, differentiate, or discriminate between scheduled services or procedures provided by a health care practitioner selected under this subchapter and performed in the scope of that practitioner's license and the same services or procedures provided by another type of health care practitioner whose services or procedures are covered by a health insurance policy, in regard to:

 (1) the payment schedule or payment provisions of the policy; or

 (2) the amount or manner of payment or reimbursement under the policy.

(b) An insurer may not deny payment or reimbursement for services or procedures in accordance with the policy payment schedule or payment provisions solely because the services or procedures were performed by a health care practitioner selected under this subchapter.

(c) Notwithstanding Subsection (a), a health insurance policy may provide for a different amount of payment or reimbursement for scheduled services or procedures performed by an advanced practice nurse, nurse first assistant, licensed surgical assistant, or physician assistant if the methodology used to compute the amount is the same as the methodology used to compute the amount of payment or reimbursement when the services or procedures are provided by a physician.

§1451.105. Selection of Acupuncturist

An insured may select an acupuncturist to provide the services or procedures scheduled in the health insurance policy that are within the scope of the acupuncturist's license.

§1451.106. Selection of Advanced Practice Nurse

An insured may select an advanced practice nurse to provide the services scheduled in the health insurance policy that are within the scope of the nurse's license.

§1451.107. Selection of Audiologist

An insured may select an audiologist to measure hearing to determine the presence or extent of the insured's hearing loss or provide aural rehabilitation services to the insured if the insured has a hearing loss and the services or procedures are scheduled in the health insurance policy.

§1451.108. Selection of Chemical Dependency Counselor

An insured may select a chemical dependency counselor to provide services or procedures scheduled in the health insurance policy that are within the scope of the counselor's license.

§1451.109. Selection of Chiropractor

An insured may select a chiropractor to provide the medical or surgical services or procedures scheduled in the health insurance policy that are within the scope of the chiropractor's license.

§1451.110. Selection of Dentist

An insured may select a dentist to provide the medical or surgical services or procedures scheduled in the health insurance policy that are within the scope of the dentist's license.

§1451.111. Selection of Dietitian

An insured may select a licensed dietitian or a provisionally licensed dietitian acting under the supervision of a licensed dietitian to provide the services scheduled in the health insurance policy that are within the scope of the dietitian's license.

Occupations Code

General Regulatory Authority Regarding Health Care Practitioners Use of Internet

§106.001. Effect of Internet Activity

(a) In this section:

(1) "*Licensing authority*" means a department, commission, board, office, or other agency of the state or a political subdivision of the state that regulates activities and persons under this title.

(2) "*Internet*" has the meaning assigned by Section 2002.001, Government Code.

(b) The fact that an activity occurs through the use of the Internet does not affect a licensing authority's power to regulate an activity or person that would otherwise be regulated under this title.

§107.001. Definitions

In this chapter:

(1) "*Health professional*" and "*physician*" have the meanings assigned by Section 1455.001, Insurance Code.

(2) "*Telehealth service*" and "*telemedicine medical service*" have the meanings assigned by Section 57.042, Utilities Code.

§107.002. Informed Consent

A treating physician or health professional who provides or facilitates the use of telemedicine medical services or telehealth services shall ensure that the informed consent of the patient, or another appropriate individual authorized to make health care treatment decisions for the patient, is obtained before telemedicine medical services or telehealth services are provided.

§107.003. Confidentiality

A treating physician or health professional who provides or facilitates the use of telemedicine medical services or telehealth services shall ensure that the confidentiality of the patient's medical information is maintained as required by applicable law.

§107.004. Rules

The Texas State Board of Medical Examiners, in consultation with the commissioner of insurance, as appropriate, may adopt rules necessary to:

(1) ensure that patients using telemedicine medical services receive appropriate, quality care;

(2) prevent abuse and fraud in the use of telemedicine medical services, including rules relating to the filing of claims and records required to be maintained in connection with telemedicine medical services;

(3) ensure adequate supervision of health professionals who are not physicians and who provide telemedicine medical services;

(4) establish the maximum number of health professionals who are not physicians that a physician may supervise through a telemedicine medical service; and

(5) require a face-to-face consultation between a patient and a physician providing a telemedicine medical service within a certain number of days following an initial telemedicine medical service only if the physician has never seen the patient.

Penal Code

Insanity—§8

§8.01. Insanity

(a) It is an affirmative defense to prosecution that, at the time of the conduct charged, the actor, as a result of severe mental disease or defect, did not know that his conduct was wrong.

(b) The term *"mental disease or defect"* does not include an abnormality manifested only by repeated criminal or otherwise antisocial conduct.

Use of force on child, student, or incompetent—§9

§9.61. Parent — Child

(a) The use of force, but not deadly force, against a child younger than 18 years is justified:

   (1) if the actor is the child's parent or stepparent or is acting in loco parentis to the child; and

   (2) when and to the degree the actor reasonably believes the force is necessary to discipline the child or to safeguard or promote his welfare.

(b) For purposes of this section, *"in loco parentis"* includes grandparent and guardian, any person acting by, through, or under the direction of a court with jurisdiction over the child, and anyone who has express or implied consent of the parent or parents.

§9.62. Educator — Student

The use of force, but not deadly force, against a person is justified:

   (1) if the actor is entrusted with the care, supervision, or administration of the person for a special purpose; and

   (2) when and to the degree the actor reasonably believes the force is necessary to further the special purpose or to maintain discipline in a group.

§9.63. Guardian — Incompetent

The use of force, but not deadly force, against a mental incompetent is justified:

   (1) if the actor is the incompetent's guardian or someone similarly responsible for the general care and supervision of the incompetent; and

(2) when and to the degree the actor reasonably believes the force is necessary:

(A) to safeguard and promote the incompetent's welfare; or

(B) if the incompetent is in an institution for his care and custody, to maintain discipline in the institution.

DEVIATE SEXUAL ACTIVITY—§21

§21.01. Definitions

In this chapter:

(1) "*Deviate sexual intercourse*" means:

(A) any contact between any part of the genitals of one person and the mouth or anus of another person; or

(B) the penetration of the genitals or the anus of another person with an object.

(2) "*Sexual contact*" means any touching of the anus, breast, or any part of the genitals of another person with intent to arouse or gratify the sexual desire of any person.

(3) "*Sexual intercourse*" means any penetration of the female sex organ by the male sex organ.

§21.06. Homosexual Conduct

(a) A person commits an offense if he engages in deviate sexual intercourse with another individual of the same sex.

(b) An offense under this section is a Class C misdemeanor.

§21.07. Public Lewdness

(a) A person commits an offense if he knowingly engages in any of the following acts in a public place or, if not in a public place, he is reckless about whether another is present who will be offended or alarmed by his:

(1) act of sexual intercourse;

(2) act of deviate sexual intercourse;

(3) act of sexual contact; or

(4) act involving contact between the person's mouth or genitals and the anus or genitals of an animal or fowl.

(b) An offense under this section is a Class A misdemeanor.

§21.08. Indecent Exposure

(a) A person commits an offense if he exposes his anus or any part of his genitals with intent to arouse or gratify the sexual desire of any person, and he is reckless about whether another is present who will be offended or alarmed by his act.

(b) An offense under this section is a Class B misdemeanor.

§21.11. Indecency with a Child

(a) A person commits an offense if, with a child younger than 17 years and not his spouse, whether the child is of the same or opposite sex, he:

(1) engages in sexual contact with the child; or

(2) exposes his anus or any part of his genitals, knowing the child is present, with intent to arouse or gratify the sexual desire of any person.

(b) It is an affirmative defense to prosecution under this section that the actor:

(1) was not more than three years older than the victim and of the opposite sex;

(2) did not use duress, force, or a threat against the victim at the time of the offense; and

(3) at the time of the offense:

(A) was not required under Chapter 62, Code of Criminal Procedure, as added by Chapter 668, Acts of the 75th Legislature, Regular Session, 1997, to register for life as a sex offender; or

(B) was not a person who under Chapter 62 had a reportable conviction or adjudication for an offense under this section.

(c) An offense under Subsection (a)(1) is a felony of the second degree and an offense under Subsection (a)(2) is a felony of the third degree.

Interference with child custody—§25

§25.03. Interference with Child Custody

(a) A person commits an offense if he takes or retains a child younger than 18 years when he:

(1) knows that his taking or retention violates the express terms of a judgment or order of a court disposing of the child's custody; or

(2) has not been awarded custody of the child by a court of competent jurisdiction, knows that a suit for divorce or a civil suit or application for habeas corpus to dispose of the child's custody has been filed, and takes the child out of the geographic area of the counties composing the judicial district if the court is a district court or the county if the court is a statutory county court, without the permission of the court and with the intent to deprive the court of authority over the child.

(b) A noncustodial parent commits an offense if, with the intent to interfere with the lawful custody of a child younger than 18 years, he knowingly entices or persuades the child to leave the custody of the custodial parent, guardian, or person standing in the stead of the custodial parent or guardian of the child.

(c) It is a defense to prosecution under Subsection (a)(2) that the actor returned the child to the geographic area of the counties composing the judicial district if the court is a district court or the county if the court is a statutory county court, within three days after the date of the commission of the offense.

(d) An offense under this section is a state jail felony.

PROBATE CODE

GUARDIANSHIP LAW

PART G. LETTERS OF GUARDIANSHIP

§659. Issuance Of Letters Of Guardianship

(a) When a person who is appointed guardian has qualified under Section 699 of this code, the clerk shall issue to the guardian a certificate under seal, stating the fact of the appointment, of the qualification, the date of the appointment and qualification, and the date the letters of guardianship expire. The certificate issued by the clerk constitutes letters of guardianship.

(b) All letters of guardianship expire one year and four months after the date of issuance unless renewed.

(c) The clerk may not renew letters of guardianship relating to the appointment of a guardian of the estate until the court receives and approves the guardian's annual accounting. The clerk may not renew letters of guardianship relating to the appointment of a guardian of the person until the court receives and approves the annual report. If the guardian's annual accounting or annual report is disapproved or not timely filed, the clerk may not issue further letters of guardianship to the delinquent guardian unless ordered by the court.

(d) Regardless of the date the court approves an annual accounting or annual report for purposes of this section, a renewal relates back to the date the original letters of guardianship are issued, unless the accounting period has been changed as provided by this chapter, in which case a renewal relates back to the first day of the accounting period.

§683. Court's Initiation Of Guardianship Proceedings

(a) If a court has probable cause to believe that a person domiciled or found in the county in which the court is located is an incapacitated person, and the person does not have a guardian in this state, the court shall appoint a guardian ad litem or court investigator to investigate and file an application for the appointment of a guardian of the person or estate, or both, of the person believed to be incapacitated.

(b) To establish probable cause under this section, the court may require:

  (1) an information letter about the person believed to be incapacitated that is submitted by an interested person and satisfies the requirements of Section 683A of this code; or

(2) a written letter or certificate from a physician who has examined the person believed to be incapacitated that satisfies the requirements of Section 687(a) of this code, except that the letter must be dated not earlier than the 120th day before the date of the filing of an application under Subsection (a) of this section and be based on an examination the physician performed not earlier than the 120th day before that date.

(c) A court that creates a guardianship for a ward under this chapter may authorize compensation of a guardian ad litem who files an application under Subsection (a) of this section from available funds of the ward's estate. If after examining the ward's assets the court determines the ward is unable to pay for services provided by the guardian ad litem, the court may authorize compensation from the county treasury.

§683A. Information Letter

An information letter under Section 683(b)(1)of this code about a person believed to be incapacitated may:

(1) include the name, address, telephone number, county of residence, and date of birth of the person;

(2) state whether the residence of the person is a private residence, health care facility, or other type of residence;

(3) describe the relationship between the interested person and the person;

(4) contain the names and telephone numbers of any known friends and relatives of the person;

(5) state whether a guardian of the person or estate of the person has been appointed in this state;

(6) state whether the person has executed a power of attorney and, if so, the designee's name, address, and telephone number;

(7) describe any property of the person, including the estimated value of that property;

(8) list any amount and source of monthly income of the person; and

(9) describe the nature and degree of the person's alleged incapacity and include a statement of whether the person is in imminent danger of serious impairment to the person's physical health, safety, or estate.

PART E. GENERAL DUTIES AND POWERS OF GUARDIANS

§767. Powers and Duties of Guardians of the Person

(a) The guardian of the person is entitled to take charge of the person of the ward, and the duties of the guardian correspond with the rights of the guardian. A guardian of the person has:

   (1) the right to have physical possession of the ward and to establish the ward's legal domicile;

   (2) the duty to provide care, supervision, and protection for the ward;

   (3) the duty to provide the ward with clothing, food, medical care, and shelter;

   (4) the power to consent to medical, psychiatric, and surgical treatment other than the in-patient psychiatric commitment of the ward; and

   (5) on application to and order of the court, the power to establish a trust in accordance with 42 U.S.C. Section 1396p(d)(4)(B), as amended, and direct that the income of the ward as defined by that section be paid directly to the trust, solely for the purpose of the ward's eligibility for medical assistance under Chapter 32, Human Resources Code.

(b) Notwithstanding Subsection (a)(4) of this section, a guardian of the person of a ward has the power to transport the ward to an inpatient mental health facility for a preliminary examination in accordance with Subchapters A and C, Chapter 573, Health and Safety Code.

§768. General Powers and Duties of Guardian of the Estate

The guardian of the estate of a ward is entitled to the possession and management of all property belonging to the ward, to collect all debts, rentals, or claims that are due to the ward, to enforce all obligations in favor of the ward, and to bring and defend suits by or against the ward; but, in the management of the estate, the guardian is governed by the provisions of this chapter. It is the duty of the guardian of the estate to take care of and manage the estate as a prudent person would manage the person's own property, except as otherwise provided by this chapter. The guardian of the estate shall account for all rents, profits, and revenues that the estate would have produced by such prudent management.

§769. Summary of Powers of Guardian of Person and Estate

The guardian of both the person of and estate of a ward has all the rights and powers and shall perform all the duties of the guardian of the person and of the guardian of the estate.

CASE LAW

Three legal decisions important for the practice of social work are included in this Section:

Jaffee v. Redmond for the first time gave the right of privacy to psychotherapy notes in federal court. *Thapar v. Zezulka* provides an excellent discussion of the duty to warn and duty to protect doctrine in Texas. We waited over 20 years in Texas to know the status of these duties. The Texas Supreme Court has now given practitioners guidance when a patient threatens another person. In this case, the Texas Supreme Court takes the position that courts should not second-guess the decision by a practitioner to tell law enforcement personnel or medical personnel about the danger presented by a patient. This gives a good deal of discretion to practitioners who are faced with a difficult situation and the decision is certainly pro-therapist.

Abrams v. Jones concerns the privacy of information between a therapist, a child client, and the child's parents and provides a remedy for parents who request but are denied access to a child's records. Practitioners can draw guidance from this case about record keeping and the duty to parents and child clients.

Confidentiality of Psychotherapy Notes

(Jaffee vs. Redmond)[1]

Background

Petitioner, the administrator of decedent Allen's estate, filed this action alleging that Allen's constitutional rights were violated when he was killed by respondent Redmond, an on-duty police officer employed by respondent village. The court ordered respondents to give petitioner notes made by Karen Beyer, a licensed clinical social worker, during counseling sessions with Redmond after the shooting, rejecting their argument that a psychotherapist-patient privilege protected the contents of the conversations. Neither Beyer nor Redmond complied with the order. At trial, the jury awarded petitioner damages after being instructed that the refusal to turn over the notes was legally unjustified and the jury could presume that the notes would have been unfavorable to respondents. The Court of Appeals reversed and remanded, finding that "reason and experience," the touchstones for acceptance of a privilege under Federal Rule of Evidence 501, compelled recognition of a psychotherapist-patient privilege. However, it found that the privilege would not apply if in the interests of justice, the evidentiary need for disclosure outweighed the patient's privacy interests. Balancing those interests, the court concluded that Beyer's notes should have been protected.

Held: The conversations between Redmond and her therapist and the notes taken during their counseling sessions are protected from compelled disclosure under Rule 501. Pp. 5-17.

(a) Rule 501 authorizes federal courts to define new privileges by interpreting "the principles of the common law . . . in the light of reason and experience."

1 *Jaffee, Special Administrator For Allen, Deceased v. Redmond et al.*518 U.S. 1 (1996)

The Rule thus did not freeze the law governing privileges at a particular point in history, but rather directed courts to "continue the evolutionary development of testimonial privileges." Trammel v. United States, 445 U.S. 40, 47. An exception from the general rule disfavoring testimonial privileges is justified when the proposed privilege "promotes sufficiently important interests to outweigh the need for probative evidence . . . ." *Id.*, at 51. Pp. 5-7.

(b) Significant private interests support recognition of a psychotherapist privilege. Effective psychotherapy depends upon an atmosphere of confidence and trust, and therefore the mere possibility of disclosure of confidential communications may impede development of the relationship necessary for successful treatment. The privilege also serves the public interest, since the mental health of the Nation's citizenry, no less than its physical health, is a public good of transcendent importance. In contrast, the likely evidentiary benefit that would result from the denial of the privilege is modest. That it is appropriate for the federal courts to recognize a psychotherapist privilege is confirmed by the fact that all 50 States and the District of Columbia have enacted into law some form of the privilege, see Trammel v. United States, 445 U.S., at 48 -50, and reinforced by the fact that the privilege was among the specific privileges recommended in the proposed privilege rules that were rejected in favor of the more open-ended language of the present Rule 501. Pp. 7-13.

(c) The federal privilege, which clearly applies to psychiatrists and psychologists, also extends to confidential communications made to licensed social workers in the course of psychotherapy. The reasons for recognizing the privilege for treatment by psychiatrists and psychologists apply with equal force to clinical social workers, and the vast majority of States explicitly extend a testimonial privilege to them. The balancing component implemented by the Court of Appeals and a few States is rejected, for it would eviscerate the effectiveness of the privilege by making it impossible for participants to predict whether their confidential conversations will be protected. Because this is the first case in which this Court has recognized a psychotherapist privilege, it is neither necessary nor feasible to delineate its full contours in a way that would govern all future questions. Pp. 13-16. 51 F. 3d 1346, affirmed.

Stevens, J., delivered the opinion of the Court, in which O'Connor, Kennedy, Souter, Thomas, Ginsburg, and Breyer, JJ., joined. Scalia, J., filed a dissenting opinion, in which Rehnquist, C. J., joined as to Part III.

OPINION

(Justice Stevens delivered the opinion of the Court.) After a traumatic incident in which she shot and killed a man, a police officer received extensive counseling from a licensed clinical social worker. The question we address is whether statements the officer made to her therapist during the counseling sessions are protected from compelled disclosure in a federal civil action brought by the family of the deceased. Stated otherwise, the question is whether it is appropriate for federal courts to recognize a "psychotherapist privilege" under Rule 501 of the Federal Rules of Evidence.

I. Petitioner is the administrator of the estate of Ricky Allen. Respondents are Mary Lu Redmond, a former police officer, and the Village of Hoffman Estates, Illinois, her employer during the time that she served on the police force.[2] Petitioner commenced this action against respondents after Redmond shot and killed Allen while on patrol duty.

On June 27, 1991, Redmond was the first officer to respond to a "fight in progress" call at an apartment complex. As she arrived at the scene, two of Allen's sisters ran toward her squad car, waving their arms and shouting that there had been a stabbing in one of the apartments. Redmond testified at trial that she relayed this information to her dispatcher and requested an ambulance. She then exited her car and walked toward the apartment building. Before Redmond reached the building, several men ran out, one waving a pipe. When the men ignored her order to get on the ground, Redmond drew her service revolver. Two other men then burst out of the building, one, Ricky Allen, chasing the other. According to Redmond, Allen was brandishing a butcher knife and disregarded her repeated commands to drop the weapon. Redmond shot Allen when she believed he was about to stab the man he was chasing. Allen died at the scene. Redmond testified that before other officers arrived to provide support, "people came pouring out of the buildings," App. 134, and a threatening confrontation between her and the crowd ensued.

Petitioner filed suit in Federal District Court alleging that Redmond had violated Allen's constitutional rights by using excessive force during the encounter at the apartment complex. The complaint sought damages under Rev. Stat. Section(s) 1979, 42 U. S. C. Section(s) 1983 and the Illinois wrongful death statute, Ill. Comp. Stat., ch. 740, Section(s) 180/1 et seq. (1994). At trial, petitioner presented testimony from members of Allen's family that conflicted with Redmond's version of the incident in several important respects. They testified, for example, that Redmond drew her gun before exiting her squad car and that Allen was unarmed when he emerged from the apartment building.

During pretrial discovery petitioner learned that after the shooting Redmond had participated in about 50 counseling sessions with Karen Beyer, a clinical social worker licensed by the State of Illinois and employed at that time by the Village of Hoffman Estates. Petitioner sought access to Beyer's notes concerning the sessions for use in cross-examining Redmond. Respondents vigorously resisted the discovery. They asserted that the contents of the conversations between Beyer and Redmond were protected against involuntary disclosure by a psychotherapist-patient privilege. The district judge rejected this argument. Neither Beyer nor Redmond, however, complied with his order to disclose the contents of Beyer's notes. At depositions and on the witness stand both either refused to answer certain questions or professed an inability to recall details of their conversations.

In his instructions at the end of the trial, the judge advised the jury that the refusal to turn over Beyer's notes had no "legal justification" and that the jury could therefore presume that the contents of the notes would have been

2 Redmond left the police department after the events at issue in this lawsuit.

unfavorable to respondents.[3] The jury awarded petitioner $45,000 on the federal claim and $500,000 on her state-law claim.

The Court of Appeals for the Seventh Circuit reversed and remanded for a new trial. Addressing the issue for the first time, the court concluded that "reason and experience," the touchstones for acceptance of a privilege under Rule 501 of the Federal Rules of Evidence, compelled recognition of a psychotherapist-patient privilege.[4] 51 F. 3d 1346, 1355 (1995). "Reason tells us that psychotherapists and patients share a unique relationship, in which the ability to communicate freely without the fear of public disclosure is the key to successful treatment." *Id.*, at 1355-1356. As to experience, the court observed that all 50 States have adopted some form of the psychotherapist-patient privilege. *Id.*, at 1356. The court attached particular significance to the fact that Illinois law expressly extends such a privilege to social workers like Karen Beyer.[5] *Id.*, at 1357. The court also noted that, with one exception, the federal decisions rejecting the privilege were more than five years old and that the "need and demand for counseling services has skyrocketed during the past several years." *Id.*, at 1355-1356.

The Court of Appeals qualified its recognition of the privilege by stating that it would not apply if "in the interests of justice, the evidentiary need for the disclosure of the contents of a patient's counseling sessions outweighs that patient's privacy interests." *Id.*, at 1357. Balancing those conflicting interests, the court observed, on the one hand, that the evidentiary need for the contents of the confidential conversations was diminished in this case because there were numerous eyewitnesses to the shooting, and, on the other hand, that Officer Redmond's privacy interests were substantial.[6] *Id.*, at 1358. Based on this assessment, the court concluded that the trial court had erred by refusing to afford protection to the confidential communications between Redmond and Beyer.

---

3 App. to Pet. for Cert. 67.

4 Rule 501 provides as follows: "Except as otherwise required by the Constitution of the United States or provided by Act of Congress, or in rules prescribed by the Supreme Court pursuant to statutory authority, the privilege of a witness, person, government, State, or political subdivision thereof shall be governed by the principles of the common law as they may be interpreted by the courts of the United States in the light of reason and experience. However, in civil actions and proceedings, with respect to an element of a claim or defense as to which State law supplies the rule of decision, the privilege of a witness, person, government, State or political subdivision thereof shall be determined in accordance with State law."

5 See Illinois Mental Health and Developmental Disabilities Confidentiality Act, Ill. Comp. Stat., ch. 740, Section(s) 110/1-110/17 (1994).

6 "Her ability, through counseling, to work out the pain and anguish undoubtedly caused by Allen's death in all probability depended to a great deal upon her trust and confidence in her counselor Karen Beyer. Officer Redmond, and all those placed in her most unfortunate circumstances, are entitled to be protected in their desire to seek counseling after mortally wounding another human being in the line of duty. An individual who is troubled as the result of her participation in a violent and tragic event, such as this, displays a most commendable respect for human life and is a person well-suited 'to protect and to serve.'" 51 F. 3d, at 1358.

The United States courts of appeals do not uniformly agree that the federal courts should recognize a psychotherapist privilege under Rule 501. Compare In re Doe, 964 F. 2d 1325 (CA2 1992) (recognizing privilege); In re Zuniga, 714 F. 2d 632 (CA6), cert. denied, 464 U.S. 983 (1983) (same), with United States v. Burtrum, 17 F. 3d 1299 (CA10), cert. denied, 513 U. S. ___ (1994) (declining to recognize privilege); In re Grand Jury Proceedings, 867 F. 2d 562 (CA9), cert. denied sub nom. Doe v. United States, 493 U.S. 906 (1989) (same); United States v. Corona, 849 F. 2d 562 (CA11 1988), cert. denied, 489 U.S. 1084 (1989) (same); United States v. Meagher, 531 F. 2d 752 (CA5), cert. denied, 429 U.S. 853 (1976) (same). Because of the conflict among the courts of appeals and the importance of the question, we granted certiorari. 516 U. S. (1995). We affirm.

II. Rule 501 of the Federal Rules of Evidence authorizes federal courts to define new privileges by interpreting "common law principles . . . in the light of reason and experience." The authors of the Rule borrowed this phrase from our opinion in Wolfle v. United States, 291 U. S. 7, 12 (1934),[7] which in turn referred to the oft-repeated observation that "the common law is not immutable but flexible, and by its own principles adapts itself to varying conditions." Funk v. United States, 290 U. S. 371, 383 (1933). See also Hawkins v. United States, 358 U.S. 74, 79 (1958) (changes in privileges may be "dictated by `reason and experience'"). The Senate Report accompanying the 1975 adoption of the Rules indicates that Rule 501 "should be understood as reflecting the view that the recognition of a privilege based on a confidential relationship . . . should be determined on a case-by-case basis." S. Rep. No. 93- 1277, p. 13 (1974).[8] The Rule thus did not freeze the law governing the privileges of witnesses in federal trials at a particular point in our history, but rather directed federal courts to "continue the evolutionary development of testimonial privileges." Trammel v. United States, 445 U.S. 40, 47 (1980); see also University of Pennsylvania v. EEOC, 493 U.S. 182, 189 (1990).

The common-law principles underlying the recognition of testimonial privileges can be stated simply. "`For more than three centuries it has now been

---

7 "[T]he rules governing the competence of witnesses in criminal trials in the federal courts are not necessarily restricted to those local rules in force at the time of the admission into the Union of the particular state where the trial takes place, but are governed by common law principles as interpreted and applied by the federal courts in the light of reason and experience. Funk v. United States, 290 U. S. 371." Wolfle v. United States, 291 U. S., at 12-13.

8 In 1972 the Chief Justice transmitted to Congress proposed Rules of Evidence for United States Courts and Magistrates. 56 F. R. D. 183 (hereinafter Proposed Rules). The rules had been formulated by the Judicial Conference Advisory Committee on Rules of Evidence and approved by the Judicial Conference of the United States and by this Court. Trammel v. United States, 445 U.S. 40, 47 (1980). The proposed rules defined nine specific testimonial privileges, including a psychotherapist-patient privilege, and indicated that these were to be the exclusive privileges absent constitutional mandate, Act of Congress, or revision of the Rules. Proposed Rules 501-513, 56 F. R. D., at 230-261. Congress rejected this recommendation in favor of Rule 501's general mandate. Trammel, 445 U.S., at 47 .

recognized as a fundamental maxim that the public . . . has a right to every man's evidence. When we come to examine the various claims of exemption, we start with the primary assumption that there is a general duty to give what testimony one is capable of giving, and that any exemptions which may exist are distinctly exceptional, being so many derogations from a positive general rule.'" United States v. Bryan, 339 U.S. 323, 331 (1950) (quoting[9] J. Wigmore, Evidence Section(s) 2192, p. 64 (3d ed. 1940)). 8 See also United States v. Nixon, 418 U.S. 683, 709 (1974). Exceptions from the general rule disfavoring testimonial privileges may be justified, however, by a "`public good transcending the normally predominant principle of utilizing all rational means for ascertaining the truth.'" Trammel, 445 U.S., at 50 , quoting Elkins v. United States, 364 U.S. 206, 234 (1960) (Frankfurter, J., dissenting).

Guided by these principles, the question we address today is whether a privilege protecting confidential communications between a psychotherapist and her patient "promotes sufficiently important interests to outweigh the need for probative evidence . . . ." 445 U.S., at 51 . Both "reason and experience" persuade us that it does.

III. Like the spousal and attorney-client privileges, the psychotherapist-patient privilege is "rooted in the imperative need for confidence and trust." Trammel, 445 U.S., at 51 . Treatment by a physician for physical ailments can often proceed successfully on the basis of a physical examination, objective information supplied by the patient, and the results of diagnostic tests. Effective psychotherapy, by contrast, depends upon an atmosphere of confidence and trust in which the patient is willing to make a frank and complete disclosure of facts, emotions, memories, and fears. Because of the sensitive nature of the problems for which individuals consult psychotherapists, disclosure of confidential communications made during counseling sessions may cause embarrassment or disgrace. For this reason, the mere possibility of disclosure may impede development of the confidential relationship necessary for successful treatment.[10] As the Judicial Conference Advisory Committee observed in 1972 when it recommended that Congress recognize a psychotherapist privilege as part of the Proposed Federal Rules of Evidence, a psychiatrist's ability to help her patients "is completely dependent upon [the patients'] willingness and ability to talk freely. This makes it difficult if not impossible for [a psychiatrist] to function without being able to assure . . . patients of confidentiality and, indeed, privileged communication. Where there may be exceptions to this general rule

9 The familiar expression "every man's evidence" was a well-known phrase as early as the mid-18th century. Both the Duke of Argyll and Lord Chancellor Hardwicke invoked the maxim during the May 25, 1742, debate in the House of Lords concerning a bill to grant immunity to witnesses who would give evidence against Sir Robert Walpole, first Earl of Orford. 12 T. Hansard, Parliamentary History of England 643, 675, 693, 697 (1812). The bill was defeated soundly. *Id.*, at 711.

10 See studies and authorities cited in the Brief for American Psychiatric Association et al. as Amici Curiae 14-17, and the Brief for American Psychological Association as Amicus Curiae 12-17.

. . ., there is wide agreement that confidentiality is a sine qua non for successful psychiatric treatment." Advisory Committee's Notes to Proposed Rules, 56 F. R. D. 183, 242 (1972) (quoting Group for Advancement of Psychiatry, Report No. 45, Confidentiality and Privileged Communication in the Practice of Psychiatry 92 (June 1960)).

By protecting confidential communications between a psychotherapist and her patient from involuntary disclosure, the proposed privilege thus serves important private interests.

Our cases make clear that an asserted privilege must also "serv[e] public ends." Upjohn Co. v. United States, 449 U.S. 383, 389 (1981). Thus, the purpose of the attorney-client privilege is to "encourage full and frank communication between attorneys and their clients and thereby promote broader public interests in the observance of law and administration of justice." Ibid. And the spousal privilege, as modified in Trammel, is justified because it "furthers the important public interest in marital harmony," 445 U.S., at 53 . See also United States v. Nixon, 418 U.S., at 705 ; Wolfle v. United States, 291 U. S., at 14. The psychotherapist privilege serves the public interest by facilitating the provision of appropriate treatment for individuals suffering the effects of a mental or emotional problem. The mental health of our citizenry, no less than its physical health, is a public good of transcendent importance.[11]

In contrast to the significant public and private interests supporting recognition of the privilege, the likely evidentiary benefit that would result from the denial of the privilege is modest. If the privilege were rejected, confidential conversations between psychotherapists and their patients would surely be chilled, particularly when it is obvious that the circumstances that give rise to the need for treatment will probably result in litigation. Without a privilege, much of the desirable evidence to which litigants such as petitioner seek access-for example, admissions against interest by a party-is unlikely to come into being. This unspoken "evidence" will therefore serve no greater truth-seeking function than if it had been spoken and privileged.

That it is appropriate for the federal courts to recognize a psychotherapist privilege under Rule 501 is confirmed by the fact that all 50 States and the District of Columbia have enacted into law some form of psychotherapist privilege.[12] We have previously observed that the policy decisions of the States

11 This case amply demonstrates the importance of allowing individuals to receive confidential counseling. Police officers engaged in the dangerous and difficult tasks associated with protecting the safety of our communities not only confront the risk of physical harm but also face stressful circumstances that may give rise to anxiety, depression, fear, or anger. The entire community may suffer if police officers are not able to receive effective counseling and treatment after traumatic incidents, either because trained officers leave the profession prematurely or because those in need of treatment remain on the job.

12 Ala. Code Section(s) 34-26-2 (1975); Alaska Rule Evid. 504; Ariz. Rev. Stat. Section(s) 32-2085 (1992); Ark. Rule Evid. 503; Cal. Evid. Code Ann. Section(s) 1010, 1012, 1014 (1995); Colo. Rev. Stat. Section(s) 13-90-107(g)(1) (1987); Conn. Gen. Stat. Section(s) 52-146c (1995); Del. Uniform Rule Evid. 503; D. C. Code Ann. Section(s) 14-307 (1995); Fla. Stat. Section(s) 90.503 (Supp. 1992); Ga. Code Ann.

bear on the question whether federal courts should recognize a new privilege or amend the coverage of an existing one. See Trammel, 445 U.S., at 48 -50; United States v. Gillock, 445 U.S. 360, 368 , n. 8 (1980). Because state legislatures are fully aware of the need to protect the integrity of the fact-finding functions of their courts, the existence of a consensus among the States indicates that "reason and experience" support recognition of the privilege. In addition, given the importance of the patient's understanding that her communications with her therapist will not be publicly disclosed, any State's promise of confidentiality would have little value if the patient were aware that the privilege would not be honored in a federal court.[13] Denial of the federal privilege therefore would frustrate the purposes of the state legislation that was enacted to foster these confidential communications.

It is of no consequence that recognition of the privilege in the vast majority of States is the product of legislative action rather than judicial decision. Although common-law rulings may once have been the primary source of new developments in federal privilege law, that is no longer the case. In Funk v. United States, 290 U. S. 371 (1933), we recognized that it is appropriate to treat a consistent body of policy determinations by state legislatures as reflecting both "reason" and "experience." *Id.*, at 376-381. That rule is properly respectful of the States and at the same time reflects the fact that once a state legislature has enacted a privilege there is no longer an opportunity for common-law creation of the protection. The history of the psychotherapist privilege illustrates the latter point. In 1972 the members of the Judicial Conference Advisory Committee

---

Section(s) 24-9-21 (1995); Haw. Rules Evid. 504, 504.1; Idaho Rule Evid. 503; Ill. Comp. Stat., ch. 225 Section(s) 15/5 (1994); Ind. Code Section(s) 25-33-1-17 (1993); Iowa Code Section(s) 622.10 (1987); Kan. Stat. Ann. Section(s) 74-5323 (1985); Ky. Rule Evid. 507; La. Code Evid. Ann., Art. 510 (West 1995); Me. Rule Evid. 503; Md. Cts. & Jud. Proc. Section(s) 9-109 (1995); Mass. Gen. Laws Section(s) 233:20B (1995); Mich. Comp. Laws Ann. Section(s) 333.18237 (Supp. 1996); Minn. Stat. Ann. Section(s) 595.02 (1988 and Supp. 1996); Miss. Rule Evid. 503; Mo. Rev. Stat. Section(s) 491.060 (1994); Mont. Code Ann. Section(s) 26-1-807 (1995); Neb. Rev. Stat. Section(s) 27-504 (1995); Nev. Rev. Stat. Ann. Section(s) 49.209 (Supp. 1995); N. H. Rule Evid. 503; N. J. Stat. Ann. Section(s) 45:14B-28 (West 1995); N. M. Rule Evid. 11-504; N. Y. Civ. Prac. Law Section(s) 4507 (McKinney 1992); N. C. Gen. Stat. Section(s) 8-53.3 (Supp. 1995); N. D. Rule Evid. Section(s) 503; Ohio Rev. Code Ann. Section(s) 2317.02 (1995); Okla. Stat., Tit. 12 Section(s) 2503 (1991); Ore. Rules Evid. 504, 504.1; 42 Pa. Cons. Stat. Section(s) 5944 (1982) R. I. Gen. Laws Section(s) 5-37.3-3, 5-37.3-4 (1995); S. C. Code Ann. Section(s) 19-11-95 (Supp. 1995); S. D. Codified Laws Section(s) 19-13-6 to 19-13-11 (1995); Tenn. Code Ann. Section(s) 24-1-207 (1980); Tex. Rules Civ. Evid. 509, 510; Utah Rule Evid. 506; Vt. Rule Evid. 503; Va. Code Ann. Section(s) 8.01-400.2 (1992); Wash. Rev. Code Section(s) 18.83.110 (1994); W. Va. Code Section(s) 27-3-1 (1992); Wis. Stat. Section(s) 905.04 (1993-1994); Wyo. Stat. Section(s) 33-27-123 (Supp. 1995). ;

13 At the outset of their relationship, the ethical therapist must disclose to the patient "the relevant limits on confidentiality." See American Psychological Association, Ethical Principles of Psychologists and Code of Conduct, Standard 5.01 (Dec. 1992). See also National Federation of Societies for Clinical Social Work, Code of Ethics V(a) (May 1988); American Counseling Association, Code of Ethics and Standards of Practice A.3.a (effective July 1995).

noted that the common law "had indicated a disposition to recognize a psychotherapist-patient privilege when legislatures began moving into the field." Proposed Rules, 56 F. R. D., at 242 (citation omitted). The present unanimous acceptance of the privilege shows that the state lawmakers moved quickly. That the privilege may have developed faster legislatively than it would have in the courts demonstrates only that the States rapidly recognized the wisdom of the rule as the field of psychotherapy developed.[14]

The uniform judgment of the States is reinforced by the fact that a psychotherapist privilege was among the nine specific privileges recommended by the Advisory Committee in its proposed privilege rules. In United States v. Gillock, 445 U.S. 360, 367 -368 (1980), our holding that Rule 501 did not include a state legislative privilege relied, in part, on the fact that no such privilege was included in the Advisory Committee's draft. The reasoning in Gillock thus supports the opposite conclusion in this case. In rejecting the proposed draft that had specifically identified each privilege rule and substituting the present more open-ended Rule 501, the Senate Judiciary Committee explicitly stated that its action "should not be understood as disapproving any recognition of a psychiatrist-patient . . . privileg[e] contained in the [proposed] rules." S. Rep. No. 93-1277, at 13.

Because we agree with the judgment of the state legislatures and the Advisory Committee that a psychotherapist-patient privilege will serve a "public good transcending the normally predominant principle of utilizing all rational means for ascertaining truth," Trammel, 445 U.S., at 50 , we hold that confidential communications between a licensed psychotherapist and her patients in the course of diagnosis or treatment are protected from compelled disclosure under Rule 501 of the Federal Rules of Evidence.[15]

---

14 Petitioner acknowledges that all 50 state legislatures favor a psychotherapist privilege. She nevertheless discounts the relevance of the state privilege statutes by pointing to divergence among the States concerning the types of therapy relationships protected and the exceptions recognized. A small number of state statutes, for example, grant the privilege only to psychiatrists and psychologists, while most apply the protection more broadly. Compare Haw. Rules Evid. 504, 504.1 and N. D. Rule Evid. 503 (privilege extends to physicians and psychotherapists), with Ariz. Rev. Stat. Ann. Section(s) 32-3283 (1992) (privilege covers "behavioral health professional[s]"); Tex. Rule Civ. Evid. 510(a)(1) (privilege extends to persons "licensed or certified by the State of Texas in the diagnosis, evaluation or treatment of any mental or emotional disorder" or "involved in the treatment or examination of drug abusers"); Utah Rule Evid. 506 (privilege protects confidential communications made to marriage and family therapists, professional counselors, and psychiatric mental health nurse specialists). The range of exceptions recognized by the States is similarly varied. Compare Ark. Code Ann. Section(s) 17-46-107 (1987) (narrow exceptions); Haw. Rules Evid. 504, 504.1 (same), with Cal. Evid. Code Ann. Section(s) 1016-1027 (West 1995) (broad exceptions); R. I. Gen. Laws Section(s) 5-37.3-4 (1956) (same). These variations in the scope of the protection are too limited to undermine the force of the States' unanimous judgment that some form of psychotherapist privilege is appropriate.

15 Like other testimonial privileges, the patient may of course waive the protection.

IV. All agree that a psychotherapist privilege covers confidential communications made to licensed psychiatrists and psychologists. We have no hesitation in concluding in this case that the federal privilege should also extend to confidential communications made to licensed social workers in the course of psychotherapy. The reasons for recognizing a privilege for treatment by psychiatrists and psychologists apply with equal force to treatment by a clinical social worker such as Karen Beyer.[16] Today, social workers provide a significant amount of mental health treatment. See, e.g., U. S. Dept. of Health and Human Services, Center for Mental Health Services, Mental Health, United States, 1994 pp. 85-87, 107-114; Brief for National Association of Social Workers et al. as Amici Curiae 5-7 (citing authorities). Their clients often include the poor and those of modest means who could not afford the assistance of a psychiatrist or psychologist, id., at 6-7 (citing authorities), but whose counseling sessions serve the same public goals.[17] Perhaps in recognition of these circumstances, the vast majority of States explicitly extend a testimonial privilege to licensed social workers.[18] We therefore agree with the Court of Appeals that "[d]rawing

16 If petitioner had filed her complaint in an Illinois state court, respondents' claim of privilege would surely have been upheld, at least with respect to the state wrongful death action. An Illinois statute provides that conversations between a therapist and her patients are privileged from compelled disclosure in any civil or criminal proceeding. Ill. Comp. Stat., ch. 740, Section(s) 110/10 (1994). The term "therapist" is broadly defined to encompass a number of licensed professionals including social workers. Ch. 740, Section(s) 110/2. Karen Beyer, having satisfied the strict standards for licensure, qualifies as a clinical social worker in Illinois. 51 F. 3d 1346, 1358, n. 19 (CA7 1995).

Indeed, if only a state-law claim had been asserted in federal court, the second sentence in Rule 501 would have extended the privilege to that proceeding. We note that there is disagreement concerning the proper rule in cases such as this in which both federal and state claims are asserted in federal court and relevant evidence would be privileged under state law but not under federal law. See C. Wright & K. Graham, 23 Federal Practice and Procedure Section(s) 5434 (1980). Because the parties do not raise this question and our resolution of the case does not depend on it, we express no opinion on the matter.

17 The Judicial Conference Advisory Committee's proposed psychotherapist privilege defined psychotherapists as psychologists and medical doctors who provide mental health services. Proposed Rules, 56 F.R.D., at 240. This limitation in the 1972 recommendation does not counsel against recognition of a privilege for social workers practicing psychotherapy. In the quarter-century since the Committee adopted its recommendations, much has changed in the domains of social work and psychotherapy. See generally Brief for National Association of Social Workers et al. as Amici Curiae 5-13 (and authorities cited). While only 12 States regulated social workers in 1972, all 50 do today. See American Association of State Social Work Boards, Social Work Laws and Board Regulations: A State Comparison Study 29, 31 (1996). Over the same period, the relative portion of therapeutic services provided by social workers has increased substantially. See U. S. Dept. of Health and Human Services, Center for Mental Health Services, Mental Health, United States, 1994, pp. 85-87, 107-114.

18 See Ariz. Rev. Stat. Ann. Section(s) 32-3283 (1992); Ark. Code Ann. Section(s) 17-46-107 (1995); Cal. Evid. Code Section(s) 1010, 1012, 1014 (West 1995); Colo. Rev. Stat. Section(s) 13-90-107 (1987); Conn. Gen. Stat. Section(s) 52-146q

a distinction between the counseling provided by costly psychotherapists and the counseling provided by more readily accessible social workers serves no discernible public purpose." 51 F. 3d, at 1358, n. 19.

We part company with the Court of Appeals on a separate point. We reject the balancing component of the privilege implemented by that court and a small number of States.[19] Making the promise of confidentiality contingent upon a trial judge's later evaluation of the relative importance of the patient's interest in privacy and the evidentiary need for disclosure would eviscerate the effectiveness of the privilege. As we explained in Upjohn, if the purpose of the privilege is to be served, the participants in the confidential conversation "must be able to predict with some degree of certainty whether particular discussions will be protected. An uncertain privilege, or one which purports to be certain but results in widely varying applications by the courts, is little better than no privilege at all." 449 U.S., at 393 .

These considerations are all that is necessary for decision of this case. A rule that authorizes the recognition of new privileges on a case-by-case basis makes it appropriate to define the details of new privileges in a like manner. Because this is the first case in which we have recognized a psychotherapist privilege, it is neither necessary nor feasible to delineate its full contours in a way that would "govern all conceivable future questions in this area." *Id.*, at 386.[20]

(1991); Del. Code Ann., Tit. 24 Section(s) 3913 (1987); D. C. Code Section(s) 14-307 (1995); Fla. Stat. Section(s) 90.503 (1991); Ga. Code Ann. Section(s) 24-9-21 (1995); Idaho Code Section(s) 54-3213 (1994); Ill. Comp. Stat., ch. 225, Section(s) 20/16 (1994); Ind. Code Section(s) 25-23.6-6-1 (1993); Iowa Code Section(s) 622.10 (1987); Kan. Stat. Ann. Section(s) 65-6315 (Supp. 1990); Ky. Rule Evid. 507; La. Code Evid. Ann., Art. 510 (West 1995); Me. Rev. Stat. Ann., Tit. 32, Section(s) 7005 (1988); Md. Cts. & Jud. Proc. Code Ann. Section(s) 9-121 (1995); Mass. Gen. Laws Section(s) 112:135A (1994); Mich. Comp. Stat. Ann. 339.1610 (1992); Minn. Stat. Section(s) 595.02(g) (1994); Miss. Code Ann. Section(s) 73-53-29 (1972); Mo. Ann. Stat. Section(s) 337.636 (Supp. 1996); Mont. Code Ann. Section(s) 37-22-401 (1995); Neb. Rev. Stat. Ann. Section(s) 71-1,335 (1995); Nev. Rev. Stat. Ann. Section(s) 49.215, 49.225, 49.235 (Supp. 1995); N. H. Rev. Stat. Ann. Section(s) 330-A:19 (1995); N. J. Stat. Ann. Section(s) 45:15BB-13 (1995); N. M. Stat. Ann. Section(s) 61-31-24 (Supp. 1995); N. Y. Civ. Prac. Law Section(s) 4508 (1992); N. C. Gen. Stat. Section(s) 8-53.7 (1986); Ohio Rev. Code Ann. Section(s) 2317.02 (1995); Okla. Stat., Tit. 59, Section(s) 1261.6 (1991); Ore. Rev. Stat. Section(s) 40.250 (1991); R. I. Gen. Laws Section(s) 5-37.3-3, 5-37.3-4 (1995); S. C. Code Ann. Section(s) 19-11-95 (Supp. 1995); S. D. Codified Laws Section(s) 36-26-30 (1994); Tenn. Code Ann. Section(s) 63-23-107 (1990); Tex. Rule Civ. Evid. 510; Utah Rule Evid. 506; Vt. Rule Evid. 503; Va. Code Ann. Section(s) 8.01-400.2 (1992); Wash. Rev. Code Section(s) 18.19.180 (1994); W. Va. Code Section(s) 30-30-12 (1993); Wis. Stat. Section(s) 905.04 (1993-1994); Wyo. Stat. Section(s) 33-38-109 (Supp. 1995).

19 See, e.g., Me. Rev. Stat. Ann., Tit. 32, Section(s) 7005 (1964); N. H. Rev. Stat. Ann. Section(s) 330-A:19 (1995); N. C. Gen. Stat. Section(s) 8-53.7 (1986); Va. Code Ann. Section(s) 8.01-400.2 (1992).

20 Although it would be premature to speculate about most future developments in the federal psychotherapist privilege, we do not doubt that there are situations in which the privilege must give way, for example, if a serious threat of harm to the patient or

V. The conversations between Officer Redmond and Karen Beyer and the notes taken during their counseling sessions are protected from compelled disclosure under Rule 501 of the Federal Rules of Evidence. The judgment of the Court of Appeals is affirmed. *It is so ordered.*

DISSENT

Justice Scalia, with whom The Chief Justice joins as to Part III, dissenting.

The Court has discussed at some length the benefit that will be purchased by creation of the evidentiary privilege in this case: the encouragement of psychoanalytic counseling. It has not mentioned the purchase price: occasional injustice. That is the cost of every rule which excludes reliable and probative evidence-or at least every one categorical enough to achieve its announced policy objective. In the case of some of these rules, such as the one excluding confessions that have not been properly "Mirandized," see Miranda v. Arizona, 384 U.S. 436 (1966), the victim of the injustice is always the impersonal State or the faceless "public at large." For the rule proposed here, the victim is more likely to be some individual who is prevented from proving a valid claim-or (worse still) prevented from establishing a valid defense. The latter is particularly unpalatable for those who love justice, because it causes the courts of law not merely to let stand a wrong, but to become themselves the instruments of wrong.

In the past, this Court has well understood that the particular value the courts are distinctively charged with preserving-justice-is severely harmed by contravention of "the fundamental principle that `"the public . . . has a right to every man's evidence."'" Trammel v. United States, 445 U.S. 40, 50 (1980) (citation omitted). Testimonial privileges, it has said, "are not lightly created nor expansively construed, for they are in derogation of the search for truth." United States v. Nixon, 418 U.S. 683, 710 (1974) (emphasis added). Adherence to that principle has caused us, in the Rule 501 cases we have considered to date, to reject new privileges, see University of Pennsylvania v. EEOC, 493 U.S. 182 (1990) (privilege against disclosure of academic peer review materials); United States v. Gillock, 445 U.S. 360 (1980) (privilege against disclosure of "legislative acts" by member of state legislature), and even to construe narrowly the scope of existing privileges, see, e.g., United States v. Zolin, 491 U.S. 554, 568 -570 (1989) (permitting in camera review of documents alleged to come within crime-fraud exception to attorney-client privilege); Trammel, supra (holding that voluntary testimony by spouse is not covered by husband-wife privilege). The Court today ignores this traditional judicial preference for the truth, and ends up creating a privilege that is new, vast, and ill-defined. I respectfully dissent.

I. The case before us involves confidential communications made by a police officer to a state-licensed clinical social worker in the course of psychotherapeutic counseling. Before proceeding to a legal analysis of the case, I must observe that the Court makes its task deceptively simple by the manner in which it proceeds. It

to others can be averted only by means of a disclosure by the therapist.

begins by characterizing the issue as "whether it is appropriate for federal courts to recognize a `psychotherapist privilege,'" ante, at 1, and devotes almost all of its opinion to that question. Having answered that question (to its satisfaction) in the affirmative, it then devotes less than a page of text to answering in the affirmative the small remaining question whether "the federal privilege should also extend to confidential communications made to licensed social workers in the course of psychotherapy," ante, at 13.

Of course the prototypical evidentiary privilege analogous to the one asserted here-the lawyer-client privilege-is not identified by the broad area of advice-giving practiced by the person to whom the privileged communication is given, but rather by the professional status of that person. Hence, it seems a long step from a lawyer-client privilege to a tax advisor-client or accountant-client privilege. But if one recharacterizes it as a "legal advisor" privilege, the extension seems like the most natural thing in the world. That is the illusion the Court has produced here: It first frames an overly general question ("Should there be a psychotherapist privilege?") that can be answered in the negative only by excluding from protection office consultations with professional psychiatrists (i.e., doctors) and clinical psychologists. And then, having answered that in the affirmative, it comes to the only question that the facts of this case present ("Should there be a social worker-client privilege with regard to psychotherapeutic counseling?") with the answer seemingly a foregone conclusion. At that point, to conclude against the privilege one must subscribe to the difficult proposition, "Yes, there is a psychotherapist privilege, but not if the psychotherapist is a social worker." Relegating the question actually posed by this case to an afterthought makes the impossible possible in a number of wonderful ways. For example, it enables the Court to treat the Proposed Federal Rules of Evidence developed in 1972 by the Judicial Conference Advisory Committee as strong support for its holding, whereas they in fact counsel clearly and directly against it. The Committee did indeed recommend a "psychotherapist privilege" of sorts; but more precisely, and more relevantly, it recommended a privilege for psychotherapy conducted by "a person authorized to practice medicine" or "a person licensed or certified as a psychologist," Proposed Rule of Evidence 504, 56 F. R. D. 183, 240 (1972), which is to say that it recommended against the privilege at issue here. That condemnation is obscured, and even converted into an endorsement, by pushing a "psychotherapist privilege" into the center ring. The Proposed Rule figures prominently in the Court's explanation of why that privilege deserves recognition, ante, at 12-13, and is ignored in the single page devoted to the sideshow which happens to be the issue presented for decision, ante, at 13-14.

This is the most egregious and readily explainable example of how the Court's misdirection of its analysis makes the difficult seem easy; others will become apparent when I give the social-worker question the fuller consideration it deserves. My initial point, however, is that the Court's very methodology-giving serious consideration only to the more general, and much easier, question-is in violation of our duty to proceed cautiously when erecting barriers between us and the truth.

II. To say that the Court devotes the bulk of its opinion to the much easier question of psychotherapist-patient privilege is not to say that its answer to that question is convincing. At bottom, the Court's decision to recognize such a privilege is based on its view that "successful [psychotherapeutic] treatment" serves "important private interests" (namely those of patients undergoing psychotherapy) as well as the "public good" of "[t]he mental health of our citizenry." Ante, at 7-9. I have no quarrel with these premises. Effective psychotherapy undoubtedly is beneficial to individuals with mental problems, and surely serves some larger social interest in maintaining a mentally stable society. But merely mentioning these values does not answer the critical question: are they of such importance, and is the contribution of psychotherapy to them so distinctive, and is the application of normal evidentiary rules so destructive to psychotherapy, as to justify making our federal courts occasional instruments of injustice? On that central question I find the Court's analysis insufficiently convincing to satisfy the high standard we have set for rules that "are in derogation of the search for truth." Nixon, 418 U.S., at 710 .

When is it, one must wonder, that the psychotherapist came to play such an indispensable role in the maintenance of the citizenry's mental health? For most of history, men and women have worked out their difficulties by talking to, inter alios, parents, siblings, best friends and bartenders-none of whom was awarded a privilege against testifying in court. Ask the average citizen: Would your mental health be more significantly impaired by preventing you from seeing a psychotherapist, or by preventing you from getting advice from your mom? I have little doubt what the answer would be. Yet there is no mother-child privilege.

How likely is it that a person will be deterred from seeking psychological counseling, or from being completely truthful in the course of such counseling, because of fear of later disclosure in litigation? And even more pertinent to today's decision, to what extent will the evidentiary privilege reduce that deterrent? The Court does not try to answer the first of these questions; and it cannot possibly have any notion of what the answer is to the second, since that depends entirely upon the scope of the privilege, which the Court amazingly finds it "neither necessary nor feasible to delineate," ante, at 16. If, for example, the psychotherapist can give the patient no more assurance than "A court will not be able to make me disclose what you tell me, unless you tell me about a harmful act," I doubt whether there would be much benefit from the privilege at all. That is not a fanciful example, at least with respect to extension of the psychotherapist privilege to social workers. See Del. Code Ann., Tit. 24, Section(s) 3913(2) (1987); Idaho Code Section(s) 54-3213(2) (1994).

Even where it is certain that absence of the psychotherapist privilege will inhibit disclosure of the information, it is not clear to me that that is an unacceptable state of affairs. Let us assume the very worst in the circumstances of the present case: that to be truthful about what was troubling her, the police officer who sought counseling would have to confess that she shot without reason, and wounded an innocent man. If (again to assume the worst) such an act constituted the crime of negligent wounding under Illinois law, the officer would of course have the absolute right not to admit that she shot without reason in criminal court. But I see no reason why she should be enabled both not to admit it in criminal court (as a good citizen should), and to get the benefits of psychotherapy by admitting it to a therapist who cannot tell anyone else. And even less reason why she should be enabled to deny her guilt in the criminal trial-or in a civil trial for negligence-while yet obtaining the benefits of psychotherapy by confessing guilt to a social worker who cannot testify. It seems to me entirely fair to say that if she wishes the benefits of telling the truth she must also accept the adverse consequences. To be sure, in most cases the statements to the psychotherapist will be only marginally relevant, and one of the purposes of the privilege (though not one relied upon by the Court) may be simply to spare patients needless intrusion upon their privacy, and to spare psychotherapists needless expenditure of their time in deposition and trial. But surely this can be achieved by means short of excluding even evidence that is of the most direct and conclusive effect.

The Court confidently asserts that not much truth-finding capacity would be destroyed by the privilege anyway, since "[w]ithout a privilege, much of the desirable evidence to which litigants such as petitioner seek access . . . is unlikely to come into being." Ante, at 10. If that is so, how come psychotherapy got to be a thriving practice before the "psychotherapist privilege" was invented? Were the patients paying money to lie to their analysts all those years? Of course the evidence-generating effect of the privilege (if any) depends entirely upon its scope, which the Court steadfastly declines to consider. And even if one assumes that scope to be the broadest possible, is it really true that most, or even many, of those who seek psychological counseling have the worry of litigation in the back of their minds? I doubt that, and the Court provides no evidence to support it.

The Court suggests one last policy justification: since psychotherapist privilege statutes exist in all the States, the failure to recognize a privilege in federal courts "would frustrate the purposes of the state legislation that was enacted to foster these confidential communications." Ante, at 11. This is a novel argument indeed. A sort of inverse pre-emption: the truth-seeking functions of federal courts must be adjusted so as not to conflict with the policies of the States. This reasoning cannot be squared with Gillock, which declined to recognize an evidentiary privilege for Tennessee legislators in federal prosecutions, even though the Tennessee Constitution guaranteed it in state criminal proceedings. Gillock, 445 U.S., at 368 . Moreover, since, as I shall discuss, state policies regarding the psychotherapist privilege vary considerably from State to State, no uniform federal policy can possibly honor most of them. If furtherance of state policies is the name of the game, rules of privilege in federal courts should vary from State to State, a la Erie.

The Court's failure to put forward a convincing justification of its own could perhaps be excused if it were relying upon the unanimous conclusion of state courts in the reasoned development of their common law. It cannot do that, since no State has such a privilege apart from legislation.[21] What it relies upon, instead, is "the fact that all 50 States and the District of Columbia have 1. enacted into law 2. some form of psychotherapist privilege." Ante, at 10 (emphasis added). Let us consider both the verb and its object: The fact 1. that all 50 States have enacted this privilege argues not for, but against, our adopting the privilege judicially. At best it suggests that the matter has been found not to lend itself to judicial treatment-perhaps because the pros and cons of adopting the privilege, or of giving it one or another shape, are not that clear; or perhaps because the rapidly evolving uses of psychotherapy demand a flexibility that only legislation can provide. At worst it suggests that the privilege commends itself only to decision making bodies in which reason is tempered, so to speak, by political pressure from organized interest groups (such as psychologists

21 The Court observes: "In 1972 the members of the Judicial Conference Advisory Committee noted that the common law `had indicated a disposition to recognize a psychotherapist-patient privilege when legislatures began moving into the field.' Proposed Rules, 56 F. R. D., at 242 (citation omitted)." Ante, at 12. The sole support the Committee invoked was a student Note entitled Confidential Communications to a Psychotherapist: A New Testimonial Privilege, 47 Nw. U. L. Rev. 384 (1952). That source, in turn, cites (and discusses) a single case recognizing a common-law psychotherapist privilege: the unpublished opinion of a judge of the Circuit Court of Cook County, Illinois, Binder v. Ruvell, No. 52-C-2535 (June 24, 1952)-which, in turn, cites no other cases.

I doubt whether the Court's failure to provide more substantial support for its assertion stems from want of trying. Respondents and all of their amici pointed us to only four other state-court decisions supposedly adopting a common-law psychotherapist privilege. See Brief for the American Psychiatric Association et al. as Amici Curiae 8, n. 5; Brief for the American Psychoanalytic Association et al. as Amici Curiae 15-16; Brief for the American Psychological Association as Amicus Curiae 8. It is not surprising that the Court thinks it not worth the trouble to cite them: (1) In In re "B", 482 Pa. 471, 394 A. 2d 419 (1978), the opinions of four of the seven Justices explicitly rejected a nonstatutory privilege; and the two Justices who did recognize one recognized, not a common-law privilege, but rather (mirabile dictu) a privilege "constitutionally based," "emanat[ing] from the penumbras of the various guarantees of the Bill of Rights, . . . as well as from the guarantees of the Constitution of this Commonwealth." *Id.*, at 484, 394 A. 2d, at 425. (2) Allred v. State, 554 P. 2d 411 (Alaska 1976), held that no privilege was available in the case before the court, so what it says about the existence of a common-law privilege is the purest dictum. (3) Falcon v. Alaska Pub. Offices Comm'n, 570 P. 2d 469 (1977), a later Alaska Supreme Court case, proves the last statement. It rejected the claim by a physician that he did not have to disclose the names of his patients, even though some of the physician's practice consisted of psychotherapy; it made no mention of Allred's dictum that there was a common-law psychiatrist-patient privilege (though if that existed it would seem relevant), and cited Allred only for the proposition that there was no statutory privilege, id., at 473, n. 12. And finally, (4) State v. Evans, 104 Ariz. 434, 454 P. 2d 976 (1969), created a limited privilege, applicable to court-ordered examinations to determine competency to stand trial, which tracked a privilege that had been legislatively created after the defendant's examination.

In light of this dearth of case support-from all the courts of 50 States, down to the county-court level-it seems to me the Court's assertion should be revised to read: "The common law had indicated scant disposition to recognize a psychotherapist-patient privilege when (or even after) legislatures began moving into the field."

and social workers), and decision making bodies that are not overwhelmingly concerned (as courts of law are and should be) with justice.

And the phrase 2. "some form of psychotherapist privilege" covers a multitude of difficulties. The Court concedes that there is "divergence among the States concerning the types of therapy relationships protected and the exceptions recognized." Ante, at 12, n. 13. To rest a newly announced federal common-law psychotherapist privilege, assertable from this day forward in all federal courts, upon "the States' *unanimous judgment* that some form of psychotherapist privilege is appropriate," *ibid.* (emphasis added), is rather like announcing a new, immediately applicable, federal common law of torts, based upon the States' "unanimous judgment" that some form of tort law is appropriate. In the one case as in the other, the state laws vary to such a degree that the parties and lower federal judges confronted by the new "common law" have barely a clue as to what its content might be.

III. Turning from the general question that was not involved in this case to the specific one that is: The Court's conclusion that a social-worker psychotherapeutic privilege deserves recognition is even less persuasive. In approaching this question, the fact that five of the state legislatures that have seen fit to enact "some form" of psychotherapist privilege have elected not to extend any form of privilege to social workers, see ante, at 15, n. 17, ought to give one pause. So should the fact that the Judicial Conference Advisory Committee was similarly discriminating in its conferral of the proposed Rule 504 privilege, see supra. The Court, however, has "no hesitation in concluding . . . that the federal privilege should also extend" to social workers, ante, at 13- and goes on to prove that by polishing off the reasoned analysis with a topic sentence and two sentences of discussion, as follows (omitting citations and non-germane footnote):

"The reasons for recognizing a privilege for treatment by psychiatrists and psychologists apply with equal force to treatment by a clinical social worker such as Karen Beyer. Today, social workers provide a significant amount of mental health treatment. Their clients often include the poor and those of modest means who could not afford the assistance of a psychiatrist or psychologist, but whose counseling sessions serve the same public goals." Ante, at 13-14.

So much for the rule that privileges are to be narrowly construed.

Of course this brief analysis-like the earlier, more extensive, discussion of the general psychotherapist privilege-contains no explanation of why the psychotherapy provided by social workers is a public good of such transcendent importance as to be purchased at the price of occasional injustice. Moreover, it considers only the respects in which social workers providing therapeutic services are similar to licensed psychiatrists and psychologists; not a word about the respects in which they are different. A licensed psychiatrist or psychologist is an expert in psychotherapy-and that may suffice (though I think it not so clear that this Court should make the judgment) to justify the use of extraordinary means to encourage counseling with him, as opposed to counseling with one's rabbi, minister, family or friends. One must presume that a social worker does not bring this greatly heightened degree of skill to bear, which is alone a reason for not encouraging that consultation as generously. Does a social worker bring to bear at least a significantly heightened degree of skill-more than a minister or rabbi, for example? I have no idea, and neither does the Court. The social worker in the present case, Karen Beyer, was a "licensed clinical social worker" in Illinois, App. 18, a job title whose training requirements consist of "master's degree in social work from an approved program," and "3,000 hours of satisfactory, supervised clinical professional experience." Ill. Comp. Stat., ch. 225, Section(s) 20/9 (1994). It is not clear that the degree in social work requires any training in psychotherapy. The "clinical professional experience" apparently will impart some such training, but only of the vaguest sort, judging from the Illinois Code's definition of "[c]linical social work practice," viz., "the providing of mental health services for the evaluation, treatment, and prevention of mental and emotional disorders in individuals, families and groups based on knowledge and theory of psychosocial development, behavior, psychopathology, unconscious motivation, interpersonal relationships, and environmental stress." Ch. 225, Section(s) 20/3(5). But the rule the Court announces today-like the Illinois evidentiary privilege which that rule purports to respect, Ch. 225, Section(s) 20/16.[22] -is not limited to "licensed clinical social workers," but includes all "licensed social workers." "Licensed social workers" may also provide "mental health services" as described in Section(s) 20/3(5), so long as it is done under supervision of a licensed clinical social worker. And the training requirement for a "licensed social worker" consists of either (a) "a degree from a graduate program of social work" approved by the State, or (b) "a degree in social work from an undergraduate program" approved by the State, plus "3 years of supervised professional experience." Ch. 225, Section(s) 20/9A. With due respect, it does not seem to me that any of this training is comparable in its rigor (or indeed in the precision of its subject) to the training of the other experts (lawyers) to whom this Court has accorded a privilege, or even of the experts (psychiatrists and psychologists) to whom the Advisory Committee and this Court proposed extension of a privilege in 1972. Of course these are only Illinois' requirements for "social workers." Those of other States, for all we know, may be even less demanding. Indeed, I am not even sure there is a nationally accepted definition of "social worker," as there is of psychiatrist and psychologist. It seems to me

22 Section 20/16 is the provision of the Illinois Statutes cited by the Court to show that Illinois has "explicitly extend[ed] a testimonial privilege to licensed social workers." Ante, at 15, and n. 17. The Court elsewhere observes that respondent's communications to Beyer would have been privileged in state court under another provision of the Illinois Statutes, the Mental Health and Developmental Disabilities Confidentiality Act, Ill. Comp. Stat., ch. 740, Section(s) 110/10 (1994). Ante, at 14, n. 15. But the privilege conferred by Section(s) 110/10 extends to an even more ill-defined class: not only to licensed social workers, but to all social workers, to nurses, and indeed to "any other person not prohibited by law from providing [mental health or developmental disabilities] services or from holding himself out as a therapist if the recipient reasonably believes that such person is permitted to do so." Ch. 740, Section(s) 110/2.

quite irresponsible to extend the so-called "psychotherapist privilege" to all licensed social workers, nationwide, without exploring these issues.

Another critical distinction between psychiatrists and psychologists, on the one hand, and social workers, on the other, is that the former professionals, in their consultations with patients, do nothing but psychotherapy. Social workers, on the other hand, interview people for a multitude of reasons. The Illinois definition of "[l]icensed social worker," for example, is as follows:

"Licensed social worker" means a person who holds a license authorizing the practice of social work, which includes social services to individuals, groups or communities in any one or more of the fields of social casework, social group work, community organization for social welfare, social work research, social welfare administration or social work education." Ch. 225, Section(s) 20/3(9).

Thus, in applying the "social worker" variant of the "psychotherapist" privilege, it will be necessary to determine whether the information provided to the social worker was provided to him in his capacity as a psychotherapist, or in his capacity as an administrator of social welfare, a community organizer, etc. Worse still, if the privilege is to have its desired effect (and is not to mislead the client), it will presumably be necessary for the social caseworker to advise, as the conversation with his welfare client proceeds, which portions are privileged and which are not.

Having concluded its three sentences of reasoned analysis, the Court then invokes, as it did when considering the psychotherapist privilege, the "experience" of the States-once again an experience I consider irrelevant (if not counter-indicative) because it consists entirely of legislation rather than common-law decision. It says that "the vast majority of States explicitly extend a testimonial privilege to licensed social workers." Ante, at 15. There are two elements of this impressive statistic, however, that the Court does not reveal.

First-and utterly conclusive of the irrelevance of this supposed consensus to the question before us-the majority of the States that accord a privilege to social workers do not do so as a subpart of a "psychotherapist" privilege. The privilege applies to all confidences imparted to social workers, and not just those provided in the course of psychotherapy.[23] In Oklahoma, for example, the social-

23 See Ariz. Rev. Stat. Ann. Section(s) 32-3283 (1992); Ark. Code Ann. Section(s) 17-46-107 (1995); Del. Code Ann., Tit. 24, Section(s) 3913 (1987); Idaho Code Section(s) 54-3213 (1994); Ind. Code Section(s) 25-23.6-6-1 (1993); Iowa Code Section(s) 154C.5 and Section(s) 622.10 (1987); Kan. Stat. Ann. Section(s) 65-6315 (Supp. 1990); Me. Rev. Stat. Ann., Tit. 32, Section(s) 7005 (1988); Mass. Gen. Laws Section(s) 112:135A (1994); Mich. Comp. Laws Ann. Section(s) 339.1610 (1992); Miss. Code Ann. Section(s) 73-53-29 (1995); Mo. Rev. Stat. Section(s) 337.636 (1994); Mont. Code Ann. Section(s) 37-22-401 (1995); Neb. Rev. Stat. Section(s) 71-1,335 (Supp. 1994); N. J. Stat. Ann. Section(s) 45:15BB-13 (1995); N. M. Stat. Ann. Section(s) 61-31-24 (1993); N. Y. Civ. Prac. Section(s) 4508 (McKinney 1992); N. C. Gen. Stat. Section(s) 8-53.7 (1986); Ohio Rev. Code Ann. Section(s) 2317.02(G)(1) (1995); Okla. Stat., Tit. 59 Section(s) 1261.6 (1991); Ore. Rev. Stat. Section(s) 40.250 (1991); S. D. Codified Laws Section(s) 36-26-30 (1994); Tenn. Code Ann. Section(s) 63-23-107 (1990); Wash. Rev. Code Section(s) 18.19.180 (1994); W. Va. Code Section(s) 30-30-12 (1993); Wyo. Stat. Section(s) 33-38-109 (Supp. 1995).

worker-privilege statute prohibits a licensed social worker from disclosing, or being compelled to disclose, "any information acquired from persons consulting the licensed social worker in his or her professional capacity" (with certain exceptions to be discussed infra). Okla. Stat., Tit. 59, Section(s) 1261.6 (1991) (emphasis added). The social worker's "professional capacity" is expansive, for the "practice of social work" in Oklahoma is defined as:

"[T]he professional activity of helping individuals, groups, or communities enhance or restore their capacity for physical, social and economic functioning and the professional application of social work values, principles and techniques in areas such as clinical social work, social service administration, social planning, social work consultation and social work research to one or more of the following ends: Helping people obtain tangible services; counseling with individuals families and groups; helping communities or groups provide or improve social and health services; and participating in relevant social action. The practice of social work requires knowledge of human development and behavior; of social economic and cultural institutions and forces; and of the interaction of all of these factors. Social work practice includes the teaching of relevant subject matter and of conducting research into problems of human behavior and conflict." Tit. 59, Section(s) 1250.1(2) (1991).

Thus, in Oklahoma, as in most other States having a social-worker privilege, it is not a subpart or even a derivative of the psychotherapist privilege, but rather a piece of special legislation similar to that achieved by many other groups, from accountants, see, e.g., Miss. Code Ann. Section(s) 73-33-16(2) (1995) (certified public accountant "shall not be required by any court of this state to disclose, and shall not voluntarily disclose" client information), to private detectives, see, e.g., Mich. Comp. Laws Section(s) 338.840 (1979) ("Any communications . . . furnished by a professional man or client to a [licensed private detective], or any information secured in connection with an assignment for a client, shall be deemed privileged with the same authority and dignity as are other privileged communications recognized by the courts of this state").[24] These social-worker statutes give no support, therefore, to the theory (importance of psychotherapy) upon which the Court rests its disposition.

Second, the Court does not reveal the enormous degree of disagreement among the States as to the scope of the privilege. It concedes that the laws of four States are subject to such gaping exceptions that they are "`little better than no privilege at all,'" ante, at 16 and n. 18, so that they should more appropriately be categorized with the five States whose laws contradict the action taken today. I would add another State to those whose privilege is illusory. See Wash. Rev. Code Section(s) 18.19.180 (1994) (disclosure of information required "[i]n response to a subpoena from a court of law"). In adopting any sort of a social worker privilege, then, the Court can at most claim that it is following the legislative "experience" of 40 States, and contradicting the "experience" of 10.

---

24 These ever-multiplying evidentiary-privilege statutes, which the Court today emulates, recall us to the original meaning of the word "privilege." It is a composite derived from the Latin words "privus" and "lex": private law.

But turning to those States that do have an appreciable privilege of some sort, the diversity is vast. In Illinois and Wisconsin, the social-worker privilege does not apply when the confidential information pertains to homicide, see Ill. Comp. Stat., ch. 740, Section(s) 110/10(a)(9) (1994); Wis. Stat. Section(s) 905.04(4)(d) (1993-1994), and in the District of Columbia when it pertains to any crime "inflicting injuries" upon persons, see D. C. Code Section(s) 14-307(a)(1) (1995). In Missouri, the privilege is suspended as to information that pertains to a criminal act, see Mo. Rev. Stat. Section(s) 337.636(2) (1994), and in Texas when the information is sought in any criminal prosecution, compare Tex. Rule Civ. Evid. 510(d) with Tex. Rule Crim. Evid. 501 et seq. In Kansas and Oklahoma, the privilege yields when the information pertains to "violations of any law," see Kan. Stat. Ann. Section(s) 65-6315(a)(2) (Supp. 1990); Okla. Stat., Tit. 59, Section(s) 1261.6(2) (1991); in Indiana, when it reveals a "serious harmful act," see Ind. Code Ann. Section(s) 25-23.6-6-1(2) (1995); and in Delaware and Idaho, when it pertains to any "harmful act," see Del. Code Ann., Tit. 24, Section(s) 3913(2) (1987); Idaho Code Section(s) 54-3213(2) (1994). In Oregon, a state-employed social worker like Karen Beyer loses the privilege where her supervisor determines that her testimony "is necessary in the performance of the duty of the social worker as a public employee." See Ore. Rev. Stat. Section(s) 40.250(5) (1991). In South Carolina, a social worker is forced to disclose confidences "when required by statutory law or by court order for good cause shown to the extent that the patient's care and treatment or the nature and extent of his mental illness or emotional condition are reasonably at issue in a proceeding." See S. C. Code Ann. Section(s) 19-11-95(D)(1) (Supp. 1995). The majority of social-worker-privilege States declare the privilege inapplicable to information relating to child abuse.[25] And the States that do not fall into any of the above categories provide exceptions for commitment proceedings, for proceedings in which the patient relies on his mental or emotional condition as an element of his claim or defense, or for communications made in the course of a court-ordered examination of the mental or emotional condition of the patient.[26]

25 See, e.g., Ariz. Rev. Stat. Ann. Section(s) 32-3283 (1992); Ark. Code Ann. Section(s) 17-46-107(3) (1995); Cal. Evid. Code Ann. Section(s) 1027 (West 1995); Colo. Rev. Stat. Section(s) 19-3-304 (Supp. 1995); Del. Rule Evid. 503(d)(4); Ga. Code Ann. Section(s) Code Evid. Ann., Art. 510(B)(2)(k) (West 1995); Md. Cts. & Jud. Proc. Code Ann. Section(s) 9-121(e)(4) (1995); Mass. Gen. Laws, Section(s) 119:51A (1994); Mich. Comp. Laws Ann. Section(s) 722.623 (1992 Supp. Pamph.); Minn. Stat. Section(s) 595.02.2(a) (1988); Miss. Code Ann. Section(s) 73-53-29(e) (1995); Mont. Code Ann. Section(s) 37-22-401(3) (1995); Neb. Rev. Stat. Section(s) 28-711 (1995); N. M. Stat. Ann. 4508(a)(3) (McKinney 1992); Ohio Rev. Code Ann. Section(s) 2317.02(G)(1)(a) (1995); Ore. Rev. Stat. Section(s) 40.250(4) (1991); R. I. Gen. Laws Section(s) 5-37.3-4(b)(4) (1995); S. D. Codified Laws Section(s) 36-26-30(3) (1994); Tenn. Code Ann. Section(s) 63-23-107(b) (1990); Vt. Rule Evid. 503(d)(5); W. Va. Code Section(s) 30-30-12(a)(4) (1993); Wyo. Stat. Section(s) 14-3-205 (1994).

26 See, e.g., Fla. Stat. Section(s) 90.503(4) (Supp. 1992) (all three exceptions); Ky. Rule Evid. 507(c) (all three); Nev. Rev. Stat. Section(s) 49.245 (1993) (all three); Utah Rule Evid. 506(d) (all three); Conn. Gen. Stat. Section(s) 52-146q(c)(1) (1995) (commitment proceedings and proceedings in which patient's mental condition at

Thus, although the Court is technically correct that "the vast majority of States explicitly extend a testimonial privilege to licensed social workers," ante, at 15, that uniformity exists only at the most superficial level. No State has adopted the privilege without restriction; the nature of the restrictions varies enormously from jurisdiction to jurisdiction; and 10 States, I reiterate, effectively reject the privilege entirely. It is fair to say that there is scant national consensus even as to the propriety of a social-worker psychotherapist privilege, and none whatever as to its appropriate scope. In other words, the state laws to which the Court appeals for support demonstrate most convincingly that adoption of a social-worker psychotherapist privilege is a job for Congress.

The question before us today is not whether there should be an evidentiary privilege for social workers providing therapeutic services. Perhaps there should. But the question before us is whether (1) the need for that privilege is so clear, and (2) the desirable contours of that privilege are so evident, that it is appropriate for this Court to craft it in common-law fashion, under Rule 501. Even if we were writing on a clean slate, I think the answer to that question would be clear. But given our extensive precedent to the effect that new privileges "in derogation of the search for truth" "are not lightly created," United States v. Nixon, 418 U.S., at 710 , the answer the Court gives today is inexplicable.

In its consideration of this case, the Court was the beneficiary of no fewer than 14 amicus briefs supporting respondents, most of which came from such organizations as the American Psychiatric Association, the American Psychoanalytic Association, the American Association of State Social Work Boards, the Employee Assistance Professionals Association, Inc., the American Counseling Association, and the National Association of Social Workers. Not a single amicus brief was filed in support of petitioner. That is no surprise. There is no self-interested organization out there devoted to pursuit of the truth in the federal courts. The expectation is, however, that this Court will have that interest prominently, indeed, primarily in mind. Today we have failed that expectation, and that responsibility. It is no small matter to say that, in some cases, our federal courts will be the tools of injustice rather than unearth the truth where it is available to be found. The common law has identified a few instances where that is tolerable. Perhaps Congress may conclude that it is also tolerable for the purpose of encouraging psychotherapy by social workers. But that conclusion assuredly does not burst upon the mind with such clarity that a judgment in favor of suppressing the truth ought to be pronounced by this honorable Court. I respectfully dissent.

---

issue); Iowa Code Section(s) 622.10 (1987) (proceedings in which patient's mental condition at issue).

Duty to Warn/Protect

(Thapar vs. Zezulka)[1]

Background

The primary issue in this case is whether a mental-health professional can be liable in negligence for failing to warn the appropriate third parties when a patient makes specific threats of harm toward a readily identifiable person. In reversing the trial court's summary judgment, the court of appeals recognized such a cause of action.[2] Because the Legislature has established a policy against such a common-law cause of action, we refrain from imposing on mental-health professionals a duty to warn third parties of a patient's threats. Accordingly, we reverse the court of appeals' judgment and render judgment that Zezulka take nothing.

Because this is an appeal from summary judgment, we take as true evidence favorable to Lyndall Zezulka, the nonmovant.[3] Freddy Ray Lilly had a history of mental-health problems and psychiatric treatment. Dr. Renu K. Thapar, a psychiatrist, first treated Lilly in 1985, when Lilly was brought to Southwest Memorial Hospital's emergency room. Thapar diagnosed Lilly as suffering from moderate to severe post-traumatic stress disorder, alcohol abuse, and paranoid and delusional beliefs concerning his stepfather, Henry Zezulka, and people of certain ethnic backgrounds. Thapar treated Lilly with a combination of psychotherapy and drug therapy over the next three years.

For the majority of their relationship, Thapar treated Lilly on an outpatient basis. But on at least six occasions Lilly was admitted to Southwest Memorial Hospital, or another facility, in response to urgent treatment needs.

Often the urgency involved Lilly's problems in maintaining amicable relationships with those with whom he lived. Lilly was also admitted on one

1 Thapar vs. Zezulka, 994 S.W.2d 635 (Tex. 1999)

2 961 S.W.2d 506.

3 See Science Spectrum, Inc. v. Martinez, 941 S.W.2d 910, 911 (Tex. 1997).

occasion after threatening to kill himself. In August 1988, Lilly agreed to be admitted to Southwest Memorial Hospital. Thapar's notes from August 23, 1988, state that Lilly "feels like killing" Henry Zezulka. These records also state, however, that Lilly "has decided not to do it but that is how he feels." After hospitalization and treatment for seven days, Lilly was discharged. Within a month Lilly shot and killed Henry Zezulka.

Despite the fact that Lilly's treatment records indicate that he sometimes felt homicidal, Thapar never warned any family member or any law enforcement agency of Lilly's threats against his stepfather. Nor did Thapar inform any family member or any law enforcement agency of Lilly's discharge from Southwest Memorial Hospital.

Lyndall Zezulka, Henry's wife and Lilly's mother, sued Thapar for negligence resulting in her husband's wrongful death. Zezulka alleged that Thapar was negligent in diagnosing and treating Lilly and negligent in failing to warn of Lilly's threats toward Henry Zezulka. It is undisputed that Thapar had no physician-patient relationship with either Lyndall or Henry Zezulka. Based on this fact, Thapar moved for summary judgment on the ground that Zezulka had not stated a claim for medical negligence because Thapar owed no duty to Zezulka in the absence of a doctor-patient relationship. The trial court overruled Thapar's motion.

Thapar filed a motion for rehearing of her summary judgment motion based largely on our decision in Bird v. W.C.W, in which we held that no duty runs from a psychologist to a third party to not negligently misdiagnose a patient's condition.[4] In light of Bird, the trial court reconsidered and granted summary judgment for Thapar. Zezulka appealed.

After concluding that Zezulka was not stopped from complaining about the trial court's judgment by her agreement to resolve the duty question through summary judgment, a conclusion with which we agree, the court of appeals reversed the trial court's judgment.[5] The court of appeals held that the no-duty ground asserted in Thapar's motion for summary judgment was not a defense to the cause of action pleaded by Zezulka.[6]

To decide this case we must determine the duties a mental-health professional owes to a nonpatient third party. Zezulka stated her claims against Thapar in negligence. Liability in negligence is premised on duty, a breach of which proximately causes injuries, and damages resulting from that breach.[7] Whether a legal duty exists is a threshold question of law for the court to decide from the facts surrounding the occurrence in question.[8] If there is no duty, there cannot be negligence liability.[9]

4 868 S.W.2d 767 (Tex. 1994).

5 See 961 S.W.2d at 510-11.

6 See id. at 511.

7 See Bird, 868 S.W.2d at 769 (citing Greater Houston Transp. Co. v. Phillips, 801 S.W.2d 523, 525 (Tex. 1990)).

8 See St. John v. Pope, 901 S.W.2d 420, 424 (Tex. 1995); Bird, 868 S.W.2d at 769.

9 See Van Horn v. Chambers, 970 S.W.2d 542, 544 (Tex. 1998); St. John, 901 S.W.2d

In her second amended petition Zezulka lists seventeen particulars by which she alleges Thapar was negligent. But each allegation is based on one of two proposed underlying duties: *(1) a duty to not negligently diagnose or treat a patient that runs from a psychiatrist to nonpatient third parties; or (2) a duty to warn third parties of a patient's threats.* In her motion for summary judgment Thapar asserted that she owed Zezulka no duty. Thus, we must determine if Thapar owed Zezulka either of these proposed duties.

Negligent Diagnosis And Treatment

First, we consider Zezulka's allegations that Thapar was negligent in her diagnosis and treatment of Lilly's psychiatric problems. Among other claims, Zezulka alleged that Thapar was negligent in releasing Lilly from the hospital in August 1988, in failing to take steps to have Lilly involuntarily committed, and in failing to monitor Lilly after his release to ensure that he was taking his medication. All of these claims are based on Thapar's medical diagnosis of Lilly's condition, which dictated the treatment Lilly should have received and the corresponding actions Thapar should have taken.[10] The underlying duty question here is whether the absence of a doctor-patient relationship precludes Zezulka from maintaining medical negligence claims against Thapar based on her diagnosis and treatment of Lilly.

In Bird we held that no duty runs from a psychologist to a third party to not negligently misdiagnose a patient's condition.[11] Since Bird, we have had occasion to consider several permutations of this same duty question.[12] Bird and our post-Bird writings answer definitively the first duty question presented by the facts before us: Thapar owes no duty to Zezulka, a third party nonpatient, for negligent misdiagnosis or negligent treatment of Lilly.[13] Accordingly, Thapar was entitled to summary judgment on all of the claims premised on Zezulka's first duty theory.

Failure to Warn

Second, we consider Zezulka's allegations that Thapar was negligent for failing to warn either the Zezulkas or law enforcement personnel of Lilly's threats. We are not faced here with the question of whether a doctor owes a duty to third parties to warn a patient of risks from treatment which may endanger

---

at 424; Graff v. Beard, 858 S.W.2d 918, 919 (Tex. 1993).

10 See, e.g., Van Horn, 970 S.W.2d at 545.

11 Bird, 868 S.W.2d at 769-70 (citing Vineyard v. Kraft, 828 S.W.2d 248, 251 (Tex. App._Houston [14th Dist.] 1992, writ denied); Wilson v. Winsett, 828 S.W.2d 231, 232-33 (Tex. App._Amarillo 1992, writ denied); Fought v. Solce, 821 S.W.2d 218, 220 (Tex. App._Houston [1st Dist.] 1991, writ denied); Dominguez v. Kelly, 786 S.W.2d 749 (Tex. App._El Paso 1990, writ denied)).

12 See Van Horn, 970 S.W.2d at 543; Edinburg Hosp. Auth. v. Trevino, 941 S.W.2d 76, 77-79 (Tex. 1997); Krishnan v. Sepulveda, 916 S.W.2d 478, 482 (Tex. 1995); see also Praesel v. Johnson, 967 S.W.2d 391, 392 (Tex. 1998); Cathey v. Booth, 900 S.W.2d 339, 342 (Tex. 1995).

13 See Van Horn, 970 S.W.2d at 545; Trevino, 941 S.W.2d at 79; Krishnan, 916 S.W.2d at 482; Bird, 868 S.W.2d at 770.

third parties.[14] Instead, we are asked whether a mental-health professional owes a duty to directly warn third parties of a patient's threats.

The California Supreme Court first recognized a mental-health professional's duty to warn third parties of a patient's threats in the seminal case Tarasoff v. Regents of University of California.[15] The court of appeals here cited Tarasoff in recognizing a cause of action for Thapar's failure to warn of her patient's threats.[16] But we have never recognized the only underlying duty upon which such a cause of action could be based -- a mental-health professional's duty to warn third parties of a patient's threats. Without considering the effect of differences in the development of California and Texas jurisprudence on the outcome of this issue, we decline to adopt a duty to warn now because the confidentiality statute governing mental-health professionals in Texas makes it unwise to recognize such common-law duty.

The Legislature has chosen to closely guard a patient's communications with a mental-health professional. In 1979, three years after Tarasoff issued, the Legislature enacted a statute governing the disclosure of communications during the course of mental-health treatment.[17] The statute classifies communications between mental-health "professional[s]" and their "patient[s]/client[s]" as confidential and prohibits mental-health professionals from disclosing them to third parties unless an exception applies.[18]

Zezulka complains that Thapar was negligent in not warning members of the Zezulka family about Lilly's threats. But a disclosure by Thapar to one of the Zezulkas would have violated the confidentiality statute because no exception in the statute provides for disclosure to third parties threatened by the patient.[19] We considered a similar situation in Santa Rosa Health Care Corp. v. Garcia,[20] in which we concluded there is no duty to disclose confidential information

14 See Gooden v. Tips, 651 S.W.2d 364, 365-66 (Tex. App._Tyler 1983, no writ) (holding doctor owed duty to third party to warn patient not to drive after prescribing the drug Quaalude to patient); see also Flynn v. Houston Emergicare, Inc., 869 S.W.2d 403, 405-06 (Tex. App._Houston [1st Dist.] 1994, writ denied) (holding doctor owed no duty to third party to warn patient not to drive after patient was treated for cocaine use because doctor did not create impairment that resulted in injury).

15 551 P.2d 334, 345-47 (Cal. 1976).

16 961 S.W.2d at 511 n.2. The court of appeals also cited four Texas cases that considered whether to adopt a Tarasoff duty but did not. See 916 S.W.2d at 511 n.2 (citing Limon v. Gonzaba, 940 S.W.2d 236, 238-41 (Tex. App._San Antonio 1997, writ denied); Kehler v. Eudaly, 933 S.W.2d 321, 329-32 (Tex. App._Fort Worth 1996, writ denied); Kerrville State Hosp. v. Clark, 900 S.W.2d 425, 435-36 (Tex. App._Austin 1995), rev'd on other grounds, 923 S.W.2d 582 (Tex. 1996);Williams v. Sun Valley Hosp., 723 S.W.2d 783, 785-86 (Tex. App._El Paso 1987, writ ref'd n.r.e.)).

17 See Act of May 9, 1979, 66th Leg., R.S., ch. 239, 1979 Tex. Gen. Laws 512 (amended 1991) (current version at Tex. Health & Safety Code § 611.002 (1996)).

18 See § 2(a), 1979 Tex. Gen. Laws at 513.

19 See § 4, 1979 Tex. Gen. Laws at 514.

20 964 S.W.2d 940, 941 (Tex. 1998) (involving disclosure of HIV test under Tex. Rev. Civ. Stat. art. 4419b-1, § 9.03).

when disclosure would violate the confidentiality statute.[21] The same reasoning applies here. Under the applicable statute, Thapar was prohibited from warning one of his patient's potential victims and therefore had no duty to warn the Zezulka family of Lilly's threats.

Zezulka also complains that Thapar was negligent in not disclosing Lilly's threats to any law enforcement agency. There is an exception in the confidentiality statute that provides for disclosure to law enforcement personnel in certain circumstances.[22] The statute, however, permits these disclosures but does not require them:

(b) Exceptions to the privilege of confidentiality, in other than court proceedings, allowing disclosure of confidential information by a professional, exist only to the following:...

(2) to medical or law enforcement personnel where the professional determines that there is a probability of imminent physical injury by the patient/client to himself or to others, or where there is a probability of immediate mental or emotional injury to the patient/client....[23]

The term "allowing" in section 4(b), quoted above, makes clear that disclosure of confidential information under any of the statute's exceptions is permissive but not mandatory. Imposing a legal duty to warn third parties of patient's threats would conflict with the scheme adopted by the Legislature by making disclosure of such threats mandatory.

We consider legislative enactments that evidence the adoption of a particular public policy significant in determining whether to recognize a new common-law duty.[24] For example, in recognizing the existence of a common-law duty to guard children from sexual abuse, we found persuasive the Legislature's strongly avowed policy to protect children from abuse.[25] The statute expressing this policy, however, makes the reporting of sexual abuse mandatory[26] and makes failure to report child abuse a crime.[27] Further, under the statute, those who report child abuse in good faith are immune from civil and criminal liability.[28]

---

21 Id. at 944.

22 See § 4(b), 1979 Tex. Gen. Laws at 514.

23 See § 4, 1979 Tex. Gen. Laws at 514 (emphasis added). Current Tex. Health & Safety Code § 611.004(a)(2) adopts the same standard: (a) A professional may disclose confidential information only:... (2) to medical or law enforcement personnel if the professional determines that there is a probability of imminent physical injury by the patient to the patient or others or there is a probability of immediate mental or emotional injury to the patient...

24 See Gibbs v. Jackson, ___ S.W.2d ___, ___ (Tex. 1999); Smith v. Merritt, 940 S.W.2d 602, 604-05 (Tex. 1997) (citing Graff, 858 S.W.2d at 919).

25 See Golden Spread Council, Inc. v. Akins, 926 S.W.2d 287, 291 (Tex. 1996).

26 Tex. Fam. Code § 261.101(a) states: "A person having cause to believe that a child's physical or mental health or welfare has been adversely affected by abuse or neglect by any person shall immediately make a report as provided by this subchapter."

27 See Tex. Fam. Code § 261.109.

28 See Tex. Fam. Code § 261.106.

Thus, imposing a common law duty to report was consistent with the legislative scheme governing child abuse.

The same is not true here. The confidentiality statute here does not make disclosure of threats mandatory nor does it penalize mental-health professionals for not disclosing threats. And, perhaps most significantly, the statute does not shield mental-health professionals from civil liability for disclosing threats in good faith. On the contrary, mental-health professionals make disclosures at their peril.[29] Thus, if a common-law duty to warn is imposed, mental-health professionals face a Catch-22. They either disclose a confidential communication that later proves to be an idle threat and incur liability to the patient, or they fail to disclose a confidential communication that later proves to be a truthful threat and incur liability to the victim and the victim's family.

The confidentiality statute here evidences an intent to leave the decision of whether to disclose confidential information in the hands of the mental-health professional. In the past, we have declined to impose a common-law duty to disclose when disclosing confidential information by a physician has been made permissible by statute but not mandatory.[30] We have also declined to impose a common-law duty after determining that such a duty would conflict with the Legislature's policy and enactments concerning the employment-at-will doctrine.[31] Our analysis today is consistent with the approach in those cases.

Because of the Legislature's stated policy, we decline to impose a common law duty on mental-health professionals to warn third parties of their patient's threats. Accordingly, we conclude that Thapar was entitled to summary judgment because she owed no duty to Zezulka, a third-party nonpatient. We reverse the court of appeals' judgment and render judgment that Zezulka take nothing.

---

29 See § 5, 1979 Tex. Gen. Laws at 514.

30 See Praesel, 967 S.W.2d at 396-98.

31 See Austin v. HealthTrust, Inc._The Hosp. Co., 967 S.W.2d 400, 403 (Tex. 1998); see also Winters v. Houston Chronicle Pub. Co., 795 S.W.2d 723, 724-25 (Tex. 1990).

Confidentiality of a Child's Mental Health Records

(Abrams vs. Jones)[1]

This case presents issues of statutory construction. We are called upon to determine if either section 153.072 of the Family Code or section 611.0045 of the Health and Safety Code allows a parent to demand access to detailed notes of his or her child's conversations with a mental health professional when that parent is not acting on behalf of the child or when the mental health professional believes that releasing the information would be harmful to the child's physical, mental, or emotional health. The Legislature has balanced a child's need for effective treatment and a parent's rights and has imposed some limits on a parent's right of access to confidential mental health records. Accordingly, we reverse the judgment of the court of appeals and render judgment that Jones take nothing.

Background

The child whose records are at issue is Karissa Jones. Her parents, Donald and Rosemary Jones, divorced when she was about seven years old. Both parents remarried sometime before the present controversy erupted, and Rosemary Jones is now Rosemary Droxler. In the original decree, Karissa's parents were appointed joint managing conservators of her and her younger sister. Two years after the divorce, her father initiated further court proceedings to become the sole managing conservator of his daughters. Litigation ensued for two more years. Karissa's parents ultimately agreed to a modification of the original order, but both parents were retained as joint managing conservators. The modified decree gave Jones certain rights of access to his children's psychological records.

Several months after the modification proceedings were concluded, Rosemary Droxler sought the professional services of a psychologist, Dr. Laurence Abrams,

1 Abrams vs. Jones, 35 S.W.3d 620 (Tex. 2000)

for Karissa. The uncontroverted evidence is that Karissa, who by this time was eleven years old, was agitated and showed signs of sleeplessness and worry. At the time the trial court heard this case, Abrams had seen Karissa six times for about fifty minutes on each occasion.

At the beginning of Abrams's first consultation with Karissa, she was reluctant to talk to him. When Abrams explored that reluctance with her, she told him that she was concerned that he would relate what she had to say to her parents. Abrams responded that he would have to provide a report to her parents, but that he could give them a general description of what was discussed without all the specifics. Abrams and Karissa reached an understanding about what he would and would not tell her parents, and he was thereafter able to establish a rapport with her.

Shortly after Karissa began seeing Abrams, her father (Jones) and his legal counsel met with Abrams and requested that he release all of her records. Abrams gave Jones and his counsel a verbal summary of information, sharing with them the basic subject matter of his consultations with Karissa. Abrams related that Karissa had told him that Jones's new wife (who formerly was Karissa's nanny) had said to Karissa that when she turned twelve, she would have to choose where she lived. Karissa told Abrams that she was afraid there would be more conflict in court between her parents because of this choice. Abrams described Karissa as in a "panic" when he first saw her over what she believed to be her impending decision and an ensuing battle between her parents. Abrams also told Jones that Karissa had said that she leaned toward choosing to live with her father and that she was at times unhappy living with her mother because her mother was away from home more than Karissa liked.

After Abrams had related this information about his sessions with Karissa, Jones told Abrams that no conversations of the nature Abrams had described had occurred between Jones and Karissa or between Karissa and her stepmother. At some point in the dialogue among Abrams, Jones, and Jones's attorney, Abrams either agreed with Jones's counsel or said in response to a question from counsel that Karissa's mother had taken Karissa to see Abrams "to get a leg up on" Jones in court.

A few days after the meeting among Jones, his counsel, and Abrams, Jones's counsel again pressed for Abrams's records in two letters to Abrams. Abrams responded verbally and in writing that releasing the detailed notes about his conversations with Karissa would not be in her best interest. Abrams offered to give his notes to any other psychologist that Jones might choose to replace Abrams as Karissa's counselor, and Abrams explained that Karissa's new psychologist could then determine whether it was in Karissa's best interest to give Abrams's notes to Jones. Jones did not seek another counselor for Karissa, and Abrams did not release his notes to Jones. Abrams continued to treat Karissa until this suit was filed by Jones to compel Abrams to release his notes. The record is silent as to whether Abrams was to continue treatment after this suit was resolved.

Droxler, Karissa's mother, entered an appearance in the suit against Abrams, and she agreed with Abrams that neither parent should have access to his notes of conversations with Karissa. A hearing was held before the trial court. Abrams testified that a sense of protection and closeness is an integral part of psychotherapy and that without some expectation of confidentiality, Karissa would not have opened up to him. He said that Karissa had several discussions with him about the confidentiality of their sessions. Abrams testified that in his opinion the release to either parent of his detailed notes of what Karissa had said was not in her best interest.

Jones took the position in the trial court that as a parent, he was unconditionally entitled to see all of Abrams's records regarding his daughter. He further represented to the trial court that based on his conversations with Karissa, he was of the opinion that she did not object to the release of her records. Abrams testified, however, that Karissa had asked him not to reveal the details of their conversations, and that during the week before the hearing, her mother delivered a note which Karissa had written to Abrams again asking that he maintain the confidentiality of their discussions.

Abrams's detailed notes about what Karissa had told him during his professional consultations with her were provided to the trial court. The court, however, stated on the record at the conclusion of the hearing that it had not reviewed them and did not intend to. There is no indication that it ever did so.

The trial court held that Jones was entitled to Abrams's notes. Abrams appealed, and Karissa's mother (Droxler) filed briefing in the court of appeals in support of Abrams's position. The court of appeals affirmed the trial court's judgment with one justice dissenting. Abrams v. Jones, 983 S.W.2d 377 (Tex. App.-Houston [14th Dist.] 1999). We granted Abrams's petition for review, which was supported by Karissa's mother.

There are three questions of statutory construction that we must decide. They are (1) whether section 153.073 of the Family Code gives a divorced parent greater rights of access to mental health records than parents in general have under chapter 611 of the Texas Health and Safety Code, (2) whether section 611.0045(b) of the Health and Safety Code allows a professional to deny a parent access to portions of mental health records if the professional concludes that their release would harm the child, and (3) whether a parent is always deemed to be acting on behalf of his or her child when requesting mental health records.

Rights of Divorced Parents for Access to Records

Do divorced parents have greater rights of access to records than parents in general? As indicated above, the first question that we must resolve is whether section 153.073 of the Family Code or chapter 611 of the Health and Safety Code governs this matter. TEX. FAM. CODE § 153.073; TEX. HEALTH & SAFETY CODE §§611.001 to 611.008. We conclude that chapter 611 provides the framework within which this case must be decided.

Section 153.073 of the Family Code addresses parental rights upon dissolution of the parents' marriage to one another. It provides that unless a court orders otherwise, a parent who is appointed a conservator "has at all times the right... as specified by court order... of access to medical, dental, psychological, and educational records of the child." TEX. FAM. CODE §153.073(a)(2). Jones contends that this section of the Family Code mandates that a parent who is appointed a conservator has access at all times to all psychological records of the child. We disagree.

We interpret section 153.073 to ensure that a court may grant a parent who is divorced and who has been named a conservator the same rights of access to his or her child's psychological records as a parent who is not divorced. We do not interpret section 153.073 to override the provisions of chapter 611 of the Health and Safety Code that specifically address parents' rights to the mental health records of their children. The legislative history of section 153.073 indicates that it was enacted to equalize the rights of nonmanaging-conservator parents in comparison to managing-conservator parents. See HOUSE COMM. ON JUDICIAL AFFAIRS, BILL ANALYSIS, Tex. H.B. 1630, 73d Leg., R.S. (1993) (explaining that this provision was needed to remedy (1) previous limitations on nonmanaging conservators during periods of possession, when the child might need health care, and (2) the fact that managing conservators were not required to consult with the other parent about important decisions affecting the child's health, education, or welfare). The Legislature did not intend in section 153.073 to give greater rights to divorced parents than to parents who are not divorced. We turn to chapter 611 of the Health and Safety Code.

Denying Parental Access to Records

Can a professional deny parents access to a child's mental health records if such access is harmful? The Legislature has determined that a patient's right of access to his or her own mental health records is not absolute. Section 611.0045 of the Health and Safety Code says that a "professional may deny access to any portion of a record if the professional determines that release of that portion would be harmful to the patient's physical, mental, or emotional health." TEX. HEALTH & SAFETY CODE § 611.0045(b).

There are, however, checks and balances on a professional's decision not to disclose portions of a mental health record to a patient. A patient may select another professional for treatment of the same or related condition, and the professional denying access must allow the newly retained professional to examine and copy the records that have not been released to the patient. Id. § 611.0045(e). The newly retained professional may then decide whether to release the records to the patient.

There are provisions in chapter 611 of the Health and Safety Code that deal specifically with the mental health records of a minor. Section 611.0045(f) provides that the "content of a confidential record shall be made available to a [parent] who is acting on the patient's behalf." Id. § 611.0045(f). n1 Jones contends that a parent necessarily acts on behalf of his or her child when seeking access to a child's mental health records under section 611.0045(f). The court of appeals agreed. It held that "by requesting that Abrams turn over Karissa's mental health records, Jones was necessarily 'acting on behalf' of Karissa as contemplated by section 611.0045(f) of the Code." Abrams v. Jones, 983 S.W.2d 377, 381 (Tex. App.-Houston [14th Dist.] 1999).

In construing a statute, we must attempt to give effect to every word and phrase if it is reasonable to do so. See City of Amarillo v. Martin, 971 S.W.2d 426, 430 (Tex. 1998); see also TEX. GOV'T CODE § 311.021(2) (stating that in enacting a statute, it is presumed that the entire statute is intended to be effective). If the Legislature had intended for a parent to have access to all aspects of a child's mental health records by simply proving that he or she is indeed the child's parent, the Legislature would not have needed to add the phrase "who is acting on the patient's behalf" in section 611.0045(f).

We agree with the dissent in the court of appeals that, unfortunately, parents cannot always be deemed to be acting on the child's behalf. See Abrams, 983 S.W.2d at 382 (Edelman, J., dissenting). An obvious example is when a parent has sexually molested a child and later demands access to the child's mental health treatment records. A court would not presume that the parent is acting on the child's behalf in such circumstances. Similarly, parents embroiled in a divorce or other suit affecting the parent/child relationship may have motives of their own for seeking the mental health records of the child and may not be acting "on the patient's [child's] behalf." TEX. HEALTH & SAFETY CODE § 611.0045(f). We therefore conclude that a mental health professional is not required to provide access to a child's confidential records if a parent who requests them is not acting "on behalf of" the child.

Request for Records and "Acting on Behalf of the Child"

Is a parent always deemed to be acting on behalf of his or her child when requesting mental health records? When a parent is acting on behalf of his or her child, the question that then arises is whether, under section 611.0045(b), a professional may nevertheless deny access to a portion of a child's records if their release would be harmful to the patient's physical, mental, or emotional health. TEX. HEALTH & SAFETY CODE § 611.0045(b). Jones contends that subsection (b) only applies when "the patient" seeks his or her own records and not when a parent seeks a child's records. We disagree.

Section 611.0045(f) contemplates that when a parent seeks a child's mental health records "on the patient's behalf," the parent steps into the shoes of the patient. Id. § 611.0045(f). Subsection (f) affords third parties, including a parent, no greater rights than those of the patient. This is evident when section 611.0045(f) is considered in its entirety. It applies not only to parents, but to "a person who has the written consent of the patient." Id. §§ 611.004(a)(4), 611.0045(f). It would be unreasonable to construe subsection (f) to allow a patient to obtain through a third person a record that a mental health professional has determined under subsection (b) would be harmful if released to the patient. Because subsection (b) may limit a patient's rights to his or her own records, subsection (b) can also limit a parent's or third party's right to a patient's records when the third party or parent stands in the patient's stead.

In construing a statute or code provision, a court may consider, among other matters, the (1) object sought to be attained by the statute, (2) circumstances under which the statute was enacted, (3) legislative history, (4) consequences of a particular construction, and (5) laws on similar subjects. See Tex. Gov't Code § 311.023. This Court has recently recognized that, through Chapter 611, "the Legislature has chosen to closely guard a patient's communications with a mental-health professional." Thapar v. Zezulka, 994 S.W.2d 635, 638 (Tex. 1999). One purpose of confidentiality is to ensure that individuals receive therapy when they need it. See R.K. v. Ramirez, 887 S.W.2d 836, 840 (Tex. 1994) (describing the purposes of the physician-patient privilege under the Texas Rules of Evidence). Although a parent's responsibilities with respect to his or her child necessitate access to information about the child, if the absence of confidentiality prevents communications between a therapist and the patient because the patient fears that such communications may be revealed to their detriment, neither the purposes of confidentiality nor the needs of the parent are served.

If a professional does deny a parent access to part of a child's records, the parent has recourse under section 611.0045(e).Tex. Health & Safety Code §611.0045(e). First, the professional denying access must allow examination and copying of the record by another professional selected by the parent acting on behalf of the patient to treat the patient for the same or a related condition. Id. Second, a parent denied access to a child's records has judicial recourse. See id. § 611.005(a). We therefore conclude that the court of appeals erred in construing sections 611.0045(b) and (f) of the Health and Safety Code as giving a parent totally unfettered access to a child's mental health records irrespective of the child's circumstances or the parent's motivation.

We turn to the facts of this case and the interplay between section 611.045 and section 611.005 of the Health and Safety Code, which provides a remedy to a parent if a child's mental health records have been improperly withheld.

Recourse When a Child's Records Improperly Withheld

What recourse is there for a parent when a child's mental health records have been improperly withheld? As already indicated above, a person who is aggrieved by a professional's improper "failure to disclose confidential communications or records" may petition a district court for appropriate relief. Tex. Health & Safety Code §611.005(a). A professional who denies access has "the burden of proving that the denial was proper." Id. § 611.005(b). Accordingly, Abrams bore the burden of proving in these proceedings that he properly denied access to his notes about his conversations with Karissa.

The trial court ruled against Abrams. Abrams did not request and the trial court did not make any findings of fact or conclusions of law. But because the reporter's record is part of the record on appeal, the legal sufficiency of the trial court's implied finding in support of the judgment, which was that Abrams failed to meet his burden of proof, may be challenged in the same manner as jury findings. See Roberson v. Robinson, 768 S.W.2d 280, 281 (Tex. 1989). We must examine the entire record to determine whether Abrams established as a matter of law that his denial of access was proper either because Abrams established that (1) Jones was not acting on Karissa's behalf, or (2) access to the notes would be harmful to Karissa's mental or emotional health.

Jones never indicated that he was seeking the notes on behalf of Karissa, as distinguished from his own behalf. At the hearing, Jones testified that his motivation for obtaining Abrams's notes was in part the indication that Karissa's mother had hired Abrams "to get a leg up on me in court." Although this is some evidence that Jones was not acting on behalf of Karissa but was acting in his own interest, it is not conclusive. Jones's testimony that he was "partially" motivated by what he perceived to be his former wife's custody tactics indicated that there were additional reasons for seeking Karissa's records. Abrams did not prove conclusively that Jones was not acting on behalf of Karissa.

But even if Jones were acting on behalf of Karissa, Abrams testified that in his professional opinion it would be harmful to her to release his notes detailing their conversations. When Abrams first saw Karissa, she would not talk to him. He was unable to establish a rapport with her until they discussed confidentiality. Abrams asked her "what it would take to get her to talk," and he explained at the hearing that "it came down to, she needed protection.... She needed protection against anyone knowing what she said. She simply couldn't talk if there was a chance either parent would know what she said." Abrams made the decision during the first session with Karissa not to give his notes to either of her parents. He testified, "I had to in order to be able to treat the girl." He told Karissa at that session that he would not disclose his notes to her parents unless required to do so by a court. Karissa thereafter opened up to Abrams. Abrams explained at the hearing that an integral part of psychotherapy is that the patient have a sense of protection and security and that she drop defensive mechanisms. Abrams continued to treat Karissa after he had denied her father access to the notes, and she responded positively to treatment after Abrams assured her that the details of her conversations would be confidential. Treatment continued until this suit was filed. None of this testimony was contradicted or even challenged. See Allright, Inc. v. Strawder, 679 S.W.2d 81, 82 (Tex. App.-Houston [14 Dist.] 1984, writ ref'd n.r.e.) (observing that "uncontroverted testimony, even from a witness categorized as an expert, may be taken as true as a matter of law if it is clear, direct and positive, and is free from contradictions, inconsistencies, inaccuracies and circumstances tending to cast suspicion thereon"). This testimony, in the absence of contrary evidence, is sufficient to establish as a matter of law that release of Karissa's records would have been harmful to her.

Jones's testimony that in his opinion, Karissa did not object to the release of Abrams's notes does not raise a fact question of whether their release would be harmful to her. Karissa was a layperson—an eleven-year-old layperson. She was not qualified to make a determination of whether release of her records would be harmful to her physical, mental, or emotional health. See TEX. HEALTH

& SAFETY CODE § 611.0045(b). The uncontradicted evidence established as a matter of law that Abrams's denial of access to his detailed notes was proper.

Conclusion and Dissenting Opinions

The trial court erred in holding that Jones was entitled to the detailed notes about his daughter's conversations with her mental health professional under the facts of this case. Accordingly, we reverse the judgment of the court of appeals and render judgment that Jones take nothing.

—Priscilla R. Owen, Justice

***DISSENT: JUSTICE BAKER*, dissenting.**

I believe that the court of appeals majority correctly construed the statutory scheme and properly applied the law to the facts to reach the result it reached. Accordingly, I respectfully dissent from the Court's decision in this case.

—James A. Baker, Justice

***JUSTICE HECHT*, dissenting.**

In this Term's decisions construing the Parental Notification Act,[2] the Court has exhibited a disturbing lack of regard for the rights of parents to raise and care for their children;[3] This case continues in that vein, holding that under chapter 611 of the Texas Health and Safety Code, mental health care professionals — who, as defined by statute,[4] include everyone from physicians to pretenders — have broad discretion to deny parents access to their children's mental health records, broader discretion than even a district judge has to order disclosure. As eager as the Court has been to find justification for allowing a child to have an abortion without telling her parents, contrary to a trial court's view of the evidence, it will come as no surprise that the Court has no difficulty keeping parents ignorant of their children's mental health records, contrary to the trial court's conclusion. As in the parental notification cases, the Court casts responsibility for its decision in this case on the Legislature. But this steady erosion of parental authority is judicial, not legislative; it results from the Court's view of statutory language through a prism of presumed diminution in parental authority. I respectfully dissent.

It should go without saying that parents generally need to know information contained in their children's health records in order to make decisions for their well-being. To remove any doubt that this is true, even after divorce, for any

---

2 TEX. FAM. CODE §§ 33.001-.011.

3 In re Doe 1(I), 19 S.W.3d 249, 2000 Tex. LEXIS 21 (Tex. 2000); In re Doe 2, 19 S.W.3d 278, 2000 Tex. LEXIS 25 (Tex. 2000); In re Doe 3, 19 S.W.3d 300, 2000 Tex. LEXIS 26 (Tex. 2000); In re Doe 4(I), 19 S.W.3d 322, 2000 Tex. LEXIS 27 (Tex. 2000); In re Doe 4(II), 19 S.W.3d 337, 2000 Tex. LEXIS 34 (Tex. 2000); In re Doe 1(II), 19 S.W.3d 346, 2000 Tex. LEXIS 67 (Tex. 2000).

4 TEX. HEALTH & SAFETY CODE § 611.001(2) ("'Professional' means: (A) a person authorized to practice medicine in any state or nation; (B) a person licensed or certified by this state to diagnose, evaluate, or treat any mental or emotional condition or disorder; or (C) a person the patient reasonably believes is authorized, licensed, or certified as provided by this subsection.").

parent with custodial responsibility for a child, section 153.073(a)(2) of the Texas Family Code states that "unless limited by court order, a parent appointed as a conservator of a child has at all times the right... of access to medical, dental, psychological, and educational records of the child...." A parent's right to this information is not an insignificant matter and should not be restricted absent compelling reasons.

Section 611.0045 of the Texas Health and Safety Code, the pertinent parts of which are quoted in the margin,[5] permits a mental health care "professional", broadly defined as stated above, to deny a patient access to his own mental health records if disclosure would harm the patient's physical, mental, or emotional health. For the same reason, access may be denied to a patient's representative, including a parent if the patient is a child.[6] In a suit to obtain the records, the professional has the burden of proving that denial of access is proper.[7] Nothing in the statute suggests that this burden should be anything but substantial. Certainly, a patient should not be denied access to his own mental health records absent solid, credible evidence that disclosure will cause him real, demonstrable harm. A general concern that disclosure to the patient would not be in his best interest should not be enough to deny him access. The statute sets no different harm standard for denying a parent access to a child's records. Denial of access

5 Section 611.0045. Right to Mental Health Record: (a) Except as otherwise provided by this section, a patient is entitled to have access to the content of a confidential record made about the patient; (b) The professional may deny access to any portion of a record if the professional determines that release of that portion would be harmful to the patient's physical, mental, or emotional health; (c) If the professional denies access to any portion of a record, the professional shall give the patient a signed and dated written statement that having access to the record would be harmful to the patient's physical, mental, or emotional health and shall include a copy of the written statement in the patient's records. The statement must specify the portion of the record to which access is denied, the reason for denial, and the duration of the denial; (d) The professional who denies access to a portion of a record under this section shall redetermine the necessity for the denial at each time a request for the denied portion is made. If the professional again denies access, the professional shall notify the patient of the denial and document the denial as prescribed by Subsection (c); (e) If a professional denies access to a portion of a confidential record, the professional shall allow examination and copying of the record by another professional if the patient selects the professional to treat the patient for the same or a related condition as the professional denying access; (f) The content of a confidential record shall be made available to a person listed by Section 611.004(a)(4) or (5) who is acting on the patient's behalf; (h) If a summary or narrative of a confidential record is requested by the patient or other person requesting release under this section, the professional shall prepare the summary or narrative.

6 The persons referred to in section 611.0045(f) who can act on behalf of a patient are "a person who has the written consent of the patient, or a parent if the patient is a minor, or a guardian if the patient has been adjudicated as incompetent to manage the patient's personal affairs", id. §611.004(a)(4), or "the patient's personal representative if the patient is deceased", id. §611.004(a)(5).

7 Id. § 611.005(b) ("In a suit contesting the denial of access under Section 611.0045, the burden of proving that the denial was proper is on the professional who denied the access.").

cannot be based on some general concern that the child may be displeased or discomfited, even severely, about the disclosure. Rather, denial must be grounded on evidence of actual impairment to the child's health.

As the parental notification cases recently demonstrate, the meaning the Court gives a statutory standard is best demonstrated not by the words used to describe it but by its application in specific circumstances. This case illustrates how little evidence the Court believes is necessary not simply to raise the issue of whether a parent should be denied a child's mental health records but to conclusively establish -- so that no court can rule otherwise -- that a parent is not entitled to the records. The Court's decision to deny access to the records in this case rests entirely on the testimony of Abrams, a licensed clinical psychologist, who stated at a hearing in the district court: that Jones's former wife brought their eleven-year-old daughter, Karissa, to him in February 1996 because Karissa was agitated and showed signs of worry and sleeplessness; that Karissa refused to open up to him until he promised her that he would not reveal the details of their conversations to her parents, even though she understood that a judge might later order disclosure; that Karissa then told him she was troubled that if when she turned twelve in October she had to express a preference for living with one parent or the other, as her stepmother (her former nanny) had suggested she might,[8] it would provoke more hostility between her parents; that after meeting with Karissa six times in five months, she seemed much better; that Karissa had reiterated her desire for confidentiality in their last meeting four months earlier in June 1996, and in a note her mother had brought to him a few days before the October 15 hearing; and that he had told Karissa's father, Jones, that his former wife had hired him to "get a leg up on" Jones in their continuing court proceedings. On the specific issue of whether disclosing Karissa's records to Jones would harm Karissa's health, Abrams's testimony in its entirety is as follows:

Q: Is it your opinion at this time that the release of those records would be physically or emotionally harmful to Karissa?

A: Yes, sir.

Q: And what is that opinion?

A: That would have harmed her, as a matter of fact. It would be the very essence, it would make her get better, to give her protection.

Q: As we sit here on October 15th of 1996, is it still your opinion

8 Cf. TEX. FAM. CODE § 153.134(a)(6) ("If a written agreement of the parents is not filed with the court, the court may render an order appointing the parents joint managing conservators only if the appointment is in the best interest of the child, considering the following factors:... (6) if the child is 12 years of age or older, the child's preference, if any, regarding the appointment of joint managing conservators...."); id. § 153.008 ("If the child is 10 years of age or older, the child may, by writing filed with the court, choose the managing conservator, subject to the approval of the court."); id. § 153.009(b) ("When the issue of managing conservatorship is contested, on the application of a party, the court shall interview a child 10 years of age or older and may interview a child under 10 years of age.").

that it would be harmful to her mental or emotional health if these records are released?

A: Yes, sir.

Q: And can you tell the Judge why you believe that?

A: I've had no communications from her to be otherwise. I asked her the last time I saw her, in June about it, she reaffirmed her need for it. I received a note from her last week asking for it again.

The Court holds that this testimony, which did not persuade the district judge, conclusively established that Karissa's health would be harmed by disclosing her records to her father. The Court not only denies the trial court any meaningful role in determining credibility and weighing evidence, it reaches a conclusion, as a matter of law, on evidence that is inconclusive. Assuming that Abrams's testimony established that Karissa's health would have been harmed in February 1996 if he could not have promised her a measure of confidentiality because she would not have opened up to him and he could not have counseled her, the only evidence that disclosure of the records would harm Karissa's health in October 1996, when Abrams was no longer seeing her, was that she continued to request confidentiality. Jones disputed whether Karissa still wanted Abrams's records kept from him, testifying that based on his conversations with his daughter, his opinion was that she wanted him to have the records.

The Court concludes that Jones's testimony is no evidence that disclosure would not harm Karissa because an eleven-year-old is not qualified to say what would be harmful to her health. But if that is true, as I agree it is, then Abrams's testimony that Karissa continued to request confidentiality must likewise be disregarded. Karissa is no more qualified to say that disclosure of her records to her father would harm her health than that it would not. If Abrams's opinion cannot be based on Karissa's wishes, then it has no basis at all. Asked why he believed that disclosure would harm Karissa's health, Abrams answered, "I've had no communications from her to be otherwise."

Surely the Court does not think that a need for confidentiality at one point in time precludes disclosure of information forever. Nothing in the evidence before us suggests that Abrams would ever see Karissa again. Her twelfth birthday was three days after the hearing, and her anxieties about any choices she would have to make at that point were soon to be resolved one way or the other. No reason that Abrams gave for denying Jones access to his daughter's records remained valid. Had the trial judge found from this evidence that there might yet be some lingering need for nondisclosure, I could understand this Court's deference to that finding. But I do not understand how this Court can conclude that no reasonable trial judge could find from this evidence that Karissa's health would not be harmed by allowing her father access to her records.

It is no answer to say, as the Court seems to, that section 611.0045 allows a parent to take a child to other professionals until one is found who will release the records. True, Jones could simply have taken his daughter to one professional or another until he found one willing to turn over her records, and the statute gives Abrams no way to object. But the statute is not a full-employment guarantee for mental health care professionals, and no parent should be forced to shop a child as a patient merely to obtain the child's records. More importantly, I see no justification for applying section 611.0045 to permit one professional to trump another, regardless of their relative qualifications, and yet let any professional trump a district judge.

The Court's determination to restrict parental access to mental health records despite and not because of the statute is further demonstrated by its conclusion that section 611.0045 authorizes nondisclosure not only when the child's health may be harmed but when a parent is not "acting on the patient's behalf" as provided in subsection (f) of the statute. These words cannot, in my view, be sensibly read to create a separate standard for access to records. One might think that a parent could easily meet such a standard by stating that his or her request for a child's records was motivated out of love and concern for the child, but the Court concludes that evidence that parents are hostile to one another is enough by itself to support an inference that they are selfishly motivated and therefore not acting on their child's behalf.

The evidence the Court points to in this case is especially problematic. Abrams told Jones — Jones did not merely have his suspicions — that he believed he had been hired by Karissa's mother to counsel Karissa in order to give the mother "a leg up" in her ongoing disputes with Jones over custody of Karissa and her sister. The Court is troubled by Jones's frank admission in the October hearing that Abrams's statement to him was part of his motivation for obtaining Karissa's records, even though it could not have been important to Jones when he first went to meet with Abrams the preceding February — which was before Abrams had expressed the view that he himself was being used by Karissa's mother. It is difficult to imagine any reasonable, candid parent who would not acknowledge a similar motivation under the circumstances; indeed, one might have been less inclined to believe Jones if he had denied any such motivation. To rest denial of access to a child's medical records merely on inferences drawn from disputes between the parents conflicts with their rights under section 153.073(a)(2) of the Texas Family Code.

By construing section 611.0045 as establishing an acting-on-behalf-of standard for gaining access to a child's mental health records, the Court requires inquiry into, and inevitable disputes over, a parent's subjective motivations, instead of focusing on the more objective harm-to-the-patient's-health standard. I do not read section 611.0045 to require such an inquiry, which will almost always exacerbate difficulties between divorced parents.

While Abrams appears to have been professional in his dealings with the parties, and the district court did not suggest the contrary, the court was not bound by Abrams's views. Today's decision, coming as it does four years after the events at issue, cannot be of much importance to these parties. Karissa will soon be sixteen. Its importance lies in the difficulties it will cause future parties and in its further deterioration of parents' rights to raise their children.

—Justice Hecht

HIPAA

Texas Law and the Federal Health Insurance Portability and Accountability Act

The Health Insurance Portability and Accountability Act (HIPAA) was signed into law in 1996 as a surviving vestige of the Clinton Administration effort to overhaul the health care system. HIPAA was intended to create a more cost efficient health care system by facilitating electronic communication of health information among health care providers, health plans (including employer-sponsored group plans, Medicaid, Medicare, etc.), health care clearinghouses, and a variety of business associates that are indirectly involved in the health care enterprise (accountants, billing services, attorney's, etc.). In order to encourage the use of electronic transmission of health care information, Congress approved the bill, acknowledged that patient privacy would be of paramount concern in the electronic era of health care, and shifted responsibility to the Department of Health and Human Services (HSS) for promulgating certain rules for protecting privacy and to assume ultimate regulatory authority for enforcement. HIPAA became effective in 2001, though compliance implementation did not begin until two years later.

As of this writing, actual enforcement of HIPAA in regards to an individual health care provider practice has been limited to one case involving Medicare fraud by a non-psychologist. It seems reasonable, on the short term, to assume HHS will likely engage in more educative rather than legal intervention with individual practitioners, with the exception of those cases involving egregious crimes or serious fraudulent events. Further, it is more likely that HHS will devote its policing activity to larger health care entities, such as insurance companies and managed care companies, where protected health care information may be compromised on a large scale. For the independent psychologist or small group practice, HIPAA will serve as the "standard of practice" in civil court actions initiated against service providers by disgruntled patients. Nevertheless, it is worth noting that violation of HIPAA carries civil penalties of not more than

$100 for each violation, not to exceed $25,000 in a calendar year, fines of up to $250,000, and imprisonment for up to 10 years, or both.

There are three basic HIPAA rules germane to the typical Texas social worker engaged in health care practice: the Privacy, Transaction, and Security Rules. Please note that HIPAA is not intended to address forensic or other forms of non-health service related psychological records or communications. Briefly, the HIPAA Privacy Rule describes in some considerable detail when and to whom individually identifiable health information can be disclosed. The electronic transmission of protected health information (PHI) triggers the Privacy Rule and requires that the psychologist's entire health care practice be in compliance with HIPAA regulations. Therefore, a clinician may not segment or segregate certain patient files as being non-HIPAA compliant simply because there has been no electronic transmission of patient health care information.

There is little about the Privacy Rule that has dramatically changed the practice of social work in Texas. With patient confidentiality serving as a cornerstone to the profession and firmly underscored in the APA and NASW ethics codes, Texas law, and Texas licensure regulations, most social workers are practicing well above the minimum standards established by the HIPAA Privacy Rule. One important provision of the Privacy Rule that has been of considerable importance and assistance to social workers and their clients has been the federal mandate limiting the information that third party payers may require for payment of services. Specifically, the release of psychotherapy process notes may not be demanded as a condition for payment of services. However, clinicians are cautioned that a court ordered subpoena will likely open these records for review in a court of law and that patient access to their personal health care records was one of the specific aims of HIPAA. We strongly suggest adherence to the standards for record keeping outlined by theAmerican Psychological Association and the National Association of Social Workers. It is also important to note that HIPAA specifies that health care records be preserved for a period of six years, however, for psychological records Texas law specifies ten years, and for another ten years past age of majority for health care records for minors. As HIPAA was intended to establish a minimal floor for protected patient information, the federal act specifically indicates that when the various health care entities, including practitioners, determine a conflict or inconsistency exists between this federal law and state statue, adherence to the "higher standard" should be followed. In the case of maintenance of patient records, Texas law prevails.

The Transaction Rule with a compliance date of October 16, 2003, addresses more technical aspects of the electronic health care transaction process and requires the use of standardized formats relevant to health care claims when sent electronically. There appears to be two primary aspects of this HIPAA rule impacting clinical practice. First, HIPAA specifies use of a standard diagnostic code set, the IDC of Diseases, 9th edition (ICD-9 CM) Vol. 1 & 2. Hence, social workers may have to use a billing service or clearinghouse to convert DSM codes to ICD codes. Second, as part of the transaction standards, the Current

Procedural Terminology (CPT) must be used but will not otherwise require a conversion. Currently, there is no regulatory address of these "transaction" issues in Texas law.

The HIPAA Security Rule was the last of the three primary rules to be finalized, largely because it is the most complex due to the constantly changing world of technology. The reader should note that compliance with the HIPAA Privacy and Transaction Rules *does not* ensure compliance with the HIPAA Security Rule. The Security Rule requires assurance that confidential electronic patient health information (EPHI) is kept secure from inappropriate or incidental disclosure. The rule addresses administrative, physical, and technical procedures and processes regarding office space, files (hardcopy and electronic), computers and other electronic gadgetry (PDA'S , cell phones, electronic tablets). Compliance with the Security Rule requires a process called a "risk analysis." This risk analysis is painstaking, will likely involve at least several hours of time to complete by the typical private practitioner, and must be thoroughly documented. Essentially, a risk analysis requires psychologists to determine the physical, procedural, and administrative security risks inherent in their maintenance and communication of protected health information. We anticipate that the HIPAA Security Rule will effectively define the minimally acceptable standards of practice in this regard.

Finally, it is also important to underscore that the HIPAA Privacy, Transaction and Security Rules do not require social workers to use electronic means for the communication of health care information, including billing. Indeed, some clinicians have made effort to arrange an electronic–free practice in order to dodge HIPAA regulatory authority. Unfortunately for these technologically defiant clinicians, they may soon find that most third party payers will require them to submit billings electronically. As well, as discussed earlier, the HIPAA security rule will likely define the appropriate standard of care regarding the protection of patient records, whether or not they are stored or communicated electronically. Social workers are encouraged to become more familiar with these HIPAA rules with understanding that HIPAA may at least set standards for the security and accessibility of patient records.

Much of the material presented here was derived directly from materials provided by the American Psychological Association's Practice Directorate and the National Association of Social Workers. A more thorough description of HIPAA rules and its implications for clinical practice, as well as helpful web-based products designed to facilitate compliance with HIPAA, may be found at *http://www.apapractice.org* and at *http://www.socialworkers.org*.

OPINIONS FROM THE ATTORNEY GENERAL

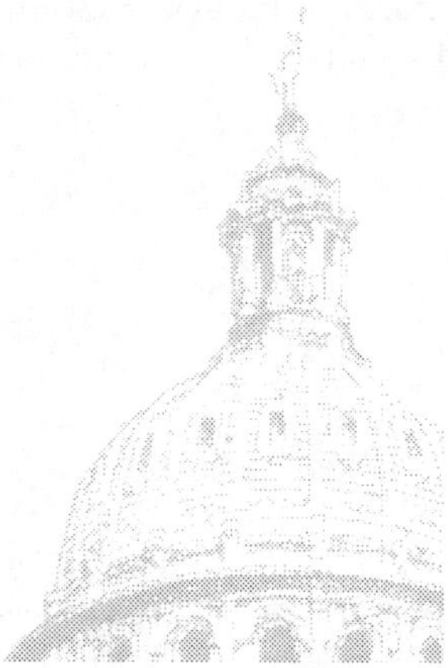

Attorney General Opinion Letters and Open Record Opinions

This section contains selected letters from the archive of Attorney General Opinions and Open Records Opinions that are relevant to the practice of social work. These opinions are relatively difficult to research because of the way they are indexed on the website of the Texas Attorney General. We hope that this archive will assist practitioners who have questions related to these decisions, such as whether there is a conflict of interest when agency employees provide services to the general public outside of departmental work hours (LO 90-043), whether social workers can be relicensed without examination (JC-0049), or whether the Texas Department of Human Resources may prohibit workers from performing court ordered social studies on their own time (JM-188)

Services Outside of Agency—Conflict of Interest?

OFFICE OF THE ATTORNEY GENERAL

STATE OF TEXAS

JIM MATTOX
ATTORNEY GENERAL

July 11, 1990

Mr. Ron Lindsey
Commissioner
Department of Human Services
P.O. Box 149030
Austin, Texas 78714-9030

Letter Opinion No. 90-043

Re: Possible conflict of interest when agency employees provide services to the general public outside of departmental work hours.

Dear Mr. Lindsey:

You express concern that conflicts of interest may exist when employees of the Department of Human Services (the department) provide counseling services to the general public outside of their department work hours. You ask whether the department "could adopt a personnel policy prohibiting its employees from engaging in social work counseling activities with the general public in a private capacity." If not, you ask if the department could prohibit such activity for employees who provide counseling services for the department?

An administrative agency "may only exercise those powers granted by statute, together with those necessarily implied from the statutory authority conferred or duties imposed." *City of Sherman v. Public Util. Comm'n*, 643 S.W.2d 681, 686 (Tex.1983). The department may establish "reasonable personnel policies for which there is an adequate showing of need" pursuant to its implied statutory authority. Attorney General Opinion JM-188 (1984), at 2; accord Attorney General Opinion JM-93 (1983), at 2. *See also Bishop v. Wood*, 426 U.S. 341 (1976); *Perry v. Sindermann*, 408 U.S. 593 (1972); *Schware v. Bd. of Bar Examiners*, 353 U.S. 232 (1957) (right to work may be curtailed for legitimate state interest).

In Attorney General Opinion JM-188, this office upheld the validity of a rule adopted by your agency that prohibited child protective service workers from performing court-ordered social studies on their own time, because such activity "would compete with the department for court appointments and revenue under [certain specified] sections of the Family Code or would ... have other adverse affects on the department." *Id.* In contrast, Attorney General Opinion H-1317

(1978) determined that a department rule prohibiting all departmental personnel from being licensed as real estate brokers or salesmen was overbroad.

You have not suggested any basis for prohibiting department employees, regardless of their job classification or duties, from conducting counseling services on their own time. Nor have you offered any basis to support a rule prohibiting department counselors from performing private counseling services. Absent a showing that the prohibitions are reasonably related to some interest of the department, the department may not adopt the suggested prohibitions.

SUMMARY

In summary, the Department of Human Services may not prohibit employees, regardless of their job classification or duties, from conducting counseling services on their own time unless it can show that there would be an adverse affect on the department.

Very truly yours,

Karen C. Gladney
Assistant Attorney General
Opinion Committee

APPROVED

Rick Gilpin, Chairman
Opinion Committee

Sarah Woelk, Chief
Letter Opinion Section

Relicensure without Examination

OFFICE OF THE ATTORNEY GENERAL - STATE OF TEXAS

JOHN CORNYN

May 17, 1999

Ms. Deborah Hammond, LMSW-ACP
Chair, Texas State Board
of Social Worker Examiners
1100 West 49th Street
Austin, Texas 78756-3183

Opinion No. JC-0049

Re: *Whether section 50.023(e) of the Human Resources Code permits a person originally licensed without an examination, whose license has expired for more than a year, to reapply for a new license without an examination (RQ-1172)*

Dear Ms. Hammond

You ask about the licensing of a person as a social worker by the Texas State Board of Social Worker Examiners under section 50.023(e) of the Human Resources Code. Specifically, you ask whether section 50.023(e) permits a person originally licensed without an examination, whose license has expired for more than a year, to reapply for a new license without an examination. Because the plain language of the statute so provides, we conclude in the affirmative. Accordingly, we also conclude that the Board's rule on reapplication, to the extent it requires an applicant originally licensed without an examination to take an examination, is invalid.

You advise us of the following facts giving rise to your question. On April 24, 1998, an individual whose license expired more than fourteen years ago reapplied for a license contending that she is eligible to be licensed without an examination. You tell us this individual was originally certified[1] on August 31, 1983, under a "grandfather" provision which allowed her to be certified without taking an examination.[2] She did not renew the annual certification which

1 Prior to 1993, social workers were "certified" rather than "licensed." *See* Act of May 25, 1993, 73d Leg., R.S., ch. 605, §§ 1, 12, 1993 Tex. Gen. Laws 2277, 2285.

2 Prior to 1993, *qualified persons could be granted social worker certification without examination. See* Act of June 1, 1981, 67th Leg., R.S., ch. 776, § 1, 1981 Tex. Gen. Laws 2923, 2928 (authorizing certifications of persons meeting educational and other requirements of Act without examination until August 31, 1982), *amended by* Act of May 2, 1983, 68th Leg., R.S., ch. 87, § 8, 1983 Tex. Gen. Laws 417, 424 (authorizing certification without examination of persons meeting requirements of Act until December 31, 1985, and Act's work experience requirements after December 31, 1985) (eff. Sept. 1, 1983), *amended by* Act of May 25, 1993, 73d

expired on September 30, 1984. The applicant's request for licensing without an examination has prompted the Texas State Board of Social Worker Examiners in turn to request an opinion from this office as to whether section 50.023(e) of the Human Resources Code permits this.

The Texas Professional Social Work Act, sections 50.001-50.034 of the Human Resources Code (the "Act"), creates the Texas State Board of Social Worker Examiners (the "Board") and authorizes it to license and regulate social workers. *See* TEX. HUM. RES. CODE ANN. §§ 50.004(a), .006 (Vernon Supp. 1999). Unless licensed under the Act, a person may not hold himself or herself out as a social worker or use a title that implies licensure or certification in professional social work services. *Id.* § 50.010. To be eligible for licensure, a person must submit an application stating the person's education, experience and other information required by the Board; be at least eighteen years of age "and worthy of the public trust and confidence," *Id.*§ 50.013; and have the requisite educational degree. *Id.*§§ 50.015, .017. An eligible applicant must also take an examination administered by the Board. *Id.*§ 50.014(a). Upon satisfactory completion of the examination, an applicant may be granted a license as a licensed master social worker, licensed social worker, or a social work associate. *Id.* § 50.014(b).

The licenses expire on staggered dates during the year and may be renewed before the expiration date or within one year of the expiration date simply by paying renewal and examination fees. *Id.* §50.023(a)-(d). A different procedure must be followed if a license has expired for more than a year, however. Section 50.023(e), which you ask about, requires these licensees to reapply providing as follows:

> If a person's license or certificate or order of recognition has been expired for one year or longer, the person may not renew the license or order of recognition. The person may obtain a new license or order of recognition by *submitting to reexamination, if an examination was originally required*, and complying with the requirements and procedures for obtaining an original license or certificate or order of recognition. However, the board may renew without reexamination an expired license or certificate or order of recognition of a person who was licensed in this state, moved to another state, and is currently licensed or certified and has been in practice in the other state for the two years preceding application. The person must pay to the department a fee that is equal to the examination fee for the license or order of recognition.[3]

Leg., R.S., ch. 605, §§ 1, 21, 1993 Tex. Gen. Laws 2277, 2287-88 (deleting grandfather provision); *see also* Tex. Att'y Gen. LO-89-104 (discussing 1983 grandfather provision)

3 TEX. HUM. RES. CODE ANN. § 50.023(E) (*emphasis added*)

Section 50.023(e) by its plain terms requires a person whose license has expired for a year or longer applying for a new license to submit to an examination only if the person was originally required to take an examination. Like a court, we must give effect to each word and phrase in subsection (e). *See Eddins-Walcher Butane Co. v. Calvert*, 298 S.W.2d 93, 96 (Tex. 1957). Subsection (e) provides that an applicant may obtain a new license *"by submitting to reexamination, if an examination was originally required . . . ."* The emphasized language is clear and unambiguous, and we must ascribe to that language its common everyday meaning. *Commissioners Court of Titus County v. Agan*, 940 S.W.2d 77, 80 (Tex. 1997); *see also Monsanto Co. v. Cornerstones Mun. Util. Dist.*, 865 S.W.2d 937, 939 (Tex. 1993) (where language in statute is unambiguous, court must seek legislative intent in plain and common meaning of words and terms used in statute); TEX. GOV'T CODE ANN. § 311.011(a) (Vernon 1998) (words and phrases shall be read in context and construed according to rules of grammar and common usage).

The ordinary meaning of "reexamination," is to retake or resubmit to an examination and the term necessarily presupposes the existence of a prior examination. Thus, only an applicant previously subject to an examination, by definition, may be subject to a reexamination. More importantly, the phrase providing that reexamination is required "if an examination was originally required" emphasizes that it is conditioned on a previously required examination. Accordingly, if an examination was not originally required, then a reexamination is not required. Additionally, we have found no indication in the Act or its legislative history that the legislature intended otherwise. Therefore, based on the legislative language, we conclude that section 50.023(e) permits a person originally licensed without an examination, whose license has expired for more than a year, to reapply for a new social work license without an examination.

You have advised us that the Board's "policy has been, if a person allows their license to expire for more than one year, then the person is required to reapply under the rules that are in effect at the time of reapplication" and that "[n]o person has ever been allowed to reapply and be licensed after allowing their license to lapse, to be relicensed without taking an examination which has been required since January 1, 1986." By policy, we understand you to refer to the Board's interpretation as embodied in the relevant Board rule. That rule provides as follows: "On or after one year from the expiration date, a person may no longer renew the license and must reapply by submitting a new application, paying the required fees, and meeting the current requirements for the license including passing the licensure examination." 22 TEX. ADMIN. CODE § 781.504(g). This interpretation is inconsistent with the plain language of the statute. *See Monsanto*, 865 S.W.2d at 939 (where language in statute is unambiguous, court must seek legislative intent in plain and common meaning of words and terms used in statute).

As the agency charged with executing the Act, the Board's construction of the statute is entitled to serious consideration, but only as long as such construction is reasonable and does not contradict the plain language of the statute. *Tarrant*

County Appraisal Dist. v. Moore, 845 S.W.2d 820, 823 (Tex. 1993); *see also* TEX. GOV'T CODE ANN. § 311.023(6) (Vernon 1998). As a general matter, a construction that imposes additional burdens, conditions, or restrictions in excess of or inconsistent with the statutory provisions cannot be upheld. *See*, e.g., *RAILROAD COMM'N OF TEX. v. ARCO OIL & GAS CO.*, 876 S.W.2d 473, 481 (Tex. App.-Austin 1994, writ denied) (agency rule may not impose additional burdens, conditions, or restrictions in excess of or inconsistent with statutory provisions); *Hollywood Calling v. Public Util. Comm'n of Tex.*, 805 S.W.2d 618, 620 (Tex. App.-Austin 1991, no writ) (same). Specifically, a licensing agency for a business or profession cannot enforce standards that are more burdensome than those of the controlling statute, even though they may be reasonable and may be administered reasonably. *Bloom v. Texas State Bd. of Exam'rs of Psychologists*, 492 S.W.2d 460, 462 (Tex. 1973); *Murphy v. Mittlelstadt*, 199 S.W.2d 478, 481-82 (Tex. 1947); TEX. ATT'Y GEN. OP. No. JM-650 (1987) at 5. Notwithstanding that the Board's interpretation of section 50.023(e) may be consistent with the Act's general objective of setting high standards for social worker qualifications and protecting the public,[4] it is inconsistent with the plain language of section 50.023(e).

The Board's interpretation reads out of the statute the phrase "by *submitting to reexamination, if an examination was originally required*" and gives effect only to the remaining provision, *i.e.*, the language requiring the applicant to comply with the procedures for a new license, including examination. This interpretation imposes the burden of taking an examination on an applicant reapplying for a license who was not originally required to take an examination when the statute plainly exempts such applicant from examination and, thus, is inconsistent with section 50.023(e). Accordingly, we also conclude that the Board's rule on reapplication, to the extent it requires an applicant originally licensed without an examination to take an examination, is invalid. *See Bloom*, 492 S.W.2d at 462; *ARCO*, 876 S.W.2d at 481.

---

4 *See* Tex. Hum. Res. Code Ann. § 50.014(a) (Vernon Supp. 1999) ("At least once each calendar year the board shall prepare and administer an examination to determine the qualifications of applicants for licenses under this chapter."); Sunset Commission Recommendations to 68th Legislature (1982) at 19 (noting that the "state generally should only regulate a profession when the unregulated practice can clearly harm or endanger the public," describing tasks commonly performed by social workers, and concluding as follows: "From this description it can be seen that the social worker is often involved in areas in which professional judgment can have significant impact on the well-being of clients. Thus, substantial harm to the public could result from incompetent or unqualified social workers."); see also Letter from Helen Fisher, President, National Association of Social Workers, Texas, to Sarah J. Shirley, Chair, Opinion Committee (Aug. 25, 1998) (on file with Opinion Committee) (social workers licensed to protect credibility of profession and to establish safeguards for public; exempting applicant reapplying for license from examination detrimental for profession).

SUMMARY

Section 50.023(e) of the Human Resources Code permits a person originally licensed without an examination whose license has expired for more than a year to reapply for a new social work license without an examination. The Texas State Board of Social Worker Examiners' rule on reapplication, to the extent it requires an applicant originally licensed without an examination to take an examination, is invalid.

Yours very truly,

JOHN CORNYN
Attorney General of Texas

ANDY TAYLOR
First Assistant Attorney General

CLARK KENT ERVIN
Deputy Attorney General - General Counsel

ELIZABETH ROBINSON
Chair, Opinion Committee

Prepared by Sheela Rai
Assistant Attorney General

Court-Ordered Social Studies on Personal Time

OFFICE OF THE ATTORNEY GENERAL

STATE OF TEXAS

JIM MATTOX ATTORNEY GENERAL	August 13, 1984
Honorable Lloyd Doggett Texas State Senate P.O. Box 12068, Capitol Station Austin, Texas 78711	Opinion No. JM-188 Re: *Whether the Texas Department of Human Resources may prohibit workers from performing court ordered social studies on their own time*

Dear Senator Doggett:

You have requested an opinion on the validity of a policy of the Texas Department of Human Resources under which its child protective service workers are prohibited from performing court ordered social studies on their own time in disputed custody suits, even though the department has no official relationship with the parties involved in the proposed study. The existence of a conflict of interest in dual employment is a question of fact which ordinarily must be determined by the agency on a case-by-case basis, but we believe the department may find that a conflict of interest exists for all of its employees who would compete with the department for appointments and revenue under sections 11.12 and 11.18(c) of the Family Code or would perform services which may have other adverse affects on the department.

Section 11.12 of the Family Code provides, in pertinent part:

> (a) In a suit affecting the parent-child relationship, the court may order the preparation of a social study into the circumstances and condition of the child and of the home of any person seeking managing conservatorship or possession of the child.
>
> (b) The social study may be made by any state agency, including the Texas Department of Human Resources, or any private agency, *or any person appointed by the court* .... (Emphasis added).

House Bill No. 642 of the Sixty-eighth Legislature amended section 11.18 of the Family Code by adding subsection (c), which reads as follows:

> (c) If the court orders the Texas Department of Human Resources to

> prepare the social study prescribed by Section 11.12 of this code, the court *shall* award a reasonable fee for the preparation of the study to the department. The department's fee shall be taxed as costs, and shall be paid directly to the department. The department may enforce the order for the fee in its own name. (Emphasis added).

A conference committee for House Bill No. 642 intentionally determined that the language of section 11.18(c) is mandatory instead of permissive. The conference committee bill analysis and the bill's fiscal note estimate that the bill will result in sizeable revenue gains to the department's Welfare Administration Operating Fund, with corresponding reductions in the state and federal funds required for the operation of the department.

The Department of Human Resources has the powers expressly granted to it by statute together with those necessarily implied from the authority conferred or duties imposed. *See Stauffer v. City of San Antonio*, 344 S.W.2d 158, 160 (Tex.1961). The Texas Board of Human Resources is responsible for the adoption of policies and rules for the government of the department. Human Resources Code, § 21.003(a). The commissioner of Human Resources may employ personnel necessary for the administration of the department's duties. Sec. 21.005(c). We believe that reasonable personnel policies for which there is an adequate showing of need are authorized under the department's implied powers. Attorney General Opinion JM-93 (1983) expressed the opinion that a necessary concomitant of the authority to employ persons needed by an agency to perform its duties is the power to adopt reasonable employment policies calculated to insure the achievement of its objectives.

A public employee is not prohibited per se from simultaneously holding two different state employments or from simultaneously holding both state and private employments. *See* Attorney General Opinions JM-22 (1983); MW-415 (1981). Under the Department of Human Resources' policy for dual employment, activity presenting a possible conflict of interest with the employee's job duties must be reviewed and approved by the department. Rule 7200 of the department's personnel procedures prescribes the following:

7200 Other Employment

> Department employees may wish to become involved with employment or activities outside the department. This practice is generally acceptable to the department as long as the additional employment or activity is compatible with the department's work. Employees must not participate in employment or activity that violates the standards of conduct as prescribed in TEX.REV.CIV. STAT.ANN., art. 6252-9b, Section 8, known as the ethics code.
>
> ....
>
> All requests for participation in dual employment or activities are considered on an individual basis except that:
>
> 1. Employees of the department may not hold positions in both

county and state protective services programs.

2. Employees may not participate in those political activities listed in Item 7112, Political Activities Prohibited.

All other requests for participation in dual employment or activities are carefully reviewed to determine if they are compatible with the employee's assigned responsibilities in the department. The dual employment or activity may not conflict with the employee's relationship with department clients, contractors, providers, persons regulated by the Licensing Branch, or the employee's job in the department. Employees approved to participate in dual employment or activities must not use clients' or licensees' names or other information from any department files in connection with the part-time employment or activity. Employees must not use their official position or identification to influence, threaten, or coerce any person in connection with part-time employment. Employees approved to engage in off-duty employment or activities must not conduct any non-departmental business activity during duty hours. The only way an employee may conduct business for an outside activity during duty hours is for the activity to be department-related, such as councils of government, child welfare boards, or various advisory boards. The activity must be approved at the regional or state office level. Employees who violate these instructions may be subject to dismissal.

Personnel committees responsible for approving dual employment or activity requests should carefully consider the following outside activities:

....

9. Engaging in the independent activity of providing court-ordered social studies. (This type of request should be referred to the state office Personnel Committee.)

It is not suggested that Rule 7200 is per se an unreasonable procedure for screening dual employment activity that may involve conflicts of interest. The question is its present application to certain of the department's employees. We understand that since the effective date of section 11.18(c), the department has held that a conflict of interest exists in all cases involving child protective service workers who wish to perform court-ordered social studies on their own time.

Whether a conflict of interest exists is a question of fact which ordinarily must be determined by the agency on a case-by-case basis in light of the specific duties performed by the employee. However, *we cannot say* that the department may not validly determine that a conflict of interest exists in every instance in which a child protective service worker in his individual capacity competes with his employer, the Department of Human Resources, for court appointments and revenue anticipated by the department and the legislature under the recently enacted section 11.18(c) of the Family Code or adversely affects other aspects of the department, such as its anticipated workload or its credibility if the courts confuse the source of studies prepared by workers in their individual capacities.

One's right to work and earn an income, whether characterized as a liberty or a property interest, is a valuable right which should not be curtailed without legitimate state interest. *See Bishop v. Wood*, 426 U.S. 341 (1976); *The Board of Regents of State Colleges v. Roth*, 408 U.S. 564 (1972); *Perry v. Sindermann*, 408 U.S. 593 (1972); *Schware v. Board of Bar Examiners of the State of New Mexico*, 353 U.S. 232 (1957); Attorney General Opinion H-1317 (1978). It is our opinion that a prohibition against outside employment will be upheld by the courts inasmuch as the prohibition is reasonably related to the legitimate interest of the state in prohibiting outside employment that creates a conflict of interest. *See Gosney v. Sonora Independent School District*, 603 F.2d 522 (5th Cir.1979); Attorney General Opinion JM-93 (1983).

SUMMARY

The Texas Department of Human Resources may prohibit workers from performing court-ordered social studies on their own time when the workers' dual employment creates a conflict of interest by competing with the department for court appointments and revenue under sections 11.12 and 11.18(c) of the Family Code or by adversely affecting other aspects of the department.

Very truly yours,

Jim Mattox
Attorney General of Texas

TOM GREEN
First Assistant Attorney General

DAVID R. RICHARD
Executive Assistant Attorney General

Prepared by NANCY SUTTON
Assistant Attorney General

Appendix

NASW/TX Resources

General Counsel Law Note Series

The General Counsel Law Note Series provides information to social workers about legal topics of concern to the social work profession. The Law Notes are developed with the support and financial assistance of the NASW Legal Defense Fund (LDF). The topics addressed in the Law Note series include the following:

- **Client Confidentiality and Privileged Communications**

  <https://www.socialworkers.org/ldf/lawnotes/confidentiality.asp>

  Many problems arise in the application of the concepts of confidentiality and privilege to the professional services provided by social workers. This paper discusses the two principles and outlines some of the exceptions applicable to them, particularly in the context of clinical social work practice.

- **Social Workers and Subpoenas**

  <https://www.socialworkers.org/ldf/lawnotes/subpoenas.asp>

  Social workers are becoming involved in clients' lawsuits more frequently than they would like. Domestic relations matters, drunk driving accidents, and sexual harassment or other work-related problems can lead to litigation for clients who are in family counseling, therapy, or employee assistance programs. In addition, social workers are required to report acts or suspicions of child or elder abuse and may have to testify about these reports. Further, troubled clients may be involved in legal proceedings such as child custody contests, workers' compensation hearings, civil damage suits, or criminal matters including domestic violence and violation of probation orders.

  These and similar mattes may result in litigation involving social workers and the subpoena of their records. The type of subpoena, whether it must be obeyed, whether the client has provided a valid written release of information, and whether original records must be provided are some issues that must be addressed. The first step in sorting out how to treat a subpoena is to understand the concepts and rules on which a subpoena is based. Armed with some information about the purpose of a subpoena and the legal and ethical rules that generally apply, social workers can analyze how to respond and also can formulate legal questions for an attorney.

- ❑ **Social Workers and Alternative Dispute Resolution**

  <https://www.socialworkers.org/ldf/lawnotes/dispute.asp>

  An important part of a social worker's professional responsibility is to manage conflict in a productive manner. "Whether advocating for clients, dealing with conflict within organizations, or helping people learn more-effective ways of coping with conflict in their lives, . . ." resolving conflict in employment settings or related to the delivery of services to clients, social workers are involved with conflict resolution daily. Social workers are increasingly compelled to follow disputes into court, whether as fact witnesses, expert witnesses, or parties to lawsuits. The many tensions and negative feelings associated with litigation leave social workers and others asking whether there is a better method for conflict resolution. The courtroom can be both costly and time consuming, sometimes taking years for the simplest case to go to trial. The process of resolving disputes in the courtroom is being replaced or assisted in many areas by alternative dispute resolution (ADR) processes. The courts, state and federal agencies, and employers have all begun providing private and less adversarial methods of dispute resolution than litigation. "ADR is perceived as the solution to problems of runaway jury verdicts, expensive discovery proceedings and protracted litigation. Accordingly, courts, legislatures, government agencies, and private organizations are endorsing various forms of ADR."

  ADR is a process by which parties to a dispute resolve their differences without litigation. Social workers participate in ADR both as providers and as parties. This law note describes the three principle methods of voluntary alternative dispute resolution - negotiation, arbitration, and mediation - and discusses traditional and evolving uses for these processes within the social work profession.

- ❑ **Social Workers as Expert Witnesses**

  <https://www.socialworkers.org/ldf/lawnotes/expert.asp>

  Courts of law rely upon information offered in evidence as the basis for decisions rendered. Evidence comes in many forms, including photographs, recordings, devices, forensic evidence, documents, and individual testimony. Oral testimony by witnesses is, however, often the major source of evidence at a trial.

  Witnesses who testify as experts play an important role in interpreting data, explaining complex material, and drawing knowledgeable inferences based upon their training and experience. Social workers are called to testify as expert witnesses on a variety of subjects. This Law Note discusses the role of the expert witness and reviews case law confirming the role of social workers as expert witnesses in a variety of settings.

- ❑ **Social Workers, Managed Care and Antitrust Issues**

  <https://www.socialworkers.org/ldf/lawnotes/antitrust.asp>

  Managed care organizations (MCOs), in conjunction with employers who provide employment-based health insurance programs, play a large and growing role in the health care options made available to health plan participants.

MCOs have been placed in positions of bargaining strength vis-à-vis social workers as providers of mental health care or other covered services. Federal and state antitrust laws are being used by other health care professionals to challenge MCO practices that limit or interfere with the right to practice, to be members of provider panels, and to make appropriate decisions on behalf of their patients. Social workers should understand the issues and arguments raised in antitrust health care cases to be able to evaluate the business practices of the MCOs with which they are dealing.

To assist social workers in these efforts, this law note describes federal antitrust laws, the type of conduct that could be actionable under those laws, and health care cases in which MCO conduct is being challenged as violating antitrust laws. The note identifies the steps that might be taken by social workers to evaluate their own fact situation under antitrust laws, including obtaining assistance from federal and state antitrust authorities, state insurance regulators, state legislatures, and Congress. Finally, precautions that should be observed by social workers in their work and as NASW members to minimize their own risk of antitrust liability are reviewed. A sample protest letter to an MCO is also included.

❑ **The Social Worker and Protection of Privacy**

<https://www.socialworkers.org/ldf/lawnotes/privacy.asp>

Clients receiving psychotherapy risk social stigma should their "private" mental health information be disclosed. Disclosures may affect many aspects of a client's life including the ability to obtain gainful employment or run for public office. Harm may be inflicted through the very fact of disclosure-that is, simply through other people's coming to know facts or feelings that a client and psychotherapist expected to be kept confidential. "The [client] may feel embarrassed, vulnerable, or otherwise violated, as well as feel betrayed by the [psychotherapist], and personal or other relationships may suffer." Access to medical and mental health records is currently "safeguarded" under a patchwork of case law, statutes, regulations, federal and state constitutional law, and personal injury tort law. No overriding federal rule of law directly controls or protects the privacy of all persons in the United States, although some state constitutions guarantee privacy for citizens in a particular state. An invasion of privacy in the exposure of confidential mental health treatment records may have no legal recourse.

The purpose of this paper is to provide social workers with a brief overview of the current state of privacy law and how it impacts on the provision of mental health services and treatment. With an informed understanding of the many issues affecting privacy, social workers will be able to engage in the debate taking place regarding comprehensive federal legislation as well as recognize issues within their states that require response and appropriate action to ensure that client privacy is properly protected.

❑ **Social Workers and Child Abuse Reporting: A Review of State Mandatory Reporting Requirements**

<https://www.socialworkers.org/ldf/lawnotes/abuse.asp>

"Reporting [child abuse] frequently becomes an ethical dilemma as a result

of complex interactions among several factors including diverse professional contexts, legal requirements, professional-ethical standards, and the circumstances of suspected abuse. The reporting dilemma also reflects the fact that breaching confidentiality and breaking the law both constitute unethical behavior." However, beyond the professional difficulties in dealing with child abuse and neglect, there is a distinct need to intervene on behalf of the children victimized by abuse. Currently, an estimated one million children are victims of child abuse and neglect each year. In 1996, child protective services in all states investigated more than two million reports and substantiated just under one million, child abuse victims. Approximately 1,000 victims, who were previously known by child protective services, died as a result of abuse and neglect. Because of legal requirements, over fifty percent of all investigated reports of child abuse came from professionals, including medical personnel, law enforcement, educators and social service workers.

This law note discusses issues social workers confront when dealing with child abuse and neglect situations. First, this note provides a brief history of the federal legislation that mandated child protective services and the reporting of suspected child abuse at the federal level then surveys state statutes and case law, providing an overview of the current state of mandatory reporting. Third, it identifies ethical considerations mandated reporters face. Finally, it provides practical steps in reporting child abuse and, in addition, an appendix summarizing each state's reporting requirements.

- ❑ **Social Workers and Managed Care Contracts**

<https://www.socialworkers.org/ldf/lawnotes/contracts.asp>

This law note was developed to aid clinical social workers who work in a managed care environment as independent practitioners in evaluating managed care agreements. For social workers new to managed care and for those who are assessing their provider status, it is helpful to have some understanding of the legal issues related to managed care contracts. Social workers involved in health policy development or legislative initiatives may also find the law note useful to identify particular aspects of managed care provider relationships in need of state or national legislative reforms. A three-stage process for analyzing managed care concerns is presented. First, social workers are urged to evaluate fully, in advance, the organizations with which they will be doing business. Second, analytical tools are provided for social workers to review critically the language presented in managed care provider agreements. Social workers are directed to seek out other resources where appropriate, including the advice of legal counsel. Third, social workers are presented with some general considerations if a formal means of redress is necessary to resolve conflicts between the parties to the contract. In addition, a glossary of managed care terms and acronyms is provided. Finally, model contract provisions are offered for those who are in a position to revise provider agreements to form the strongest fit between social workers' ethical obligations and managed care restrictions. In some instances, this law note suggests options for social workers that may be available in only a few, optimal circumstances; however, consideration of how managed care companies and social workers "should" act is instructive and anticipates the future direction of public and private standards in the managed care industry.

A dynamic flow of ideas and information moves between legislatures, government agencies, the courts, and private standard-setting organizations. As the "best practices" of the managed care industry emerge in any one of these bodies, new measures are quick to be adopted by others. Options available to a few social workers one year may be widespread within five. Social workers need to be informed about the general trends in the world of managed care to make wise decisions about what reforms to support, when to litigate, and when to wait patiently for the storm to pass.

❑ **Social Workers and Clinical Notes**

<https://www.socialworkers.org/ldf/lawnotes/notes.asp>

This law note reviews legal issues specifically germane to social workers' clinical notes or "psychotherapy notes." However, a discussion of clinical notes takes place under various categories of guiding principles, including the NASW Code of Ethics, state medical records acts, social work licensing laws, specific federal and state psychotherapy privacy protection statutes, and state regulations applicable to social work case records in general. The definition and even the existence of clinical notes as distinct from medical or case records has been a matter of some disagreement among states, while recently issued federal regulations recognize psychotherapy notes as a distinct part of the mental health record accorded special privacy protection. This law note reviews legal opinions, statutory and regulatory language, and ethical principles that control the creation, handling, protection, and release of clinical notes within social work practice. It provides guideposts for professional practice, but does not aim to resolve particular legal problems. Consultation with an attorney, a social work licensing board representative, and other mental health professionals is necessary to resolve particular issues related to clinical notes.

The legal precedent and statutory support discussed in detail in this law note should cement social workers' understanding that it is essential to maintain accurate and timely clinical notes. Clinical notes facilitate the delivery of mental health services, ensure continuity of care, protect clients' privacy, and ensure reasonable future access to client treatment history. Contemporaneous clinical notes are an important part of the client record, as are evaluations, treatment plans, prognoses, collateral contacts, contact dates, and payment plans. Clinical notes often contain the most private client information as well as the therapist's observations, clinical concerns, and relevant anecdotal information. Social workers sometimes hold the view that the obligation to keep such records is a discretionary one. Although discretion is required when determining what to include and how to phrase comments, this law note provides abundant support for the proposition that clinical notes are necessary to create an accurate treatment record and demonstrate commitment to professional practice standards.

❑ **Social Workers and Work Issues**

<https://www.socialworkers.org/ldf/lawnotes/workIssues.asp>

This law note surveys various work-related legal problems faced by social workers who provide professional services. Some of the issues discussed are specific to social workers as a class of employees, and others apply to social workers as independent contractors. Problems common to both groups are also examined. This law note will also highlight potential legal remedies for addressing work-related problems.

LEGAL ISSUE OF THE MONTH

The "Legal Issue of the Month" provides an overview of a specific legal topic of relevance to social workers from the perspective of a particular legal decision. Topics are updated monthly and previous topics remain available for viewing.

May 2006 **Children's' Rights to Confidentiality**
<https://www.socialworkers.org/ldf/legal_issue/200605.asp>

April 2006 **Social Workers and the CIGNA Managed Care Settlement**
<https://www.socialworkers.org/ldf/legal_issue/200604.asp>

March 2006 **Overview of the LDF Amicus Brief Database**
<https://www.socialworkers.org/ldf/legal_issue/200603.asp>

Feb 2006 **Social Workers and End-of-Life Decisions**
<https://www.socialworkers.org/ldf/legal_issue/200602.asp>

Jan 2006 **Social Workers and Post-Disaster Record Keeping Questions**
<https://www.socialworkers.org/ldf/legal_issue/200601.asp>

Nov 2005 **Parental Rights and Responsibilities for Lesbian and Gay Parents**
<https://www.socialworkers.org/ldf/legal_issue/200511.asp>

Oct 2005 **Social Workers and Record Retention Requirements**
<https://www.socialworkers.org/ldf/legal_issue/200510.asp>

Sep 2005 **Social Workers and Disaster Relief Services**
<https://www.socialworkers.org/ldf/legal_issue/200509.asp>

July 2005 **Psychotherapist-Patient Privilege in the Military**
<https://www.socialworkers.org/ldf/legal_issue/200507.asp>

June 2005 **Social Work Licensure: Practice and Title Protection Reviewed**
<https://www.socialworkers.org/ldf/legal_issue/200506.asp>

May 2005 **Social Workers, Medication, and Scope of Practice**
<https://www.socialworkers.org/ldf/legal_issue/200505.asp>

April 2005 **Social Workers and HIPAA Security Standards**
<https://www.socialworkers.org/ldf/legal_issue/200504.asp>

March 2005 **Social Workers and Psychotherapist-Patient Privilege: Jaffee v. Redmond Revisited**
<https://www.socialworkers.org/ldf/legal_issue/200503.asp>

Feb 2005 **Social Workers and the Duty to Warn**
<https://www.socialworkers.org/ldf/legal_issue/200502.asp>

Jan 2005 **Review of State Balloting on Marriage for Same-Sex Couples**
<https://www.socialworkers.org/ldf/legal_issue/200501.asp>

Nov 2004 **Are Public Social Workers Liable for Failing to Prevent Child Abuse?**
<https://www.socialworkers.org/ldf/legal_issue/200411.asp>

Oct 2004 **What Do the Courts Say about Same-Sex Marriage?**
<https://www.socialworkers.org/ldf/legal_issue/200410.asp>

Sep 2004 **Social Workers and the USA PATRIOT Act**
<https://www.socialworkers.org/ldf/legal_issue/200409.asp>

July 2004 **Legal Developments in Treating and Prosecuting Pregnant Substance Abusers**
<https://www.socialworkers.org/ldf/legal_issue/200407.asp>

June 2004 **Business Expense Deductions for Psychotherapy**
<https://www.socialworkers.org/ldf/legal_issue/200406.asp>

May 2004 **HIPAA for Social Work Employers and Administrators**
<https://www.socialworkers.org/ldf/legal_issue/200405.asp>

April 2004 **Social Workers and International Human Rights**
<https://www.socialworkers.org/ldf/legal_issue/200404.asp>

March 2004 **Social Workers' Rights as Probationary Employees**
<https://www.socialworkers.org/ldf/legal_issue/200403.asp>

Feb 2004 **Social Workers and Civil Liability for Failure to Report Child Abuse**
<https://www.socialworkers.org/ldf/legal_issue/200402.asp>

Jan 2004 **Social Workers and Capital Punishment for Juveniles**
<https://www.socialworkers.org/ldf/legal_issue/200401.asp>

Nov 2003 **Social Workers and Legal Developments in Gay Rights**
<https://www.socialworkers.org/ldf/legal_issue/200311.asp>

Oct 2003 **Megan's Law: Protecting the Public or Branding Offenders?**
<https://www.socialworkers.org/ldf/legal_issue/200310.asp>

Sep 2003 **Social Workers as Death Penalty Mitigation Specialists**
<https://www.socialworkers.org/ldf/legal_issue/200309.asp>

July 2003 **Social Workers, HIPAA, and Subpoenas**
<https://www.socialworkers.org/ldf/legal_issue/200307.asp>

June 2003 **Is it Necessary for Protective Services Social Workers to Obtain a Warrant to Investigate a Child Abuse or Neglect Complaint**
<https://www.socialworkers.org/ldf/legal_issue/200306.asp>

May 2003 **Social Workers and "Any Willing Provider" Laws**
<https://www.socialworkers.org/ldf/legal_issue/200305.asp>

April 2003 **A First Look at the HIPAA Security Regulations**
<https://www.socialworkers.org/ldf/legal_issue/200304.asp>

March 2003 **HIPAA Compliance Toolkit**
<https://www.socialworkers.org/ldf/legal_issue/200303.asp>

Feb 2003 **Social Work Ethics and Non-Compete Clauses in Employment Contracts and Independent Contractor Agreements**
<https://www.socialworkers.org/ldf/legal_issue/200302.asp>

INDEX

A

B

C

D

E

F

J

L

M

Q

R

ORDERING INFORMATION

Additional copies of ***Texas Law for the Social Worker*** are available from the publisher. Orders may be placed by phone, by mail, by FAX, or directly on the web. Purchase orders from institutions are welcome.

- ❑ *To order by mail:* Complete this order form and mail it (along with check or credit card information) to Bayou Publishing, 2524 Nottingham, Houston, TX 77005-1412.
- ❑ *To order by phone:* Call (800) 340-2034.
- ❑ *To order by FAX:* Fill out this order form (including credit card information) and fax to (713) 526-4342.
- ❑ *To place a secure online order:* Visit http://www.bayoupublishing.com.

Name: ______________________________

Address: ______________________________

____

City: ____________________ ST: ___ Zip: ________

Ph: ______________________________

FAX: ______________________________

❑ VISA ❑ MasterCard ❑ American Express

Charge Card #: ______________________________

Expiration Date: ______________________________

Signature: ______________________________

Please send me ____ copies at $35.00 each __________

Sales Tax (Texas residents) __________

plus $4.50 postage and handling *(per order)* _____$4.50

Total $ __________

Bayou Publishing
2524 Nottingham, Suite 150
Houston, TX 77005-1412
Ph: (713) 526-4558/ FAX: (713) 526-4342
Orders: (800) 340-2034
http://www.bayoupublishing.com

Bayou Publishing

NASW · TEXAS CHAPTER

National Association of Social Workers

For additional resources provided by the
National Association of Social Workers—Texas Chapter, visit the
NASW/TX website at http://www.naswtx.org,
or the national website at http://www.socialworkers.org.

National Association of Social Workers
Texas Chapter
810 West 11th Street., Suite 410
Austin, TX 78701-2010
(512) 474-1454